"A strong, clearly organised study which [...]
work and provides helpful direction for stu[...]
to approach her writing" – **Daniel Lea, O**[...]

Since the publication of her high profile de[...]
has cemented her place within the flourish[...]
In this first full-length introduction to her [...]
criticism and offers new perspectives, posi[...] in the context of
both contemporary English and postcolonial traditions.

Student friendly and thought-provoking, *Zadie Smith* includes:

- A supporting timeline of key dates
- Biographical and cultural analysis of key texts
- Discussion of the full range of Smith's work, including her short stories and novels
- A survey of selected landmark interviews
- A comprehensive overview of the critical reception of Smith's work to date

PHILIP TEW is Professor of English (post-1900 Literature) at Brunel University, Director of the Brunel Centre for Contemporary Writing and Founding Director of the UK Network for Modern Fiction Studies. He is an internationally acknowledged expert in contemporary British fiction and has published widely in the field.

Each volume in this series offers a well-researched and clear introduction to a key novelist from an exciting new generation that has emerged during and after the 1970s. A user-friendly format will guide the reader through a clear and theoretically informed overview of a significant British writer. The series provides biographical information, a range of critical readings, and an informed exploration of relevant literary and cultural contexts. These guides will enable readers to contextualize and so deepen their understanding of New British Fiction.

NEW BRITISH FICTION

Series editors:
Philip Tew
Rod Mengham

Published
Sonya Andermahr: **Jeanette Winterson**
Bradley Buchanann: **Hanif Kureishi**
Frederick M. Holmes: **Julian Barnes**
Kaye Mitchell: **A. L. Kennedy**
Robert Morace: **Irvine Welsh**
Stephen Morton: **Salman Rushdie**
Philip Tew: **Zadie Smith**

Forthcoming
Gerard Barrett: **Graham Swift**
Sebastian Groes: **Martin Amis**
Rod Mengham: **Jonathan Coe**
Mark Rawlinson: **Pat Barker**
Lynn Wells: **Ian McEwan**
Mark Wormald: **Kazuo Ishiguro**

New British Fiction Series
Series Standing Order

ISBN 1–4039–4274–9 hardback
ISBN 1–4039–4275–7 paperback
(*outside North America only*)

You can receive future titles in this series as they are published by placing a standing order. Please contact your bookseller or, in the case of difficulty, write to us at the address below with your name and address, the title of the series and the ISBN quoted above.

Customer Services Department, Palgrave Ltd
Houndmills, Basingstoke, Hampshire RG216XS, England

NEW BRITISH FICTION

Zadie Smith

Philip Tew

palgrave
macmillan

First published 2010 by
PALGRAVE MACMILLAN

Palgrave Macmillan in the UK is an imprint of Macmillan Publishers Limited,
registered in England, company number 785998, of Houndmills, Basingstoke,
Hampshire RG21 6XS.

Palgrave Macmillan in the US is a division of St Martin's Press LLC,
175 Fifth Avenue, New York, NY 10010.

Palgrave Macmillan is the global academic imprint of the above companies
and has companies and representatives throughout the world.

Palgrave® and Macmillan® are registered trademarks in the United States,
the United Kingdom, Europe and other countries.

ISBN-13: 978–0–230–51675–5 hardback
ISBN-13: 978–0–230–51676–2 paperback

This book is printed on paper suitable for recycling and made from fully
managed and sustained forest sources. Logging, pulping and manufacturing
processes are expected to conform to the environmental regulations of the
country of origin.

A catalogue record for this book is available from the British Library.

A catalog record for this book is available from the Library of Congress.

10   9   8   7   6   5   4   3   2   1
19 18 17 16 15 14 13 12 11 10

Printed and bound in China

Balj Bhinder
recalling Bengal Spice 'banquet' nights and Euro road trips:
long may they continue.

CONTENTS

GENERAL EDITORS' PREFACE

This series highlights with its very title two crucial elements in the nature of contemporary British fiction, especially as a field for academic research and study. The first term indicates the originality and freshness of such writing expressed in a huge formal diversity. The second evokes the cultural identity of the authors included, who nevertheless represent through their diversity a challenge to any hegemonic or narrow view of Britishness. As regards the fiction, many of the writers featured in this series continue to draw from and adapt long traditions of cultural and aesthetic practice. Such aesthetic continuities contrast starkly with the conditions of knowledge at the end of the twentieth century and the beginning of the twenty-first, a period that has been characterized by an apprehension of radical presentness, a sense of unprecedented forms of experience and an obsession with new modes of self-awareness. This stage of the survival of the novel may perhaps be best remembered as a millennial and postmillennial moment, a time of fluctuating reading practices and of historical events whose impact is largely still unresolved. The new fiction of these times reflects a rapidly changing cultural and ideological reality, as well as a renewal of the commitment of both writers and readers to both the relevance and utility of narrative forms of knowledge.

Each volume in this series will serve as an introductory guide to an individual author chosen from a list of those whose work has proved to be of general interest to reviewers, academics, students and the general reading public. Each volume will offer information concerning the life, work and literary and cultural contexts appropriate to the chosen subject of each book; individual volumes will share the same overall structure with a largely common organization of materials. The result is intended to be suitable for both academic and general readers: putting accessibility at a premium, without compromising an ambitious series of readings of today's most vitally interesting British novelists, interpreting their work, assessing their influences and exploring their relationship to the times in which they live.

Philip Tew and Rod Mengham

ACKNOWLEDGEMENTS

I wish to highlight the many contributions of a number of individuals and institutions, variously for assistance, guidance and practical support during what proved to be a far longer project than I had anticipated, and a substantial part of which book was first drafted and revised during two summers at my chalet or 'dacha' in Bélatelep on Lake Balaton, Hungary. Thanks to all staff at Palgrave Macmillan, especially first Kate Haines (then Wallis) for 'volunteering' me for this study, and for her editorial support, and second the work of Sonya Barker and Kitty van Boxel. Praise goes to Priya Venkat (of Integra) for great patience exhibited during the extended phase of proof corrections and indexing. I must add acknowledgement of Anna Fleming (then Sandeman) for originally discussing and putting forward the overall series, before editing my numerous other projects elsewhere.

Others who deserve recognition include: Dr Nicola Allen, Birmingham City University; Dr Gavin Budge, University of Hertfordshire; Prof. Steve Dixon, Brunel University; Dr Nick Hubble, Brunel University; Dr John McLeod, Leeds University; Michael McElroy, Office of the Public Editor, *The New York Times*; Dr Anja Müller-Wood, Mainz University; Dr Alan Munton, University of Plymouth; Dr Alex Murray, Exeter University; George Alister Tew; Dr Karin E. Westman, Kansas State University; Dr John Carter Wood, Open University; as ever staff in the Humanities Two Reading Room, British Library; and also staff of Abbázia Kávéház, Fonyód for a vital internet connection (and excellent decaffeinated coffee). Finally for personal support and sustaining my efforts, I salute my partner, Ágnes Tavacs Bartha.

A NOTE ON TEXTS CITED

Wherever possible electronic sources freely available online have been consulted, and in the bibliography where there is no pagination marked in the e-version this has been signified. However, in using such sources in the main text no page reference will be designated, thus avoiding unnecessary repetition.

PART I
Introduction

TIMELINE

1960 Harold Macmillan 'Winds of Change' speech, Cape Town,
South Africa
John F. Kennedy elected as US President
Aged six, Kazuo Ishiguro arrives in Britain

1961 Adolf Eichmann on trial in Israel for role in Holocaust
Bay of Pigs: attempted invasion of Cuba
Berlin Wall constructed
Yuri Gagarin first person in Space
Silicon chip patented
Private Eye magazine begins publication
Muriel Spark, *The Prime of Miss Jean Brodie*
Jonathan Coe born

1962 Cuban Missile Crisis
Marilyn Monroe dies
Independence for Uganda; followed this decade by Kenya
(1963), Northern Rhodesia (1964), Southern Rhodesia
(1965), Barbados (1966)

1963 John F. Kennedy assassinated in Dallas
Martin Luther King Jr delivers 'I Have a Dream' speech
Profumo Affair

1964   Nelson Mandela sentenced to life imprisonment
Commercial pirate radio challenges BBC monopoly

1965   State funeral of Winston Churchill
US sends troops to Vietnam
A. L. Kennedy born in Dundee, Scotland

1966   Ian Brady and Myra Hindley sentenced to life
imprisonment for Moors Murders
England beats West Germany 4–2 at Wembley to win
Football World Cup
Star Trek series debut on NBC television
Jean Rhys, *The Wide Sargasso Sea*

1967   Six-Day War in the Middle East
World's first heart transplant
Abortion Act legalizes termination of pregnancy in the
UK
Sergeant Pepper's Lonely Hearts Club Band album released by
The Beatles
Flann O'Brien, *The Third Policeman*

1968   Anti-Vietnam War protestors attempt to storm American
Embassy in Grosvenor Square
Martin Luther King Jr assassinated
Robert F. Kennedy assassinated
May: student protests and riots in France (les événements)
Lord Chamberlain's role as censor of plays in the UK is
abolished
Lindsay Anderson, *If* ...

1969   Civil rights march in Northern Ireland attacked by
Protestants
Apollo 11 lands on the Moon with Neil Armstrong's
famous first steps
Rock concert at Woodstock
Yvonne McLean, Zadie Smith's mother, arrives in London
aged 15 from Jamaica
Yasser Arafat becomes leader of PLO

Booker Prize first awarded; winner P. H. Newby, *Something to Answer for* Open University founded in the UK

John Fowles, *The French Lieutenant's Woman*

1970 Popular Front for the Liberation of Palestine (PFLP) hijacks five planes

Students activists and bystanders shot in anti-Vietnam War protest at Kent State University, Ohio, four killed, nine wounded

UK voting age reduced from 21 to 18 years

1971 Decimal currency introduced in the UK

Internment without trial of terrorist suspects in Northern Ireland begins

India and Pakistan in conflict after Bangladesh declares independence

1972 Miners' strike

Bloody Sunday in Londonderry, 14 protestors killed outright or fatally wounded by British troops

Aldershot barracks bomb initiates IRA campaign with seven dead

Britain enters Common Market

Massacre of Israeli athletes at Munich Olympics

Watergate scandal

Anthony Burgess, *A Clockwork Orange*

Samuel Beckett, *Not I*

1973 US troops leave Vietnam

Arab–Israeli 15-day Yom Kippur War

PM Edward Heath introduces 3-day working week

Martin Amis, *The Rachel Papers*

1974 Miners' strike

IRA bombings in Guildford (5 dead) and Birmingham (21 dead)

1975 Microsoft founded

Sex Discrimination Act

Zadie Smith born in Royal Free Hospital, Hampstead on 27 October

Malcolm Bradbury, *The History Man*

1976 Weak economy forces UK government loan from the International Monetary Fund (IMF)

Ian McEwan, *First Love, Last Rites*

1977 Star Wars released

UK unemployment tops 1,600,000

Nintendo begins to sell computer games

Sex Pistols *Anarchy in the UK* tour

1978 Soviet troops occupy Afghanistan

First test-tube baby born in Oldham, England

1979 Iranian Revolution establishes Islamic theocracy

Margaret Thatcher becomes PM after Conservative election victory

USSR invades Afghanistan

Lord Mountbatten assassinated by the IRA

1980 Iran–Iraq War starts

Iranian Embassy siege in London

CND rally at Greenham Common airbase, England

IRA hunger strike at Belfast Maze Prison over political status for prisoners

Julian Barnes, *Metroland*

1981 18 January, New Cross house fire, 14 young black people killed

Prince Charles and Lady Diana marry in St Paul's Cathedral with 750 million worldwide television audience

British Nationality Bill passed

Widespread urban riots in the UK including in Brixton, Holloway, Toxteth, Handsworth, Moss Side

AIDS identified

First IBM personal computer

Alasdair Gray, *Lanark*

Salman Rushdie, *Midnight's Children*, which wins Booker Prize for Fiction

1982   Mark Thatcher, PM's son, disappears for 3 days in Sahara during the Paris–Dakar rally
Falklands War with Argentina, costing the UK over £1.6 billion
Body of Roberto Calvi, chairman of Vatican-connected Banco Ambrosiano, found hanging beneath Blackfriars Bridge, London

1983   Klaus Barbie, Nazi war criminal, arrested in Bolivia
Beirut: US Embassy and barracks bombing, killing hundreds of members of multinational peacekeeping force, mostly US marines
US troops invade Grenada
Microsoft Word first released
Salman Rushdie, *Shame*, which wins Prix du Meilleur Livre Etranger (France)

1984   Miners' strike begins
18th June, unprovoked attacks on miners by police at Orgreave; miners' retaliation shown first on evening news to imply provocation by strikers
HIV identified as cause of AIDS
IRA bomb at Conservative Party Conference in Brighton kills four
British Telecom privatization shares sale
Thirty-eight deaths during clashes at Liverpool vs Juventus football match at Heysel Stadium, Brussels
Martin Amis, *Money: A Suicide Note*
Julian Barnes, *Flaubert's Parrot*
James Kelman, *Busconductor Hines*
Graham Swift, *Waterland*

1985   Famine in Ethiopia and Live Aid concert
Damage to ozone layer discovered
Mikhail Gorbachev becomes Soviet Premier and introduces glasnost (openness with the West) and perestroika (economic restructuring)
PC Blakelock murdered during riots on Broadwater Farm estate in Tottenham, London
My Beautiful Laundrette film released (dir. Stephen Frears, screenplay Hanif Kureishi)

Jeanette Winterson, *Oranges Are Not the Only Fruit*
Miners' strike ends in defeat for strikers

1986 Abolition of Greater London Council and other
metropolitan county councils in England
Violence between police and protestors at Wapping, East
London, after Rupert Murdoch sacks 5000 print workers
Challenger shuttle explodes
Chernobyl nuclear accident
The US bombs Libya
Peter Ackroyd, *Hawksmoor*

1987 Capsizing of RORO ferry, *Herald of Free Enterprise*, off
Zeebrugge kills 193 people
London Stock Exchange and market collapse on 'Black
Monday'
Remembrance Sunday: 11 killed by Provisional IRA bomb
in Enniskillen
Ian McEwan, *The Child in Time*, which wins Whitbread
Novel Award
Jeanette Winterson, *The Passion*
16 October, hurricane hits the UK, largest storm for 300
years; winds of 94 km/hr in London, exceeding 100 km/hr
on south coast

1988 The US shoots down Iranian passenger flight
Pan Am flight 103 bombed over Lockerbie, 270 people
killed
Soviet troop withdrawals from Afghanistan begin
Salman Rushdie, *The Satanic Verses*

1989 Fatwa issued against Rushdie by Iranian leadership
(Ayatollah Khomeini) calling on all Muslims to attempt to
kill author for claimed blasphemy
Fall of Berlin Wall
Exxon Valdez oil disaster
Student protestors massacred in Tiananmen Square,
Bejing
Hillsborough Stadium disaster in which 96 football
fans die

Kazuo Ishiguro, *The Remains of the Day*, which wins Booker
Prize for Fiction
Jeanette Winterson, *Sexing the Cherry*
Sadie Smith adopts the name Zadie

1990   London poll tax riots
Fall of Thatcher; John Major becomes Conservative PM
Nelson Mandela freed from jail
Jeanette Winterson adapts *Oranges* for BBC television film
A. S. Byatt, *Possession*
Hanif Kureishi, *The Buddha of Suburbia*, which wins
Whitbread First Novel Prize
A. L. Kennedy, *Night Geometry and the Garscadden Trains*

1991   Soviet Union collapses
First Iraq War with 12-day Operation Desert Storm
Apartheid ended in South Africa
PM Major negotiates opt-out for Britain from European
Monetary Union and rejects Social Chapter of Maastricht
Treaty
Hypertext Markup Language (HTML) helps create the
World Wide Web
Hanif Kureishi: screenplays for *Sammy and Rosie Get Laid*
and *London Kills Me*
Pat Barker, *Regeneration*

1992   'Black Wednesday' stock market crisis when the UK forced
to exit European Exchange Rate Mechanism
Adam Thorpe, *Ulverton*

1993   14 February, black teenager Stephen Lawrence murdered
in Well Hall Road, London
With Downing Street Declaration, PM John Major and
Taoiseach Albert Reynolds commit Britain and Ireland to
joint Northern Ireland resolution
Film of Ishiguro's *The Remains of the Day*, starring Anthony
Hopkins and Emma Thompson
Irvine Welsh, *Trainspotting*

1994   Tony Blair elected leader of Labour Party following death
of John Smith

Channel Tunnel opens
Nelson Mandela elected President of South Africa
Provisional IRA and loyalist paramilitary cease-fire
Homosexual age of consent for men in the UK lowered
to 18
Mike Newell (dir.), *Four Weddings and a Funeral*
Jonathan Coe, *What a Carve Up!*
James Kelman, *How late it was, how late*, which wins Booker
Prize for Fiction
Irvine Welsh, *The Acid House*

1995 Oklahoma City bombing
Srebrenica massacre during Bosnian War
Pat Barker, *The Ghost Road*
Nicholas Hytner (dir.), *The Madness of King George*
Hanif Kureishi, *The Black Album*

1996 Cases of Bovine Spongiform Encephalitis (Mad Cow
Disease) in the UK
Divorce of Charles and Diana
Breaching cease-fire, Provisional IRA bombs London's
Canary Wharf and Central Manchester
Film of Irvine Welsh's *Trainspotting* (dir. Danny Boyle),
starring Ewan McGregor and Robert Carlyle
Graham Swift, *Last Orders*, which wins Booker Prize
Zadie Smith enters King's College, Cambridge, to read
English

1997 Tony Blair becomes Labour PM after landslide victory
Princess Diana dies in Paris car crash
Hong Kong returned to China by the UK
Jim Crace, *Quarantine*
Jonathan Coe, *The House of Sleep*, which wins Prix Médicis
Etranger (France)
Ian McEwan, *Enduring Love*
Iain Sinclair and Marc Atkins, *Lights Out for the Territory*
Aged 21 Zadie Smith graduates from Cambridge;
allegedly first novel sold to Hamish Hamilton on the basis
of 80 pages for £250,000 advance

1998 Good Friday Agreement on Northern Ireland and
Northern Ireland Assembly established
Twenty-eight people killed by splinter group Real IRA
bombing in Omagh
Sonny Bono Act extends copyright to lifetime plus 70
years
BFI/Channel 4 film *Stella Does Tricks*, released (screenplay
A. L. Kennedy)
Julian Barnes, *England, England*

1999 Euro currency adopted in mainland Europe
Macpherson Inquiry into Stephen Lawrence murder
accuses London's Metropolitan Police of institutional
racism
NATO bombs Serbia over Kosovo crisis
Welsh Assembly and Scottish Parliament both open
Thirty-one passengers killed in Ladbroke Grove train
disaster

2000 Zadie Smith appointed writer in residence at the Institute
of Contemporary Arts (ICA), London
Anti-globalization protest and riots in London
Hauliers and farmers blockade oil refineries in fuel price
protest in the UK
Kazuo Ishiguro, *When We Were Orphans*
Will Self, *How the Dead Live*
Zadie Smith, *White Teeth*, which wins Whitbread First
Novel Award, Commonwealth Writers First Book Prize,
Betty Trask Award and James Tait Black Memorial Prize

2001 Zadie Smith edits *May Anthology*
Labour Party under Blair re-elected to government
9/11 Al-Qaeda attacks on World Trade Center and
Pentagon
Bombing and invasion of Afghanistan
Riots in Oldham, Leeds, Bradford, and Burnley, Northern
England
Ian McEwan, *Atonement*
Beatle George Harrison dies after fight against cancer in
December

2002   Queen Mother dies aged 101

Rowan Williams nominated as new Archbishop of Canterbury

Bali terrorist bomb kills 202 people and injures a further 209

Inquiry concludes English general practitioner Dr Harold Shipman killed around 215 patients

Zadie Smith's *White Teeth* Channel 4 television adaptation broadcast in autumn

Zadie Smith until 2003 Fellow at the Radcliffe Institute for Advanced Study, Harvard University

Zadie Smith, *The Autograph Man*

2003   Invasion of Iraq and fall of Saddam Hussein

Death of UK government scientist, Dr David Kelly, and Hutton Inquiry

Worldwide threat of Severe Acute Respiratory Syndrome (SARS)

October 22, Zadie Smith delivers the 2003 Orange Word Lecture, 'E. M. Forster's Ethical Style: Love, Failure and the Good in Fiction,' at the Gielgud Theatre, London

Monica Ali *Brick Lane* Booker Prize shortlist

2004   Zadie Smith nominated by public for Hundred Great Black Britons list (voted as 77th)

BBC Director General Greg Dyke steps down over Kelly affair

Bombings in Madrid kill 190 people and injure over 1700

Zadie Smith attends Queen's inaugural lunch celebrating female excellence at Buckingham Palace

Expansion of NATO to include seven ex-Warsaw Pact countries

European Union expands to 25 countries as 8 ex-communist states join

Jonathan Coe, *Like a Fiery Elephant: The Story of B. S. Johnson*

Alan Hollinghurst, *The Line of Beauty*, which wins Booker Prize for Fiction

Andrea Levy, *Small Island*, which wins Orange Prize for Fiction

September, Zadie Smith marries Nick Laird in the Chapel, King's College, Cambridge
30 December, Asian Tsunami disaster with over 225,000 killed

2005 UK ban on foxhunting with dogs came into force
7 July or 7/7 London suicide bombings on transport system kill 52 and injure over 700 commuters in morning rush hour
Hurricane Katrina kills at least 1836 people and floods devastate New Orleans
After four failed bombings are detected, innocent Brazilian Jean Charles de Menezes is shot and killed by Metropolitan Police officers at Stockwell Underground Station
Ian McEwan, *Saturday*
Zadie Smith, *On Beauty*; shortlisted Man Booker Prize

2006 Jeanette Winterson awarded an OBE
Airline terror plot thwarted, causes major UK airline delays
Israel–Hezbollah war in Lebanon
Saddam Hussein executed by hanging in controversial circumstances
Alexander Litvineko, former Russian spy, dies in London from radioactive Polonium 2010 poisoning
Five prostitutes killed in Ipswich in a 6-week period
Zadie Smith, *On Beauty*, which wins Orange Prize for Fiction

2007 March–April British sailors seized and held by Iran before negotiated release
Smoking ban in public places in England and Wales
July sees worst floods in the UK for 60 years; South-West England hit hardest
Salman Rushdie knighted, an honour condemned by Iranian and Pakistani ministers
Tony Blair steps down

Gordon Brown becomes Prime Minister in unopposed contest
Zadie Smith moves to live in Rome, Italy

2008   Benazir Bhutto assassinated after return to campaign in Pakistan elections
UK Banking crisis beginning with Northern Rock
Credit crisis and worldwide economic recession
Housing slump in the UK
Boris Johnson defeats Ken Livingstone in dramatic London Mayoral election
Georgia and Russia fight South Ossetia war
Summer Olympics in Beijing, China
Mugabe government in Zimbabwe conceals election result and suppresses opposition
Barack Obama elected as 44th US President

2009   Hamas-Israeli War in Gaza

1

INTRODUCTION: SMITH AS CULTURAL ICON OR PRODUCTION?

This study introduces and analyses Zadie Smith's literary oeuvre, considering an author who despite her fame has published only three novels, supplemented by a modest output of shorter fiction (considered in Chapter 8). Although there is far more to Smith, she remains largely recognized for her first book, *White Teeth* (2000), initially reviewed and read as a positive, almost rapturous evocation of multicultural Britain. Dominic Head comments in 'Zadie Smith's *White Teeth*: Multiculturalism for the Millennium' that her 'evocations of post-colonial migrant experience in post-war Britain have been haunted by a sense of social failure' (107), and in its response sees in the novel an 'exemplary instance of this new phase' (109) reflecting multicultural hybridity. The novel features three often very troubled families; initially the racially mixed Joneses (of English stock, but also incorporating through the medium of Archie Jones' marriage the Jamaican Bowdens) and the Bengali Iqbals, and later the Anglo-Jewish Chalfens. As Hadley Freeman records in 'Words Smith,' conflicted families inspire Smith, regarding them as among '"the oldest structures in the world. How can all that stuff not be utterly compelling?"' (356) Smith details their interlocking narratives and sketches various characters they encounter, largely in Willesden, north-west London, reflecting on contemporary multi-racial *mores* often satirically, exhibiting a knowing, generally interrogative quality. Formally, Smith adapts several traditional forms, the comic picaresque inter-fused with a family saga, adding narratives of identity and authenticity. She evinces other quasi-Dickensian qualities, both structurally and stylistically, highlighting cultural contradictions and oddity.

Dysfunctional personal relationships and the impossible quest for some viable sense of one's identity recur in the second novel, *The Autograph Man* (2002), set in Mountjoy, a Jewish northern London suburb.[1] The narrative is centred on Alex Li-Tandem, half Chinese through his father, Li-Jin, and half English-Jewish through his mother, Sarah, and a transatlantic, commodified trade of autographs, implicated in a much wider cult of celebrity. Alex's overriding 'instinct was to detest groupings of all kinds—social, racial, national, or political—he had never joined so much as a swimming club' (167). The overlapping and recurrent themes are broad, including the obsessional, celebrity, complex family and cultural identities, and the habitual nature of love and friendship. Enmeshed in a set of relationships retained from early adolescence, although initially Alex abjures his inherited traditions apart from hypochondriacally motivated visits to Chinese doctors, finally he explores the demands of his putative Jewishness. From early adolescence Alex (like Smith herself) has been obsessed with old films and their stars, fixating on the now reclusive celebrity, Kitty Alexander, particularly her 1952 musical *The Girl from Peking*. This obsession, his father's premature death and the recovery of the facts of Alex's drug-induced three-day memory loss (from which he emerges at the beginning) are the plot's mainsprings. Other themes include London's plural culture, the populist degradation of social and ethical frameworks, the nature and effect of celebrity, reclusive lifestyles, and the demands on a series of reluctant post-adolescent men of adulthood. Alex undergoes an epiphany after visiting Kitty in America, who returns with him to London.

Smith's third novel, *On Beauty* (2005), incorporates E. M. Forster's *Howards End* (1910) as one of its explicit intertextual models (its 'hypotext'). Jessica Murphy Moo in 'Zadie, Take Three' reports that Smith 'wanted to return to the fiction she'd been brought up on to see if it could reflect contemporary concerns.' In her acknowledgements Smith highlights Forster's influence. His novel's title provides Howard Belsey's first name. As Heller McAlpin explains in '*Howards End*, Her Beginning,' 'Howard, the son of a British butcher, fled the narrowness of his father's white working-class London for the United States, where he has married Kiki Simmonds, an imposing

African American hospital administrator from Florida: "A goddess of the everyday"' (R8). Howard is an art historian, professor at the prestigious American east-coast Wellington College. Throughout, in Forsterian fashion, parallels, intersections, ironic juxtapositions and coincidences abound. Smith's plot concerns the encounter of Howard's mixed-race family with that of Sir Monty Kipps, rival art historian, and expert on Rembrandt, on which topic he has produced a recent book. The eldest Belsey child, Jerome, serves as Monty's intern in London, living temporarily with this family of Caribbean origin near Kilburn. After a Forsterian misunderstanding concerning Howard and the putative engagement of Jerome and the Kipps' daughter, Victoria, ironically Monty is invited as visiting scholar to Wellington. Howard is contradictory, multiply paradoxical. In lecturing on visual aesthetics he deconstructs and explicitly refuses any concept of beauty. As a husband he casually betrays Kiki a second time despite his earlier contrition. He seems alienated from his three mixed-race children, unable to communicate. As many critics indicate, Smith ventriloquizes her husband's poetry in the novel. Interestingly in his poem 'On Beauty' Nick Laird writes 'Speech is beautifully useless' (43), an observation that informs Smith's narrative and its rivalries, offset by the intellectual and emotional possibilities of beauty as an ethical concept and practical code.

All three books incorporate structures and themes, many of which feature in Smith's short fiction, concerned largely with family, community and possibilities (and impossibilities) of belonging. Other intercalated overarching themes and motifs include the extremities of belief; the demands of systems of faith, both secular and theological; the vicissitudes of friendship and affection; the disruptive nature of seduction, passion and sexual love; the comic possibilities of everyday realism; the simultaneously banal and heroic qualities of such quotidian human routines; and the often unexpected contradictions of an age exploring both diversity and a liberal version of multiculturalism. Interpretatively, one can exaggerate the positive qualities of cultural identity and heritage in Smith, over-determining such themes. As Smith says concerning *White Teeth* in an interview with Kathleen O'Grady,

The characters in the book are [traumatized]. That whole kind of 60s, 70s, liberation ethic that you will be released by knowing your roots, that you will discover yourself, I just always thought was a crock basically, and it's partly true, but your roots come with baggage. And the baggage isn't always fun.

(106)

This study explores both the implications of and presumptions underlying the dynamics of various critical responses, and the relevance of certain historical and cultural contexts, for as Pierre Bourdieu reminds us in *The Field of Cultural Production: Essays on Art and Literature* (1993) 'To understand the practices of writers and artists, and not least their products, entails understanding that they are the result of the meeting of two histories: the history of the positions they occupy and the history of their dispositions' (61). I intend to examine Smith's writing in terms of Bourdieu's sense of a synthesis of elements such as influence, agency and social identity, fully contextualizing her complex takings of position.

Certain key presumptions have shaped Smith's public image, creating a profile that irks the author. An overarching, often essentialist concept of the postcolonial has dominated many readings of Smith's work, often assuming their own progressive status. Many critics regard the first novel as representing directly in uncomplicated fashion a reformulated, multicultural Britain, often assuming a cultural struggle between East and West, and that colonial and postcolonial identities have created a 'newness' regarded as unique to this recent historical phase. Claudia Buonaiuto and Maria Castella in 'A Western/Eastern Map of London' align the novel with the work of Homi K. Bhabha (103) in specifying characters 'angrily conscious of living the sadness and melancholic experience of uprootedness' (104), achieving 'a borderless space of diasporic dispersion and diffusion' (106). For Phyllis Lassner in *Colonial Strangers: Women Writing the End of the British Empire* (2004), 'Smith's narrative engraves the origins of a revolutionary postcolonial Britain on a map of history' (198). Raphael Dalleo in 'Colonization in Reverse: *White Teeth* as Caribbean Novel' admits that concepts of hybridity are 'the target of parody and critique throughout the second half [...]' (93), yet sees Smith's depiction of London as 'Caribbeanized' (93), the children's language inflections representing 'the Global Caribbean' (95). For such commentators her work's success testifies to various combinations of the following: first, the nation's successful cultural adaptation; second, an ongoing racism and inequality evidenced in its themes and contextual descriptions; or, third, the radicalization of Britain by the very progressive process of hybridity identified (but largely configured as permeation of tradition, or the mainstream). Smith's own mixed-race origins and her observations about a very mixed migrant community are prioritized. Such readings neglect many of the other explicit focal points of her work; they ignore *White Teeth*'s self-conscious equivocations, rather foregrounding certain ideological convictions of the critic. Such critical and theoretical positions often share a sense of both the weight of the past and victimhood found in migrant literature, but in Smith's case one might suggest that such takings of position are themselves subject to scepticism and comic interrogation. In ' "Happy Multicultural Land"? The Implications of an "Excess of Belonging" in Zadie Smith's *White Teeth*,' Molly Thompson points out that 'Because the narrative is predominantly written in a humorous, buoyant tone, referring several times to a "Happy Multicultural Land", it could be mistaken as a representation of a world of inter-racial equanimity' (123). Thompson argues that Smith problematizes multiculturalism (123), finding rather a sense of cultural fragmentation (134) and globalized anxiety (137). Thompson indicates dangers in reading culture through a 'conflation of roots and origin' (129), exemplified in the palpable inadequacies of such accounts in *White Teeth*. In ' "We're All English Now Mate Like It or Lump It": The Black/Britishness of Zadie Smith's *White Teeth*,' Tracey L. Walters wonders why the book and author have been regarded as 'British as opposed to Black British?' (314), suggesting that it may stem from Smith's refusal to isolate black experience.[2] Jonathan P. A. Sell in 'Chance and Gesture in Zadie Smith's *White Teeth* and *The Autograph Man*: A Model for Multicultural Identity?' refuses to gauge the 'multi- or mono-culturality' of characters or evaluate degrees of ethnicity 'because any such assessment would rely on an essentialist view of identity which Smith's novels quite plainly reject' (28). Even more importantly, Smith herself struggles with the emphases or dynamics of such essentialist interpretative parameters in a journalistic piece where she reconsiders her several assessments over time of the significance of Zora Neale Hurston, whom she identifies as a writer who needs to be judged as exhibiting aesthetic qualities primarily rather than a judgement based simply on her ethnicity and that of her characters. Smith concludes in 'What Does Soulful Mean?' that 'Like all readers, I want my limits to be drawn by my own sensibilities, not by my melanin count. These forms of criticism that make black women the privileged readers of a black woman writer go against Hurston's own grain.' In a recent essay, 'F. Kafka, Everyman,' Smith writes, 'What is Muslimness? What is Polishness? What is Englishness? These days we all find our anterior legs flailing before us. We're all insects, all *Ungeziefer*, now' (5). Moreover, Smith makes clear in a newspaper article on the white rapper Enimem that an aesthetic statement ought not to be confused with life and intentionality, particularly as Smith insists, 'novels make it easy for you; they say very clearly, and between two hardback covers, I Am A Novel' (16). For Smith, fiction is not reducible to life. In 'Fail Better,' Smith notes that for writers, 'Personality is much more than autobiographical detail, it's our way of processing the world, our way of being, and it cannot be artificially removed from our activities.' Thus she resists glib conflations of her own identity and her fiction.

In *Absolutely Postcolonial: Writing Between the Singular and the Specific* (2001), Peter Hallward argues that many postcolonial critics are prone to assumptions based on the notion of 'conformity or cultural authenticity' (335), adopting an essentialist view of history, judging everything through a differential relationship with the West, ironically rendering the latter's culture as central, at least implicitly, effectively neglecting a full range of diversities (xiii). Thus the outsider is accorded victimhood. As Vamik D. Volkan says in *The Need to Have Enemies and Allies, from Clinical Practice to International Relationships* (1994) in order to believe in and sustain their victim status, such individuals and groups must have 'chosen traumas' and 'chosen glories' (7), adopting precisely the polarized view of the world that Smith parodies in *White Teeth*. Central to this is Samad Iqbal, alternately self-pitying and arrogant, vacillating between an idealized Islamic identity (that he fails ever to sustain) and numerous indulgences seen as typifying the West's corruption. His victimhood and sense of oppression are mirrored in the figures attracted to KEVIN, an Islamic militant group, including his son, Millat. Smith rejects this view, preferring more positive paradigms of migrant selfhood, for which implicit position she has been attacked. Smith may problematize the search for identity, but suggests it is not simply a postcolonial quest, nor a longing that can be satisfied. Importantly, her novels foreground the domestic, relating directly to a far broader tradition, for as Rosemary Marangoly George says in *The Politics of Home: Postcolonial Relocations and Twentieth-Century Fiction* (1996), 'the (re)writing of home reveals the ideological struggles that are staged every day in the construction of subjects and their understanding of home-countries. The search for the location in which the self is "at home" is one of the primary objects of twentieth-century fiction in English' (3).

After Tony Blair's so-called 'Cool Britannia' rebranding of Britain, just as the celebrations for the new millennium had petered out, a new age was marked for many reviewers and literary critics by the anticipated emergence of writer-in-the-making, Zadie Smith. While Smith rushed to finish *White Teeth* as Rebecca Dyer indicates in 'Generations of Black Londoners: Echoes of 1950s Caribbean Migrants' Voices in Victor Headley's *Yardie* and Zadie Smith's *White Teeth*'. 'Excerpts of the novel began to appear in 1999 in the *New Yorker* and immediately following its publication in 2000, Smith was fêted as the voice of a "New England" [...]' (92). Her publisher engaged in a slick commercial process lubricated by author access, adopting what Bourdieu describes as 'the overt form of publicity' of the business world which has displaced the more overt, 'euphemistic' process that once characterized publishers (77). Smith's literary presence was shaped in conjunction with the media, exemplified by Stephanie Merritt who identifies in a particularly brash fashion Smith's cultural significance in her interview's suggestive title 'She's young, black, British—and the first publishing sensation of the millennium' which appeared on 16 January 2000 in Britain's leading liberal-left Sunday newspaper, the *Observer*. Merritt describes Smith and her forthcoming novel in the by-line: 'At 24 she is already being compared to the likes of Salman Rushdie. Zadie Smith talks to Stephanie Merritt about her high-profile first novel.' With double irony the journalist adds, 'The hype began in the autumn of 1997. Zadie Smith was 21 and just down from Cambridge when her first novel was sold on a mere 80 pages for an advance rumoured to be in the region of £250,000.' The grounds of a contemporary myth were being seeded, one in which those such as Merritt participated openly. Smith was being manufactured in a specific fashion first seen in the United States, as described by Joe Moran in *Star Authors: Literary Celebrity in America* (2000). 'The increasing importance of book publicity in promoting authors as "personalities" is therefore a symptom of the continuing integration of literary production into the entertainment industry, making authors and books part of the cultural pervasiveness of celebrity as a market mechanism of monopoly capitalism [. . .]' (41). Like many others Merritt was enjoined in such a process, resulting in Smith becoming culturally significant, without ever having completed a novel. She was celebrated precisely for her youth, ethnicity, intelligence, and ironically even the suddenness of her emergence from obscurity. As Moran says typically this elaborate process may evoke 'superior talent or even genius, free of external determination [. . .]' (9), but in truth is neither accidental nor a matter of luck. Rather it results from a late capitalist phase of a process that Moran drawing on the work of Bourdieu calls the well-established 'phenomenon of literary celebrity' (1), creating what he describes as 'charismatic illusion' (5). Smith's initial media presence was sustained, intense, and part of print and television culture's compulsion to create, sustain and finally undermine media-driven celebrity. Smith endured this hard sell reluctantly.

Moran suggests that around 80 per cent of books produced annually are failures, those receiving full promotional treatment largely being chosen by those managing sales (38). Creating such a high profile requires a very specific image (identity) responding to (reaffirming) the zeitgeist. Smith's youth, gender, ethnicity and intellectual and cultural credibility explain the eagerness of the marketing machine. Her life was transformed. Her first novel proved seminal. Smith (albeit unwillingly) became part of a phenomenon, which created a strong brand image, dependent on publicity processes maintaining a high profile, very akin to producing music celebrities such as the Spice Girls or singers on a plethora of reality television shows offering apparent stardom. With increasing rapidity, in each new generation publishers and the music industry use the 'rags to riches motif' to create new stars.

Many commentators highlighted Smith's mixed race or 'hybridity,' the reported 'double-first' in English from Cambridge (which she would later vehemently deny with embarrassment), her striking good looks, and her youth. Despite Smith's well-publicized reservations, ironically her first novel's very success has meant international celebrity, and for much of the media she became a cultural icon. Paradoxically towards the end of a century whose last half was characterized in the West by relative affluence, influenced by several decades where intellectual culture had been shaped by identity politics, in the 1990s the liberal intelligentsia developed a new consensus, an obsession with personal victimhood and a notion of trauma. Smith transcended these coordinates of abjection, becoming a symbol of multicultural hope and positivity. Through her image the idea (or ideal) of a reborn nation could be articulated, at least implicitly. She combines variously the new (youth and hybrid origins, the latter testament to the positive effects of migration), the ongoing radicality of gender (a young woman in the public domain) with the traditional (bookishness, Cambridge, and an explicitly traditional literariness). Add immense financial rewards to her youthful literary success and her meteoric rise begins to acquire the status of an urban myth. By September 2005 Jessica Murphy Moo in 'Zadie, Take Three' notes 'her celebrity—some might say notoriety—has taken up copious real estate in London's gossip columns.' Her presence also permeated newspapers across North America and the world, her image attaining iconicity, becoming marketable in terms of both literal and cultural capital, as the first quintessentially British twenty-first-century writer. In a Public Broadcasting Service (PBS) interview later transcribed Smith positions *White Teeth*'s immense success as part of a millennial zeitgeist: 'It was very fortunate timing. End-of-the-century books catch people in an end-of-the-century mood. The possibility of a community which involved so many different people and could be workable was a very optimistic idea.' Perhaps that moment was more about transition, renewal and rebirth.

Curiously, Smith often (but not consistently) refutes claims that her first novel, *White Teeth*, is fundamentally autobiographical despite certain clear topographical indications: first, it is set in Willesden (also used in earlier writing as we shall see), precisely the area of her upbringing; second, it begins on 1 January 1975, the year of her birth; and, third, Irie Jones, like Smith, has a Jamaican mother and white English father. Claire Squires reports in *Zadie Smith's* White Teeth: *A Reader's Guide* (2002), 'While Smith denies that her characters are direct portraits of her own experience, she makes it clear that details of her autobiography have contributed to the themes [. . .]' (9). Elsewhere it is argued that other contexts are more precisely taken from Smith's experience in Willesden, even more specific aspects than a 'mixed-race' identity and notions of cultural inheritance. In *Menace in Europe: Why the Continent's Crisis is America's Too* (2006), Claire Berlinski draws explicitly on her former relationship with Zia Rahman, brother of Smith's former boyfriend Jimmi Rahman, to interrogate and refute aspects of Smith's novel. Berlinski uses interviews with Zia to apparently demonstrate how *White Teeth* can be situated as part of a new wave of ethnic or black fiction that adopts an overly positive position towards prejudice and racism and therefore lacks a certain authenticity. However, the form of Berlinski's purported interview with her partner—with its mixture of direct and reported speech—suggests perhaps the use of judicious editing on Berlinski's part to offer a partly ventriloquized opinion.

> 'Conspicuously absent from *White Teeth*,' Zia said to me, 'is the anger. Where have all the angry books gone? These new books don't feel like Hanif Kureishi.' British novels, Zia reflected, no longer 'talk about bitter experiences, about experiences of racism, domestic violence, chauvinism, and if they do, it's made saccharine, sanitized. We do not see the very dark aspects of racism. That's something that divides the book from reality—the real experience.' And strangely, he noted, these new British novels are written by women, not men.
>
> (57–8)

Smith seems less concerned with autobiographical accuracy since far more important for her is the moral or ethical possibilities of the novel, with parallels in other familiar popular cultural forms. In an interview undertaken at the time of the PBS broadcast of *White Teeth*, when asked about the kernel of the idea for the novel, Smith refers obliquely to the kind of naïve and well-meaning characters played by James Stewart [as, for instance, in *Mr. Smith Goes to Washington* (1939) dir. Frank Capra] regarding her initial major character, Archie Jones, and the provenance of the book,

> I wanted to write a book about a man who gets through the century in a good way. He lives a good life by accident. That's where Archie came from. He's a kind of Jimmy Stewart-ish character, maybe a bit simpler than that. The rest of it formed itself around him with lots of bits and bobs from my reading and my own life. It was a kind of mishmash, as first novels tend to be. [Laughs]

Significantly, many of Smith's cultural referents and influences are broadly filmic, deriving from film culture generally as well as specific movies, an influence central to *The Autograph Man*. Smith draws from this field certain fundamental conceits including the struggle of innate virtue or goodness with cynicism and ennui, an economy of celebrity and stardom, and also from the moving image and its dialogue a cinematic precision (adapting aspects of a filmic realism rather than solely textually narrative versions). This allows the interplay of deeper underlying emotions, a visceral topography of communities. Such aspects progress through her novels, influencing certain cultural dispositions and emphases. Certainly, if one considers Smith's comparison with Jimmy Stewart cited above, in *White Teeth* Archie Jones presents a British, domestic, far more unglamorous version of Stewart's naiveté and belief in practical interventionism. Mr Smith as a leader in the Boy Rangers is drawn into being radical by corruption (the American Boy Scouts refused the filmmakers' use of their name because of their fear of being associated with a movie with radical political implications); Archie focuses on the pragmatic and practical (like an overgrown, enthusiastic Boy Scout, typified in his being in his element in preparing for apparently all contingencies for the hurricane that hits Britain and which ironically nearly kills him). He abjures radicalism amidst the confusions of his world. Despite the filmic influence his character is inflected differently in part because of both the form of this comic novel and its setting. Archie is emphatically un-heroic, exhibiting an essential Englishness, his presence incongruous and the environments he moves through quotidian and banal (contrasting and undermining some of the remarkable things he has either done or encountered).

Events subsequent to the novel's publication have served to shift its initial reception and reading. The events of 9/11, the Madrid and London bombings, and the wars in Afghanistan and Iraq, precisely 'the newly dark lights of the age,' which James Wood refers to in 'Tell Me How Does it Feel?,' allowed people a space for reflection, considering both the magnitude of historical events and their capacity to be brutish, not entirely rational and yet palpably material in their destructive effects. These refuse the local, extend like ripples far beyond the physical or psychic damage of those closely involved. In 'This is How it Feels to Me,' Smith responds to Wood's critical attack upon her by first accepting that his term 'hysterical realism' was a 'painfully accurate term for [...] novels like my own *White Teeth*,' and continues by both referring to the tenor of the times and reminding him of her acceptance of certain of his objections to certain kinds of contemporary fiction.

> These are hysterical times; any novel that aims at hysteria will now be effortlessly outstripped—this was Wood's point, and I'm with him on

it. In fact, I have agreed with him several times before, in public and in private, but I appreciate that he feared I needed extra warning; that I might be sitting in my Kilburn bunker planning some 700-page generational saga set on an incorporated McDonald's island north of Tonga. Actually, I am sitting here in my pants, looking at a blank screen, finding nothing funny, scared out of my mind like everybody else, smoking a family-sized pouch of Golden Virginia.

In her work she stresses that trauma is not culturally imbued, but can be shared empathically. Certain realities transcend difference even though interpreted at an individual level, which perspective permeates her fiction. In each novel the architectonics are interwoven with a plethora of action, dialogue and memory, creating a historiography of both personal and cultural identity, through which Smith creates a phenomenology of the tribulations of identity and the self in a highly complex, constantly changing social milieu. In myriad, apparently ephemeral details, Smith mixes symbolism with eclectic realism, social coordinates transformed by compulsiveness and repetition, creating an 'obsessional' mimesis of life's minutiae.

2

A BIOGRAPHICAL READING

Despite Smith's literary success, not only is she still young, but since publishing her first novel she has become both rich and extremely famous. *White Teeth* not only attracted great critical attention, but was nominated for and won a number of awards and prizes: the Commonwealth Writers Prize (Overall Winner, Best First Book), the *Guardian* First Book Award, the Whitbread First Novel Award, and additionally two EMMAs (or BT Ethnic and Multicultural Media Awards) for Best Book/Novel and Best Female Media Newcomer. It was also short-listed for the Author's Club First Novel Award, the Orange Prize for Fiction, and the *Mail on Sunday*/John Llewellyn Rhys Prize. The very breadth of Smith's novels and stories, particularly their intellectual and aesthetic points of reference (however one judges the success of such engagements) suggest that any autobiographical account of Smith must involve certain complexities, one being the relationship of her upbringing to her writing and identity, another being her own view of both her fiction and the fame it has attracted. She seems not to have anticipated such celebrity, and certainly its surprising and often perverse qualities are very much a central subject of her second novel which is set against a backdrop of north London suburban normality (albeit with the usual oddities and quiddities of urban life). Smith recognizes a fluid history with often paradoxical influence on individuals, much as B. S. Johnson, who observes aphoristically in *Aren't You Rather Young to be Writing Your Memoirs?* (1973), published just 2 years before Smith's birth, 'Change is a condition of life. [...] Change simply *is*' (17). In this light as will become clear to the attentive reader, various aspects of her life resonate both implicitly and explicitly in her writing.

Smith was born in the Royal Free Hospital, Hampstead, on 27 October 1975 to a relatively modest family, both in a social and financial sense. As a writer associated so intimately with London Smith, her relation to the city is a quintessential one precisely in one subtle and perhaps radically different way from even a writer like Charles Dickens, who has been traditionally so closely associated with the metropolis. On a personal level Smith experienced no epiphany of conscious arrival as Dickens had done (and to which he so often returns in his fiction). Like John Betjeman, Evelyn Waugh and Virginia Woolf among others, Smith originated in the metropolis. This offers an essential, often neglected quality to even such a diversity of writers, a point of uninterrupted origin, quite unlike the migrants Smith describes, but of course, as they insist on pointing out, so very like their offspring. Importantly, Smith's consciousness was formed within the city's bounds, which may account for a marked sense of sub-textual rootedness about her first novel, despite its being concerned with concerns and characters that would appear to have a propensity for the opposite: variously postcolonial migrants, others like Archie, Poppy Burt-Jones and Joyce Chalfen who have all moved to the city, in contrast to Irie, Ryan Topps, Millat, Magid and various other minor characters, all of whom may well deplore aspects of Britain, but seem almost intuitively to belong to its capital as new generation of Londoners. This is one central paradox underlying Smith's description of the postcolonial city. Both the narrator and this younger generation seem comfortable with the mix of locality, odd social practices and the network of public and private acquaintance that holds together urban/suburban life. This is true too of *The Autograph Man*, where a sub-culture rooted in adolescent memories and a shared culture emerging from a common Judaism thrive. Both of the first two novels exemplify this radical view of belonging, as part of their underlying, mostly unspoken network of interconnectivities (for like Dickens Smith exudes a mostly implicit set of consonances and consanguinities).

In some ways Smith's family reflects certain historical and sociological changes characterizing the post-war scene, part of a larger process which Smith describes in 'E. M. Forster, Middle Manager' as 'England's transformation from elegant playground of the fortunate few to the mass factory of everybody.' Like many others, her mother, Yvonne McLean, was a migrant to England from the old colonial possessions. Yvonne arrived aged fifteen from Jamaica in 1969, marrying at twenty-one Harvey Smith, an older Englishman. Like so many others in the last quarter of the twentieth century, Smith's mother would acquire almost unexpectedly a new bourgeois status, part of Thatcher's expansion of the professional classes and their value system through a property-owning democracy. These complex processes are undercurrents of the generational changes that are part of Smith's fiction's subtext. Smith's mother aspired in career terms through the expanding higher education system. Briefly a fashion model and subsequently a secretary, she undertook a course concerned with Youth and Community Studies at Brunel University, subsequently studying further to qualify for psychoanalytic practice. To date, she continues to work in the National Health Service (NHS) as a psychotherapist and as a consultant to parents for the charity Young Minds. Although clearly strong women influenced both Smith's ambitions and later her confident self-belief, her writing suggests that both parents moulded her character in different ways. In numerous profiles and interviews Smith is described variously as quiet, awkward and reticent as a child and adolescent, drawn to old Hollywood films and musicals. She has even referred to being inspired by the crucial central role of women in the Bloomsbury Group in her deciding upon her youthful ambition of becoming a writer.

Born in Bromley, London in 1925, Smith's father, Harvey, was for a while a commercial photographer in Soho and later a paper salesman. He was more than 20 years older than his second wife, meeting her at a party. According to the account of Kevin Patrick Mahoney, Smith finds the very idea of her father at a party somewhat unlikely, which informs the implicit incredulity of White Teeth's mapping out of Archie's epiphanic meeting with his future wife, an unlikely coupling in terms of temperament more than any difference of origin. As Smith explained in her interview with Diane Rehm, Harvey and Yvonne married within four weeks of meeting according to Smith. Like Irie, Archie's daughter, Smith grew up in Willesden, an area which is part of suburban north-west London that attracted large numbers of new migrants from the 1970s onwards. As Smith says in a radio interview on 'To the Best of Our Knowledge' broadcast on Wisconsin Public Radio and published by

PBS, 'It's a very Asian area – Pakistani and Indian. I suppose it seems exotic now, but it was a very normal London upbringing.'

Importantly, Smith does not regard herself as an immigrant. In contrast, at least for many interpreting the significance of her successes, Smith's ethnic identity offers them something that can be read as either more exotic or at least more to do with the zeitgeist of multiculturalism and hybridity. Both *White Teeth* and her mother's migrant status have encouraged the weaving of an interpretative consensus for many that assumes Smith simply articulates a narrative of marginality, of an authenticity rooted in the area in which she grew up. Smith sees her own experience as among such people, but perhaps differently inflected in certain subtle ways. In the Masterpiece Theatre PBS interview she insists,

> The people in *White Teeth* are immigrants. I'm not an immigrant, so it's a different experience. But I was around people who had that experience, who felt separated or cut in two, who had moved from one country to another, who had that sense of leading two lives.

This recognizes a defining split in people's experience, a bifurcation of their lives, which Samad makes emphatic by dividing his twin sons, sending Magid back to the subcontinent. Smith concedes that many migrants from her community do understand themselves as divided, moving from one country to another, changing culturally their emphases. They experienced in effect two lives, and judging by *White Teeth* Smith recognizes that their coordinates often vacillate between a culture of origin and a changing British culture, influenced both by migration and numerous factors of late capitalism and globalization.

According to Smith's account to Laura Barton her family's roots were 'basically sort of lower middle class' (8). She writes of her father in 'Dead Man Laughing' that he was 'a creative man whose frequent attempts at advancement were forever thwarted, or so he felt, by his accent and his background, his lack of education, connections, luck.' Moreover, Smith in 'Learning Curve,' a profile published in September 2005 in the Guardian, explains to Aida Edemariam that Smith aspired to change her social class, an impulse she incorporates as a major theme in her first novel.

> I think when I was growing up I was very very aware of not being middle-class; much more aware than of being black as an unusual thing.

I never wanted to be white, but I always wanted to be middle-class. I liked the big house, I liked the piano, I liked the cats, the cello lessons.

Impressions were important to her. The first child of her father's second marriage, she was christened Sadie and so as to appear more exotic at fourteen she decided to alter her birth name. She has a half-sister and a half-brother, and two younger brothers, Luke and Ben. Initially, she was educated in two state schools, Malorees Junior School and Hampstead Comprehensive School, completing her studies in the summer of 1994. During her time at the latter establishment her parents divorced, potentially a traumatic experience for a teenager.

Mahoney records her relative timidity at school, and an avoidance of the 'unpleasantnesses' of schooldays through reading. It is reported that among her favourite childhood books was C. S. Lewis' *The Lion, The Witch and The Wardrobe*, and even later in life she is reported to have a penchant for the work of Philip Pullman, so fantasy novels feature among her influences despite her own determinedly realist, if comic, tendencies. Clearly, she was an avid, if at first undiscriminating, reader, passionate about all kinds of fictional texts. In a gossipy (slightly scurrilous) profile which appeared in the *London Standard Lite* Sebastian Shakespeare reports in 'The Secret Life of Zadie Smith (without evidence or point of reference) perhaps apocryphally that 'Zadie was a gifted child who won a national writing competition aged eight and had a short story published in a magazine aged 12.' Smith's own literary tastes remain eclectic. She lists Kafka, Nabokov, Updike, David Foster Wallace, and especially E. M. Forster. In 'Love, actually' she attempts to assess the raw visceral impact of the latter upon her at age eleven:

> EM Forster's *A Room with a View* was my first intimation of the possibilities of fiction: how wholly one might feel for it and through it, how much it could do to you. I felt it was very good and that the reading of it had done me some good. I loved it. I was too young, at 11, to realise serious people don't speak of novels this way.

One of Smith's other early passions was Hollywood, particularly musicals, and her bedroom was plastered with different stars, many from the 1930s and 1940s. In 'Dead Man Laughing' she recalls aged nine watching with her father as comedian Tommy Cooper collapsed and died on-stage on live television. She also describes her father's comic tastes, and their common interests such as comedian Tony Hancock and the series *Fawlty Towers*.

From *White Teeth* one surmises that at least one event impacted in late childhood. On the BBC's evening weather forecast on 15 October 1987 the meteorological expert, Michael Fish, reassured a woman caller that the hurricane she feared would not occur. In the early hours of 16 October one of the largest storms for 300 years hit the United Kingdom, London included. Unusual wind velocity of 94 km/hr was recorded at Heathrow airport not far from Smith's childhood home (and in excess of 100 km/hr on the south coast). Nationwide sixteen people were killed as a direct result of the storm. Over fifteen million trees were uprooted. The events inscribed themselves onto the national consciousness, one of the historical coordinates that Smith may use comically, but she does so to suggest a notion of overlapping public and private trauma.

One presumes more minor personal irritations from her admission in 'You are in Paradise' that 'I am an allergic person by nature: cats, dogs, horses, mosquitoes, and all facial products.' Iris Jones' concerns as regards her size and weight may also reflect aspects of Smith's own early years, a self-consciousness that seems at odds with her later glamorous public image. During her teenage years Smith is reported to have been overweight, and Shakespeare claims that as a consequence even as recently as 2002 Smith was 'desperately insecure about her weight (whisper it quietly but she once used to be size 18),' something to which Smith alludes herself. Both the *Vogue* interview and that with Mahoney refer both directly and obliquely to her excessive weight as a teenager. Consequently she avoided the social aspects of school life. Yet despite this reserve, Smith demonstrated an active interest in performance, and this included specifically both jazz singing and tap dance. According to Sarah Lyall in 'A Good Start,' Smith saw her younger self as awkward and not overly clever. 'She was "a bit of a stoner" as a teenager, she says. When she announced at high school that she wanted to go on to Cambridge, the teacher literally threw a book at her in disbelief.' Interestingly, Smith found the self-confidence to make her ambition a reality, itself an indication of her perseverance and intellectual acuity at a young age.

More broadly, during Smith's childhood and adolescence Thatcherism reshaped both London and the wider nation, with its rampant individualism, its so-called free market economics, its inflationary pressures and its Little or Middle England rhetoric that contradicted its continued tacit support for the opening of the labour market to migrants even though the government introduced apparently restrictive limits enshrined in the British Nationality Bill in 1981. In the early 1980s a sense of racism was evident in the causes of the outbreak of riots in Brixton, Holloway and elsewhere, leading to some conciliatory gestures on the part of the government. However, in London life was far from harmonious generally and more specifically in terms of community race relations, the latter exhibited particularly in terms of relationship between the police and the black community in London. After 18 January 1981 that community was galvanized by New Cross house fire when fourteen young black people were killed, and others injured in a blaze which engulfed a house during a joint birthday party. At the time evidence of an accelerant (possibly the residue of a petrol bomb) appeared to have been found by investigators, but the police appeared either inept or unconcerned. Its response was felt to be racist and 2 months later an estimated 10,000 people led by Darcus Howe marched on Downing Street in protest at the perceived racist attack and the police reaction. Despite broad opposition Thatcher changed the cultural and ideological emphasis, limiting of the power of the trade unions and opposing forces such as the Greater London Council or GLC (which very publicly posted London's rising unemployment figures on the side of its headquarters, County Hall, facing directly the Houses of Parliament) that was abolished in 1985.

Although such public events are often peripheral, they are implicit (such as the influence on history of Empire and the Second World War that subtends *White Teeth*). There remain many fragmentary allusions through which cumulatively Smith demonstrates an acute historical awareness, well illustrated in several examples from *White Teeth*. Samad listens to the announcement of the assassination of Indira Gandhi on the World Service. When he dismisses her leadership and India as a 'cesspit' (197), he is reminded by Alsana of the suffering and deaths that will ensue in both India and Bangladesh (198). He also watches the bringing down of the Berlin Wall, expressing his doubts about a united Germany, referring back to his own wartime experiences (239–40). According to Nina Shen Rastogi in *Zadie Smith's White*

Teeth (2003), 'Smith makes an ironic point in showing how disconnected the Joneses and Iqbals are from the "historic occasion" they watch' despite history's impact on their lives (50). Smith has Poppy Burt-Jones, the teacher of the children of Samad and Archie Jones (his friend from shared wartime service), acknowledge the London council's part in resisting the government cuts in education spending. '"Music budgets get cut every year until this year there was nothing left to cut *from*. It's got to the point where they're putting desks in cupboards and calling them offices. If it wasn't for the GLC, there wouldn't even be a desk"' (157). In the rhetoric Samad uses to counter a mad woman on the streets he is emboldened by the GLC's leader (who incidentally lived near Willesden during Smith's early years), 'taking his inspiration now from that other great North London street-preacher, Ken Livingstone' (179).

Clearly, Smith grew up in an age of public and private contradictions, many of which haunt her work. Not only did the domestic political agenda change in Britain, but from the mid-1980s onwards there was a certain ephemeral quality that haunted this new digital age, where the provenance of television images became publicly suspect (perhaps most infamously in the BBC new coverage of Orgreave on 18 June 1984 during the Miners' Strike which was reversed to evoke unprovoked violence on the part of the strikers). Many such uncertainties inform the mood of the first novel in its apprehension of history. Smith mocks the portentousness of official, public accounts of the past, for although for instance in *White Teeth* in one section the year 1984 is paired with that of 1857 and the Indian Mutiny, in this section the narrator says there are 'No better historians, no better experts in the world than Archie and Samad when it came to *The Post-War Reconstruction and Growth of O'Connell's Pool House*' (245), which is followed by a parodic chronology outlining the major events from 1952 to 1989 (245–6). During Smith's teenage years the historical and the literary converged in one headline issue, when a fatwa (Islamic religious edict) on Salman Rushdie was proclaimed in early 1989 by Ayatollah Ruhollah Khomeini, the then Supreme Leader of Iran. He called for Rushdie to be killed for blasphemy, responding to the author's controversial fourth novel, *The Satanic Verses* (1988). Smith was thirteen at the time of this seminal event presaging some of the ideological conflicts that dominate the post-millennial world. The fatwa provoked death threats to the author and other violent protests, including public book-burnings on the part of Muslims in numerous countries. Although Rushdie remained physically unharmed, he went into hiding in 1989. Moreover, given subsequent Muslim extremism, it is easy to forget how resulting events made the fatwa hot news during the late 1980s and early 1990s, and how surprising and shocking it was. The outcome was not simply a matter of protests and increasing militancy, but resulted in various deaths and injuries of translators and publishers of Rushdie's work.[1] Smith incorporates a comic account of aspects of these events and issues (without naming Rushdie) in her first novel. One is a book-burning scene, with Millat's views becoming the subject of controversy even within his Muslim family, with his mother excoriating him. The impact is evident in Smith's view of the affair, about which she is unequivocal, reflecting in her PBS interview:

> I remember it being a constant argument at dinner parties, or in the playground, or on the bus. It would always come up one way or another. There were people who supported the fatwa very strongly and who still feel that way. Then there is the other side, who feel absolutely, as I do, that a writer deserves his personal freedoms and that any questioning of it is kind of horrific.

Fiction continued to be a major influence on Smith's consciousness throughout her adolescence. She recalls one book that impacted upon her aged fourteen as a result of her mother's intervention. In 'What Does Soulful Mean?' Smith recalls being the reluctant recipient of a parental gift of Zora Neale Hurston's *Their Eyes Were Watching God*. Smith recalls already disliking two other previous maternal recommendations, Jean Rhys' *Wide Sargasso Sea* and Toni Morrison's *The Bluest Eye*. She preferred her 'own freely chosen, heterogeneous reading list.' However, she was persuaded by the first page of Hurston's novel, with its lyricism, its use of aphorism and as she continued to read 'The second part, about women, struck home. It remains as accurate a description of my mother and me as I have ever read [. . .].' Although resistant to judging aesthetic experience in effect by prioritizing identification of the reader's identity within the text, nevertheless the novel moved her to tears. Interestingly, in contrast to her younger self, much later in life on reflection Smith is persuaded that Hurston's strengths include both an unapologetic orientation towards blackness, and additionally something far more universal:

> It is not the Black Female Literary Tradition that makes Hurston great. It is Hurston herself. Zora Neale Hurston—capable of expressing human vulnerability as well as its strength, lyrical without sentiment, romantic and yet rigorous, and one of the few truly eloquent writers of sex—is as exceptional amongst black women writers as Tolstoy is amongst white male writers. However, it is true that Hurston rejected the 'neutral universal' for her novels—she wrote unapologetically in the black-inflected dialect in which she was raised.

Smith's own literary ambitions persisted throughout her teenage years and one suspects her approach was both methodical and very prone to a bricolage of influences.

Another seminal event in London at this time was the murder of Stephen Lawrence, a black teenager killed at a bus-stop in Eltham, apparently by a racist criminal gang of five youths on 14 February 1993 when Smith was seventeen. Despite the perpetrators identities being known, no conviction has been achieved to date because of the inability to gather insufficient and inadmissible evidence (in part due to the criminal links of the suspected perpetrators). For Smith on reflection this seemed atypical, something quite outside of her own experience of London, as she indicates in the PBS Masterpiece Theatre interview:

> The people who killed Stephen Lawrence are representative not of a problem of multiculturalism in London, but a problem of economic deprivation. They're very poor white kids, and they did it to Stephen Lawrence as a kind of last-ditch attempt to make themselves significant. It's pathetic. But I don't think it's representative of multiracial London at all.

Concerning the subsequent period in 'Piece of Flesh: Introduction to this Book,' which prefaces *Piece of Flesh*, Smith reports that she lost her virginity, having sex for the first time with a ballet dancer in her mother's kitchen (11). Surviving this experience which she describes as being entirely without 'fun,' at eighteen she went to Cambridge University and studied English at King's College, intending originally an academic career. As Simon Hattenstone attests in 'White Knuckle Ride,' aged eighteen Smith was consciously researching the working methods of her favourite authors. As a student Smith continued to read avidly according to her own account, and reflects later when interviewed by Ben Greenman in *The New Yorker* that

> When I was in college, I used to ridicule the idea of the subconscious impulse in fiction, but the more I write it the more I find it significant. It's not all of fiction—there needs to be structure, some shred of moral intelligence, an organizing instinct—but it's not negligible, either.

Her choice of university may have been crucial to her future achievements, for as Nico Israel observes parenthetically in 'Tropicalizing London: British Fiction and the Discipline of Postcolonialism': '(Race per se seems less of an obstacle to literary success in Britain than does educational class status; there are relatively few Booker Prize winning writers from the UK who do not have Oxbridge credentials)' (94).

Nevertheless regarding her time at Cambridge, Smith articulates an acute sense of her cultural and class difference compared to most people she met as a student, considering that many of them came from a more elite or perhaps confident class background than her own. This is something emphasized in the subtext of her account of meeting McEwan and Amis while a student:

> Because of the posh university I attended, I first met McEwan many years ago, before I was published myself. I was nineteen, down from Cambridge for the holidays, and a girl I knew from college was going to Ian McEwan's wedding party. This was a fairly normal occurrence for her, coming from the family she did, but I had never clapped eyes on a writer in my life. She invited me along, knowing what it would mean to me. That was an unforgettable evening. I was so delighted to be there and yet so rigid with fear I could barely enjoy it. It was a party full of people from my bookshelves come to life. I can recall being introduced to Martin Amis (whom I was busy plagiarizing at the time) and being shown his new baby. Meeting Martin Amis for me, at nineteen, was like meeting God. I said: 'Nice baby.'

Arguably, Smith's upbringing represents a different nuance that became part of the middle-class culture that is central to the intellectual class notion of itself and of England. She says to Hattenstone that ' "I may have been working class once, I think once you live in a nice flat in a nice area and you've had a great education, you're really pushing it, to continue to claim to be salt of the earth. Life changes, my family is a picture of change." ' Nevertheless, Smith offers others an opportunity to promulgate certain possibilities: the idea of struggle, of an ordinariness of origin, of state education, followed by Cambridge and improbable success. Her perception of class and changing affiliation is suggestive, for the nuances of class and urban complexity seem to signify that one might read Smith's work as a reflection of class and its tentacles, as much as it ruminates about the struggle of migrants to find and sustain human dignity and meaning.

Reading English at King's College allowed Smith to absorb potential influences from both literary and critical traditions. She recalls in 'Love, actually' a phase as a student when influenced by critical debates she rejected her own earlier visceral, 'sentimental' responses to literature As she admits,

> At Cambridge at least, Roland Barthes did not fully convince my generation of readers that the text is a pleasure. We rejected the very idea that novels could either make us feel good or do us good, and along with this bathwater we threw out the baby who wailed that the ethical discussion has any relationship to the literary discussion. Our interest was analytical, not ethical.

She continued with other interests. Sebastian Shakespeare illustrates this in 'The Secret Life of Zadie Smith' with his reference to her talents and to a friend who would inspire certain essential aspects of her second novel. Another friend's comments reveal something of the contradictions in Smith's persona, her underlying insecurity which contrasts her outward confidence that has been evident since her time at university.

> She was also a good jazz singer. 'I once saw her sing at a second-year dinner,' says another friend. 'She was accompanied by her friend Adam Andrusier, an autograph hunter who is the inspiration for her latest novel. She had a lovely voice but it was interesting. In person there was so much bravado about her but when she sang, she came across as insecure. It wasn't touching but it was a lot more human.' Smith's progress was not uniformly positive. She is recorded as admitting that contrary to press reports she did not achieve a double first, admitting to a third class honours grades in her part one examinations, sat at the end of

the second year. Her final degree was an upper second class honours in English.

Smith failed an audition at the Cambridge Footlights, apparently judged by David Mitchell and Robert Webb, the pair subsequently becoming a popular television comedy double act. On a more personal front, on entering a literary competition at Cambridge, Smith met Nick Laird, the eventual prize-winner, who she would eventually marry. He is from a working-class family and grew up in a small town in County Tyrone, Northern Ireland, and trained as a solicitor after university. He has published *To a Fault*, a collection of poems, and *Utterly Monkey* (2005), a novel. One might well wonder if she is the model for the character Ellen, a tall attractive black girl with 'A posh bone-dry voice' (40) and a smile that 'revealed that beautifully crooked front tooth' (344). Ellen provides the love interest of protagonist Danny, young solicitor from Northern Ireland. Laird is acknowledged later to have helped Smith edit her fiction.

As for Smith's emergence as a writer, while at Cambridge several of her short stories were published in the *May Anthologies*, an annual collection for budding writers at Oxford and Cambridge universities. Laird was the editor of the 1996 anthology in which her second story appeared. In a biographical note Smith writes that

> Zadie A. Smith (Cambridge) is a second year English undergraduate in name only, who writes fiction for pleasure but is not averse to doing it for money. Impractically minded, technologically illiterate, and with no business sense whatsoever, she hopes to one day make her living through the noble art of literature, but knows deep down, graduation will lead her straight onto a career writing for the Guardian's obituary pages.
>
> (140)

Kathleen O'Grady in '*White Teeth*: A Conversation with Author Zadie Smith' describes her own role on the editorial board of this journal while undertaking doctoral studies at the university as an 'endurance test.' She singles out Smith at twenty as uniquely gifted among the submissions O'Grady considered, recalling the 'opening paragraphs that give readers that goosepimply sensation that starts somewhere at the base of the spine and spreads rapidly to alight the whole body' (105). Through another friend Smith had contact with a published, successful novelist who was impressed with her work, as Edemariam explains in 'Learning Curve,' which profile confirms Smith's ability as a jazz singer:

> Another friend was Josh Appignanesi, now a documentary filmmaker; he showed Zadie's work to his mother, the novelist Lisa Appignanesi, who says, 'It was quite clear Zadie was going to write, and write extremely well.' She remembers a 'bubbly, energetic, rather wonderful young woman' who had a 'histrionic side', but was much loved by the Appignanesi family for her enthusiasm, her eagerness for life.

Interestingly, during the process of writing her first two novels, as she explains in 'Love, actually,' she confronted herself incessantly by a statement of aesthetic morality excerpted from Thomas Pynchon's *Gravity's Rainbow* (1973) which she had pinned to her door, an indication of her complex and laudable ambitions:

> We have to find meters whose scales are unknown in the world, draw our own schematics, getting feedback, making connections, reducing the error, trying to learn the real function ... zeroing in on what incalculable plot? [...]

> I think I felt it issued a kind of ethical challenge to the composers of narrative, a challenge that I wanted to match as I went about my own writing, an ideal that I would try to be equal to. I wanted to be like Pynchon, to be in pursuit of hidden information; I thought it the novel's responsibility to chase and pin down the ghost in the machine. In short, I was responding to the ethical vision of another writer. As a young writer, I took it as my model until I might find my own.

The first novel represents her first steps towards a voice of her own, quasi-autobiographical, but formally ambitious and exploratory.

Wyatt Mason claims of the author in 'White Knees: Zadie Smith's Novel Problem':

> There has been little disagreement over the seriousness of her ambitions. While still an undergraduate at Cambridge, she planned and executed a 500-page novel that, with terrific humor, hopscotched over 150 years of history; told a multigenerational, multifamily saga of the intertwined friendships and amorous entanglements of its English Protestant, Bengali Muslim, Jamaican Jehovah's Witness,

and Jewish geneticist principals; and collated postcolonialism, inter-marriage, religious militancy, and the moral implications of genetic engineering.

(83)

Actually, Smith had graduated before the novel (begun as a student) attracted the influential Wylie Literary Agency, who orchestrated a bidding war for Smith's unfinished manuscript. As Mario Russo records in an early online profile that retrospectively considers the reception of this unfinished manuscript,

> The pages were circulated to London publishers, generating unusual commotion and an auction at which Hamish Hamilton, the literary imprint of Penguin in the U.K., came out victorious. 'It's very rare for 100 pages to be greeted with this much excitement,' says Simon Prosser, Smith's editor at Hamish Hamilton. 'What we saw was this work that appealed to anyone, regardless of age, gender or political position. I recently got back from a party where I ran into someone who had just given *White Teeth* to his grandmother, and she absolutely loved it!'

As Merritt reports in January 2000 before completion, 'She was asked to write a short story for the *New Yorker*'s millennial fiction issue, and in April is travelling to New York to take part in a literary festival organised by the magazine and to promote the American publication of *White Teeth*.' Unusually, even prior to completion, both *White Teeth* and its author had become part of a cultural and literary phenomenon. Smith appears genuinely not to have antic-ipated the scale of her success and the attention that ensued. In 'More's the Pity' Celia Walden comments, 'When Zadie Smith's first novel, *White Teeth*, was greeted with critical acclaim in 2000, the twenty-four-year-old found herself ill-prepared for the media frenzy surrounding her looks, talent and background' (20). Ironi-cally, while simultaneously noting Smith's reluctance Russo pur-veys all of the key elements of the bandwagon about to engulf Smith in the very title of Russo's interview, 'Girl Wonder: The Life so far of Multiracial Literary Sensation Zadie Smith.' Russo follows the 'offi-cial' line, adding, 'It's impressive that Smith wrote *White Teeth* during her senior year at Cambridge University,' before reporting Smith's advance as being £250,000.

In 2000 soon after *White Teeth* appeared, Smith was appointed writer in residence for a year at the Institute of Contemporary Arts

(ICA) in London, although at this time she is reported to have suffered writer's block. Instead, she edited *Piece of Flesh*, a collection which she describes in her introduction as 'five pornographic stories' produced by friends of hers, each commissioned for a £250 fee (7). She also acted as a judge for an art competition such was her burgeoning celebrity and reputation as part of the young artistic avant-garde. Her life was beginning to change after the hype, its coordinates more expansive than those of her early years as Jennifer Frey makes evident in 'Zadie Smith: Putting Herself into Her Work,' describing Smith being interviewed in a bookshop during a US promotional tour in 2005. 'Her world, she explains, is that of the books that populated her childhood and continue to be the greatest pleasure of her adult life. Vacations, travel? Her family's idea of a "trip" was a jaunt to Cornwall. "I've never been to Africa or India or anything like that," she says. Her biggest journey, thus far, was her first American book tour, for *White Teeth* [...]' (C1). According to Lyall, by April 2000 Smith had earned enough money to secure her future. '"Now I've made enough and I don't need any more."' Her financial independence allowed her to continue with projects either which genuinely interested her or to which she was committed. In 2001 she edited the *May Anthology*, the Oxford and Cambridge journal that had published her first writing. In her 'Introduction' she warns against exaggeration or making overly complex the appearance of characters' emotions. At around this time Smith was involved in a controversy, at least as far as the *Evening Standard*'s columnist, Shakespeare, was concerned, something he alludes to this in his profile of Smith:

> Another boyfriend was James Flint who won the Amazon Bursary prize 2001. Zadie was one of the judges, although it's claimed she forgot to mention her previous relationship with him. She and Flint insisted their affair had not influenced the decision, claiming she'd had no part in choosing Flint for the shortlist.
>
> However, a fellow judge said that while Zadie did not read Flint's submission before it was shortlisted, she had taken part in the discussion to declare it a winner.

According to Shakespeare, Smith spent around 6 months in writers' retreats in Italy and Hawthornden Castle near Edinburgh to complete her second novel, *Autograph Man*, becoming progressively more reclusive. He refers to a steady boyfriend, a poet from Northern Ireland (erroneously offering the name, James), predicting that 'this autumn they are both enrolling at Harvard University where she is doing an MA in European studies.' Of course, these plans were disrupted by the traumatic events of 9/11. She watched from London like many others, writing in response in 'This is how it feels to me,' that she had thought through the significance of these portentous events, referring to a period of writer's block. She reflects, 'Does anyone want to know the networks behind those seeming simplicities, the paths that lead from September 11 back to Saudi Arabia and Palestine, and then back to Israel, back further to the second world war, back once more to the first?' She wonders whether fiction can help or ameliorate such large-scale problems, but concludes that because as personally novels continue to offer her hope and optimism, continuing to write them is worthwhile. Significantly, she rejects the inflated notions of others concerning her first novel, commenting candidly, 'When I was 21 I wanted to write like Kafka. But, unfortunately for me, I wrote like a script editor for *The Simpsons* who'd briefly joined a religious cult and then discovered Foucault. Such is life.'

Smith's first novel made the transition to the visual, adapted for television for broadcast in autumn 2002. According to David Gritten's preview, 'An everyday story of Willesden folk: *White Teeth*, Zadie Smith's cross-cultural novel set in north-west London, is coming to our TV screens,' the adaptation, originally planned as a BBC drama series, was finally produced for Channel 4 by Company Pictures as four one-hour episodes costing £3.5 million, directed by Julian Jarrold. Gritten observes that since '*White Teeth* is so complex, intricate and stuffed with memorable characters that it seemed more logical material for television. So it has turned out.' For the academic year 2002–2003 Smith finally arrived at Harvard to become a Fellow at the Radcliffe Institute for Advanced Study at the prestigious American Ivy League Harvard University, where she wrote drafts of her third novel, *On Beauty*. More than coincidentally this novel is set in and around the campus of prestigious fictional American university, so evidently Smith's own experiences helped shape this novel which is analysed and discussed in Chapter 5. In May 2003, the series was broadcast in the United States on PBS as two longer episodes, part of the long-running and prestigious *Masterpiece Theater* slot. According to Smith's accounts of this period, while at Harvard she and Laird attended a number of anti-war marches in New York, exhibiting her sense of political engagement in protest remained undiminished.

After her return to London in October she delivered the 2003 Orange Word Lecture, entitled 'E. M. Forster's Ethical Style: Love, Failure and the Good in Fiction.' In February 2004, at the conclusion of a competition to raise awareness of the rich and diverse historical background of Black Britain by the Mayor of London, Ken Livingstone, he announced Smith had been nominated by the public as one of the Hundred Great Black Britons (she would later be voted as seventy-seventh). On 11 March 2004 she was one of 180 women invited to participate in the first lunch with the Queen at Buckingham Palace to celebrate female excellence. However, there was much negative press, and increasingly cutting and sniping reviews of her work. Many dismissed the merits of her third novel. William Deresiewicz in 'Zadie Smith's Indecision' not only finds *On Beauty* less than convincing, but attributes its failings to Smith's celebrity, suggesting she was now beyond effective editorial control, saying, 'It can't be easy to rein in a writer as successful as Smith, and with the level of acclaim she's achieved, it can't be easy to curb oneself, either' (1). Increasingly, the press subjected Smith to endless, often spiteful curiosity. Richard Simpson in the *Evening Standard* even reported on a minor complaint from an older neighbour of Smith about the noise from a spa Smith had installed, even though according to Simpson's account Brent council had already deemed this did not constitute a 'nuisance.' In September 2005 interviewed by Martha Kearney on 'Woman's Hour' on Radio 4 she had to refute widespread claims in newspapers that she had described Britain as a 'disgusting place.'[2]

The press deemed Smith's wedding in September 2004 newsworthy. Laird and Smith were married in a formal ceremony in King's College Chapel, followed by a reception in the college. The best man was actor Alan Turkington. Both of Smith's parents attended, as well as many literary friends. Laird, in her shadow, remains conscious of being somewhat in the shade of his celebrated wife, ironically referred to as 'Mr Zadie Smith' by Louise Carpenter (1). After their nuptials for a period they maintained residence in a house in Kilburn, on the same street as the flat where Zadie was born, and near to her mother's current home. According to Carpenter, Laird says of Smith, 'She's very supportive of what I do. She always has been. Poetry means a lot to her and she edits my poems, although we work very differently. She'll send 20 readers her work when it's finished, including me, in order to gather opinion. I'll show nobody until it's done, except her' (1).

Following *On Beauty* Smith seemed tired of maintaining her public presence and promoting her work. In 'Zadie, Take Three,' her telephone interviewer, Murphy Moo, suggests that Smith exhibited 'a certain knack for evading a question she doesn't intend to answer.' Murphy Moo reports the author's admission that 'She'd much prefer to leave behind the media circus and allow her new novel [...] to speak for itself.' According to Murphy Moo, Smith refused interview requests in Britain because

> I live here and I want to have a normal life. I want to be able to get on the tube and do normal things. If I were a Ph.D. student studying contemporary novelists I would only look at their foreign interviews, because they say so much more. When writers are in their home country they're cagey, terrified [...].

On Beauty was selected for the shortlist of the Man Booker Prize, and although it failed to win, according to Janice C. Simpson in 'Zadie Smith' in 2006 Scott Rudin, known for *The Hours* and *Closer*, was scheduled to produce a movie version.

In 2006 Smith visited her ailing father in a Felixstowe nursing home. He died aged eighty-one after a decade of dialysis, having lost both kidneys. Smith is reported to have stayed in Rome with her husband for much of the period from 2006 to 2007, subsequently setting up home in Rome, ostensibly to avoid media attention. However, throughout 2005–2007 she continued to attend literary and media events (arguably required to sustain her literary career and presence). One was a charity event, the Lavender Trust Speakeasy held in Claridges Hotel, London, on 14 March 2007, where accompanied on the piano by the well-known British comic, David Baddiel, Smith sang 'I Could Write a Book.' Other guests included Sophie Dahl (also singing), Nigella Lawson and Emma Thompson. And despite periods of foreign residence, Smith has neither abandoned her roots nor is she entirely carried away by wealth and fame. In 2007 she used her celebrity to draw attention to an apparent plan (later denied by Brent council) to close half of its dozen libraries. And every year from 2006, Smith has judged annually the submissions to the *Willesden Herald* International short story prize. Ironically, it became the subject of controversy in February 2008 when no prize was awarded, as reported by Bilal Ghafoor in 'Last Word on the Competition Result 2008.' Smith's own comments in a letter to the paper, under the headline 'Breaking News: Short Story Competition Result 2008,' are intriguing. 'Maybe the problem with this prize is that my name is attached to it. To be very clear: just because this prize has the words Willesden and Zadie hovering by it, does not mean that I or the other judges want to read hundreds of jolly stories of multicultural life on the streets of North London.' Clearly, she actively resists the 'typecasting' resulting from distorted readings of her first book. On the release of the collection of new short stories, *The Book of Other People*, edited by Smith, in January 2008 she took part in a reading of extracts, proceeds of the event and book sales going to 826 NYC, a non-profit organization dedicated to supporting students between six and eighteen with their creative and expository writing skills. As Deresiewicz says perceptively:

> Whatever value Smith may be thought to have as a poster girl for multiculturalism, her work is a stunning refutation of all attempts to partition culture or consciousness along any such lines: male and female; gay and straight; black, brown, yellow and white (or Christian and Muslim, for that matter, the Allies and Axis of the cultural right). The empire of the spirit brooks no Balkanization.

Smith demonstrates increasing ambivalence towards her celebrity, and attempts to constrain her aesthetic identity seem inimical to her, hence this study's suggestion that some criticism is not only and counter-factual in textual terms, but naïve in its view of the author. Media attention and perverse criticism ought not to be allowed to distort interpretation of Smith's intellect and creativity.

PART II
Major Works

3

WHITE TEETH

FUNDAMENTALLY SUBURBAN

In *White Teeth* the first wartime meeting of Archie and Samad testifies to the power of trauma in forging mutual loyalty and friendship. Both are palpably incomplete individuals. Archie is a callow, inexperienced virgin. The pompous Samad waits for a daughter to be born to the influential Begum family with whom an arrangement has been reached by his own. Subsequently, he marries his younger and far from docile wife, Alsana. Migrating to Britain, the unlikely couple produce twin boys, Magid and Millat, facing racism in the East End of London stirred by Enoch Powell's infamous 'Rivers of Blood' speech. This causality stresses that the private and public are intimately interrelated, and operates in the immediacy of such lives. Archie and Samad meet again in the mid-1970s, forging an unlikely friendship. The Iqbals have escaped Powellism, settling in Willesden, becoming neighbours of the Jones family consisting of Archie, his younger Jamaican wife, Clara, and their mixed race daughter, Irie. The three children share childhood experiences, and during adolescence do so within three highly self-conscious families, exploring both the relations of the past and present. This combination of a familial perspective and retrospection allows various multi-chronic and shifting viewpoints to become centripetal. According to Caryl Phillips the novel concerns 'struggling to find a way to stare in the mirror and accept the ebb and flow of history [. . .]' (286). Smith encompasses diverse contexts: the Indian Mutiny; the Kingston earthquake of 1907; the end of the Second World War; the iconography of the suburbs; religiosity and extreme beliefs; several strands of extremism; colonialism; different phases of migration to Britain; Thatcherism; political correctness; the great storm of 1987; and eugenics and the ethics of genetic engineering. Such contingent intersections and recurrences structure this rambunctious novel, where personal and public events past and present traverse each other, converging somewhat improbably in suburban north-west London. As Karin E. Westman says, 'The novel's dual image of "white teeth"—both the lettering on the U.K. dust jacket and the metaphor threaded throughout the novel—embodies this tension, which Smith develops across the pages of her novel: the dangers of deracination and the equally perilous pursuit of origins at the expense of the present.' Coincidences combine with the dominant comic perspective to radically disturb conventional historiography.

Location and humour are focal points, drawing on autobiographical elements, for as Claire Squires says, 'Smith's representation of the multiple identities inhabiting her native Willesden Green sets the scene for *White Teeth*'s stories of origins, roots and cultures. Smith also finds a tone in which she will deal with the complex issues of her fiction: one that is comic, sympathetic, and—essentially—optimistic' (13). For Nick Bentley in 'Re-writing Englishness: Imagining the Nation in Julian Barnes's *England, England* and Zadie Smith's *White Teeth*,' Smith recognizes the role of tradition in the dominant classic realist and comic modes (497). In fact, Smith's comedy does not simply consist of the 'Horatian' aspects that Bentley identifies as concerned with the 'unavoidable foibles, hypocrisies and moral expediencies of the main characters' (497). She foregrounds the picaresque (which Bentley sees only as secondary), the aleatory, the perversities of her characters, and an occasional humour inherent in death and suffering, an inflection of the absurd. Such elements constantly subvert her realist topography. In a cursory fashion, Squires identifies two more important elements: a generally empathic and positive rendition of character even when morally difficult to do so, and simultaneously the use of laughter (comedy) which is biting and ironic about the very same individuals. Certainly conflict, failure and paradox recur throughout. Samad's tortuous relation with Islam is one example. Irie's sense of her body is another. The various (shifting) doublings and redoublings—Archie and Samad, the two wives, Clara and Alsana, the Iqbal twins, Clara and Ryan Topps, subsequently Topps and Hortense Bowen—evoke the uncanny, part of a cartography of the grotesque and comic, one that allows Smith to sub-textually structure her complex chronology of the characters often interstitial and always unfinished (incomplete) histories. As a result unfamiliarity permeates the novel's otherwise everyday banalities, with incongruities and erroneous trajectories layering the characters' lives. The absurdist and tangential letters that Archie receives from his Scandinavian pen-pal, whom he met briefly at the Olympics, are one bizarre example. Another is when Ryan takes Clara to Parliament Hill (42), attempting to persuade her to readopt the constraints of her original beliefs. 'Somewhere in the middle of Ryan Topps's enlightening biblical exegesis, his former false idol, the Vespa GS, cracked right into a 400-year-old oak tree. Nature triumphed over the presumptions of engineering. The tree survived; the bike died; Ryan was hurled one way; Clara the other' (44). Ryan takes his survival as a sign of his being chosen by God as one of the elect to be saved (although curiously at this point the location of the accident has metamorphosed to Primrose Hill [44]). Like so much else such strategies fundamentally subvert the realist mode that appears to operate in other sections concerned with social observation. Moreover, to define personal and cultural space Smith uses both comic archetypes and archetypical reactions which serve as a substitute for expression given primary characters' visceral inarticulacy or limitedness. Alsana is the indignant wife. The children are rebellious. Archie and Samad signify a kind of ossified fatherhood retreating to the symbolically significant O'Connell's café, certainly a literal product of hybrid elements, but ones so banal and comic that this environment cannot surely be seriously conceived as one of the 'temples of hybridity and complexity' (183), identified by Pilar Cuder-Domínguez in the 'Ethnic Cartographies of London in Bernardine Everisto and Zadie Smith.'

In a neo-Dickensian tradition, Smith paradoxically affiliates humour and suffering, a quality Georges Bataille identifies in *The*

Unfinished System of Nonknowledge (2001) when he says, 'I can laugh at the impossible in humanity: the impossible leaves the essence of the project intact. Laughing at the impossible as it overcomes me, laughing knowing I am sinking [...]' (23). Éric Tabuteau in 'Marginally Correct: Zadie Smith's *White Teeth* and Sam Selvon's *The Lonely Londoners'* recognizes that 'some trivial aspects of London life are lauded,' and perceives a Swiftian undercurrent in the disparity of the newcomers' view of the world found in 'repeated and naïve comparisons with their mother country, [which] is amusing' (94). Smith's juxtapositions are even more complex than Tabuteau's account of them, inflected with a general sense of whimsy, satire *and* irony that permeates the novel throughout. As Maurice Chittenden reports in *The Sunday Times* a brother of Smith's early boyfriend claims its narrative is far from the darker realities of those living in pre-millennial Willesden.[1]

> Ziad Haider Rahman, the inspiration for Magid, one of the twin Muslim brothers at the centre of the novel, said Zadie Smith's book, which was adapted for a television series, was divorced from reality. "Conspicuously absent from *White Teeth* is the anger," he said. "We don't see the very dark aspects of racism. That's something that divides the book from reality."

Smith chooses to make the brothers twins for thematic reasons, particularly the comic and uncanny effect. Another oblique reference to the real-life brothers is when Smith describes the school playground as testament to 'the century of the great immigrant experiment. It is only this late in the day that you can walk into a playground and find Isaac Leung by the fish pond, *Danny Rahman* in the football cage, Quang O'Rourke bouncing a basketball, and Irie Jones humming a tune' [my italics] (326).

The comedy remains largely an authorial and readerly experience, a position of knowingness, of judgement, partly accounting for Ziad Rahman's objection. Apart from Alsana's confrontational (often aggressive) and bitter wit, and Archie's wry but melancholy acceptance of fate or chance (the aleatory), the characters laugh very little. They do not share humour among themselves. They suffer, seeing a world verging on the tragic. They seem troubled, conflicted, in pain. James Wood in *The Irresponsible Self: On Laughter and the Novel* (2005) sees in Smith's characterization the immediacy

(174) and some of the authorial empathy found in a Dickensian caricature, making Smith for Wood a more nuanced (and differently inflected) writer than Rushdie (175). To adopt Tabuteau's terminology if Smith's characters exhibit a 'propensity to exaggerate' it may not only derive from the 'culture shock' (94), of migration. Samad is far too knowing, Hortense Bowden too evangelical, and both characters too interrogative to be reduced simply to such trans-cultural incongruities. Moreover, Smith's central male West Indians are aged, grotesquely neo-Dickensian, and sketchily archetypal. If parodies one wonders whether such depictions undermine or reinterpret the absurdity and contradiction inherent in certain stereotypical cultural expectations, or demonstrate what Janice C. Simpson calls Smith's 'Dickensian swagger.' Samad himself is the victim of a colleague, Shiva's savage and crude mimicry:

> Round and round the kitchen he went, bending his head and rubbing his hands over and over like Uriah Heep, bowing and genuflecting to the head cook, to the old man arranging great hunks of meat in the walk-in freezer, to the young boy scrubbing the underside of the oven. 'Samad, Samad . . .' he said with what seemed infinite pity, then stopped abruptly, pulled the apron off and wrapped it round his waist. 'You are such a sad little man.'
>
> (57)

Such humour depends on the readers' recognition of the validity of Shiva's account, complicit with her neo-Dickensian grotesque, with its complex interplay of pity and humour. Shiva demands violently that Samad desist from engaging in conversations with customers concerning biology, politics, his studies at Delhi University and his time in the British army, especially if he wants tips. Shiva regards Samad as an anachronism, a resistance to change. For Wood, Samad very largely 'has really, only the one dimension, his angry defence of Islam' (180). Surely this diminishes the complexity of his inner struggles, his anger and his paradoxical sense of selfhood. Admittedly with so many shifting contexts and episodes, the novel's moral centre is evasive. As Childs indicates in *Contemporary Novelists: British Fiction Since 1970* (2005), Smith combines omniscient narration with an extensive use of free indirect discourse and a mirroring of the 'vocabulary and speech-mannerisms of her characters [. . .] to show events from their perspective' (201). This only partly situates her strategy. Smith in undermining her characters does so to cultural shibboleths such as liberalism, political correctness and multiculturalism. As Janice C. Simpson adds, 'Refugees from the era of political correctness and others who are easily offended probably should stay clear.' Bentley also recognizes Smith's uneasiness with political correctness (497) and her centring of moral authority on particular characters, most especially Irie (497) and Archie (498).

In the novel's first phase Smith emphasizes the underlying themes of deceit, abandonment and arrival. Archie languishes in his recent betrayal, traumatized by the end of his marriage to Ophelia Diagilo, whom he met in spring 1946 in Florence. As the narrator indicates at this time she has not suspected Archie's record of only short-term relationships, his dislike and mistrust of women. More-over, 'No one told Archie that lurking in the Diagilo family tree were two hysteric aunts, an uncle who talked to aubergines and a cousin who wore his clothes back to front' (8). Human imperfection and strangeness are a constant theme throughout, the text revelling in the incongruities of life, its pathos and deceit.

The novel commences at 06:27 on 1 January 1975 with Archie languishing in his car exhaust fumes, windows taped shut, on the comically suggestive Cricklewood Broadway (a place previously known by outsiders largely because of the absurdist, child-like comedy of *Goodies* television programmes) parked outside a halal butcher. Its huge owner, Mo Hussein-Ishmael, is an Elvis fan, suitably bequiffed. Mo is intent upon his ongoing battle with defecating pigeons, and irritated by his shrinking violet assistants and their failure to move the vehicle blocking his expected delivery, dismissive when they offer Archie's intended fate as an excuse or defence of their inaction. The bleak becomes ridiculous, part of the comically absurd. Smith enjoins the comic potential in dialogue, its interplay, with Mo's paradoxically indignant, suburban vocabulary emphasizing apparently incongruous intersections of cultures and ethnicities. Advancing he pulls down Archie's window with brute force, protesting ' "Do you hear that, mister? We're not licensed for suicides around here. This place halal. Kosher, understand? If you're going to die round here, my friend, I'm afraid you've got to be thoroughly bled first" ' (7). In her first six pages Smith establishes the comic tone and structure of the book, including variously: her use of a series of punch-lines; gallows humour; the oddly interrelated compaction of detail within the vignette;

and the trans-cultural encounter. There follows a brief recollection of Archie's first meeting with his first wife, divorce from whom has led to his suicide attempt. Smith establishes a multicultural community, initiating an underlying sense of difference that animates the characters. The narrative spirals into a series of moments from his past that lead to Archie's gate-crashing a party where he meets his future wife, Clara, many years his junior. Thus Smith offers a notion of improbable causality, a comic concatenation that is repeated and structurally can be charted in almost every section. The novel's method suggests an erratic, occasionally portentous and yet mundane reality underlying the various lives, a communality that although fragmented relies on certain underlying principles, with a sense of trauma and ineptitude underpinning this world.

Location may appear significant, but Smith's descriptions offer a partial view, sketching very few environments, many involving interiors. Geographically, the novel maps, for the most part, two suburbs of contemporary London, intermittently an area in the South, and repeatedly that around Willesden, actively redrafting the city through its descriptions of the interactions and experiences of a gamut of characters. Smith's domestic and localized landscapes—which are full of coincidences and overlapping patterns of life—incorporate an innate sense of certain qualities that Henri Lefebvre describes in *Everyday Life in the Modern World* (1999). First that 'Everyday life is made of recurrences: gestures of labour and leisure, mechanical movements both human and properly mechanical [. . .]' (18). Second drawing upon Lefebvre's description of remarkable possibilities inherent in the quotidian, Smith's fiction senses throughout that potentially there resides 'a power concealed in everyday life's apparent banality, a depth beneath its triviality, *something extraordinary in its very ordinariness*' (37). Through ineptitude Archie's attempted suicide becomes a site for laughter, but also emphasizes the sense of the quotidian indicated by Lefebvre. Equally in classic comic tradition it renders acute emotional suffering humorous through a kind of burlesque. Archie's first name may well in punning fashion imply a reduction of *archetypal* English status. He flips a coin to decide whether to commit suicide, which is supplemented with a narrative aside, 'In fact it was a New Year's resolution' (3), confirming that Archie is part of a post-Nietzschean 'comédie humaine.'

Another intervention stresses the incongruity of Archie's chosen location. 'This nasty urban street where he had ended up living, living alone at the age of forty-seven, in a one-bedroom flat above a deserted chip shop' (3–4), the latter symbolizing Britain's tradition in decline. Distancing herself with such scorn, Smith simultaneously establishes her intimacy with the characters' world and privileges the narrative perspective. Rather than sustain Archie as a symbol for the end of a peculiarly British, patriarchal way of life (its crisis is implied in his isolation and the closure of the quintessentially British institution below his home), Smith allows him an unexpected epiphany, and simultaneously reveals the diversity that subtends the shifting cultural customs and boundaries of contemporary London. What is already potentially visible and possible is revealed, for as Jacques Derrida comments in *The Gift of Death* (1995), that which has been concealed is nevertheless always 'within the order of visibility; it remains constructively visible' (9). Throughout Smith engages in a partial recovery of such underlying meanings, evoking what is barely visible in people, aspects obscured by the topography of the urban landscape, and by stereotypes. Moreover, as Sell insists (29) and Bentley confirms Archie remains Smith's 'unlikely hero' (498).

White Teeth charts various aspects of the history over several hundred years, much of it retrospectively, from the far colonial past through the final stages of the Second World War to the millennium, interweaving the personal, the social and political through the characters' lives and cultural baggage. In 'Revisiting Postcolonial London' John McLeod thinks the characters have two polarized responses to 'change and difference,' either a glorifying of the past, an 'ossification,' or they undertake its erasure (41). In 'New Ethnicities, the Novel and the Burdens of Representation,' James Procter believes the novel 'historicize[s] and challenge[s] the former exoticist multiculturalism that prevail[s] in the present' (113). Different periods correlate. Z. Esra Mirze in 'Fundamental Differences in Zadie Smith's *White Teeth*' feels Samad exhibits during the war a desire to serve the Empire 'which has endowed him with a colonial education and a sense of patriotic duty' (189) by being heroic, and finds himself racialized, a process he resists (190–1). However, in Kilburn Park the pregnant Clara and Alsana grow closer, puzzling over the absurd notion of their husbands as heroes, something Alsana dismisses as lies, before both deriding their jobs and Samad's failed religiosity (80–2). However, they cannot so easily dismiss the war, for the women encounter ex-park keeper, Sol Jozefowicz, whom they realize may have survived the Holocaust. Smith comprehends such hidden truths, glimpsed intermittently, for as Derrida says, 'history never effaces what it buries; it always keeps within itself the secret of whatever it encrypts, the secret of its secret' (21). Such epiphanies recur throughout, ironic secrets underlying the narrative, historical points of reference. Like Sol, Archie and Samad represent a living, if unlikely testimony to the threat of terror, the power of death and finally the sacrifice of war. Derrida regards wartime killing as 'a further experience of the gift of death [. . .]' (17), providing meaning to those taking and losing life. This precisely is the self-discovery Samad seeks, but opts to do so vicariously in his bullying insistence that Archie should sacrifice their Nazi captive, Dr Sick. Curiously, he also seeks to re-inhabit his origins vicariously when he sends Magid back to Bangladesh. Hortense Bowden, Clara's mother, represents another direct link to the historical past, not only evoking colonialism but linking the present to slavery, the middle passage and the hidden desire of a racist order, all part of the root canals of history evoked by the metaphor underlying the novel's title. Additionally, her birth invokes the deaths of the 1907 Kingston earthquake. Suffering, death, revolt, violent natural phenomena, riot and conflict generally are all periodic counter-weights and yet contributory elements to Smith's comic mode, underpinning uncomfortably the reader's own laughter. Brutality underpins many of the novel's historical events, contained by the overriding comic perspective, even with Samad's obsession with debating the role of his ancestor, Mangal Pande, in the Indian Mutiny, what Matthew Paproth in 'The Flipping Coin: The Modernist and Postmodernist Zadie Smith' calls his 'unhealthy preoccupation with revising history [. . .]' (15); one whose event refers finally to rebellion, slaughter and execution, none of which Samad regards in any sense of conciliation. Perhaps the weight of history might represent an attempted avoidance of a painful present, but results in its rediscovery in the personalization of the past. Both narrator and various characters find significance in repeated behaviour, in personal obsessions, and in people's sense of their genetic inheritance. They accept notions of uncanny recurrence. The distant and more recent pasts both haunt the present. However finally, and invariably, the pretensions of such trans-historical interconnections are undercut.

Violence also fractures the present. Mirze considers the blending of and tension between contradictory cultural elements as underlying the different identity crises of Samad, Magid and Millat, and says regarding the latter that 'Like Samad, he hopes to use religion as a coping mechanism to counter his alienation from the center' (196). However in using Islam 'as a weapon to fight back' (197), Millat rejects his brother, and adopts 'a form of Islam that offers no space for moral negotiation or individual agency' (199). McLeod describes Millat's drift into fundamentalism and how this offers him within the rhetoric frame of faith an apparent identity, but only while denying others any freedom of expression or belief. More importantly, for McLeod, Millat's attraction to a mix of styles also suggests a 'vision of vernacular cosmopolitanism' (42).

Smith seems more sceptical about such adoptions (or perversions) of faith than McLeod believes (43). Two aspects explain such misinterpretation: first, the text's comic excess sits uncomfortably with the more sombre post-9/11 zeitgeist; second, a projection onto the novel of the critic's over-optimistic sense that a social mediation of the complex conflicts between different interests and identities might be easily obtained. This is not Smith's view. As McLeod concedes, 'The identity crises and divided consciousnesses of London have *not* been so easily dismissed in the London of *White Teeth* as some critics have presumed' (42). Smith refuses easy conciliations, and those found in the novel are partial and tentative. The dominant mode is opposition, conflict. For instance, Alsana is incandescent and Clara is irritated about the perceived interference of the Chalfens in their family lives (which the children variously exploit). Samad and Alsana trade blows. Samad literally rages at his son, Magid, who on his ninth birthday is called for by 'a group of very nice-looking white boys with meticulous manners' (150–1), asking for Mark Smith:

'I GIVE YOU A GLORIOUS NAME LIKE MAGID MAHFOOZ MUR-
SHED MUBTASIM IQBAL!' Samad had yelled after Magid when he
returned home that evening and whipped up the stairs like a bullet to
hide in his room. 'AND YOU WANT TO BE CALLED MARK SMITH!'
(151)

Consistently, the Iqbal family returns to explicit rage and anger, with each other, with others, with the world. They remain conflictual, divided. Significantly, Magid doubles his own identity, in his eagerness to become not just more English, but mirroring Smith's own desires as a child, more *middle class* and *successful*. As the narrator insists, 'This was just a symptom of a far deeper malaise' (151), before outlining the qualities of life to which he aspires. He exhibits an adolescent compulsion to conform, but also another typical adolescent embarrassment concerning his warring parents. He may partly sublimate his ethnic identity, but also undergoes an oedipal struggle. He rejects Samad's obsession with the past, with legacy and traditions his father cannot sustain. Importantly, as McLeod realizes, London is not the relentless corrigible environment so attractive to postmodern critics (40–1), and he concludes, 'The example of *White Teeth* suggests that in engaging with significant literary texts, at times we need to attend closer to what they seem to say, rather than what we might want them to say' (43).

Smith's characters are not only prisms, viewpoints, but part of typology. The comedy and poignant accuracy of social observation is often explicitly dependent upon their possibilities as archetypes. And yet as Deresiewicz observes, her novel

> exhibits two great strengths, neither of them the kind one expects from so young a writer: the acuteness of its social satire and the brilliance with which it inhabits perspectives utterly different from its author's. Smith gives us aging Indian waiters, bookish teenagers, high-handed liberal moms and a dozen or two others, all with a wicked ear for dialogue and a gimlet eye for the dodges and poses of the social comedy.
>
> (1)

However, while each character represents certain key stock characteristics, they are simultaneously challenged. Dogged and practical, Archie is limited, easily swayed, and yet offers loyalty, bravery and the moral compass of an innocent naïf (or holy fool). A braggart and bully, Samad is contradictory, morally weak, and yet he exhibits great loyalty, an acerbic visionary quality, and linguistic passion. Smith uses outcomes to refute narrow categorizations. Although the characters' ethnic and cultural make-ups reflect the increasingly hybrid or multicultural nature of British society after 1945, they do not offer a simplistic, 'politically correct' or idealist worldview. Smith's humour would not function without highlighting their contradictions and imperfections. Through these she demonstrates some historical tensions. The children's secondary school, Glenard Oak, is intriguing. As Procter says, a 'burden of representation was tangible in the late 1970s, when the state identified multicultural-ism as a key initiative in educational reform; a potential solution to the growing racial tensions in Britain [...]' (104). In *Mongrel Nation* Ashley Dawson dismisses those critics who 'argue that racial difference is no longer a salient social phenomenon' (153), and Proc-ter regards the sections of the novel's set in 1984 as satirizing the permeation of such an optimistic creed in education, specifically exemplified in the parent-governor meeting actively disrupted by Samad. According to Procter this 'satirizes political correctness as it is enshrined within multicultural thinking. Ms Miniver defends the inclusion of the Harvest Festival in terms of its place in the school's broader commitment to multicultural representativeness [...]' (114). Samad's response may be amusing, even perceptive in its own way, but that too is undercut, Smith refuses the reader comfortable binaries, especially given as Procter indicates 'Samad's public performance as the devout, principled Muslim is contra-dicted after the meeting, as he flirts with (and subsequently dates) the young and attractive music teacher, Poppy Burt-Jones' (115). Anthony Quinn in 'The New England' describes Samad's comic response as demonstrating a broader comic quality, a quality of juxtaposition of elements that subvert each other. 'This confla-tion of the high and the low—biblical morality juxtaposed with the mundane details of domesticity—is key to Smith's frisky and irreverent comic attack.' Samad may complain about London 'Cold, wet, miserable; terrible food, dreadful newspapers—who would want to stay? In a place where you are never welcomed, only tol-erated. Just tolerated' (407). However, as his feisty wife, Alsana, repeatedly makes clear, Samad is prone to articulating clichés, each with a rational core, but opinionated and never truly profound. Alsana mocks his ethnic, racial categorizations as without basis, rendering them fundamentally essentialist, and that he is pompous is confirmed by his bullying dismissal of Archie when the latter (admittedly in an annoying fashion) becomes obsessed with bus tickets on their collective journey to the launch of FutureMouse© (512–14). The copyright symbol which is used throughout satirizes the copyrighting of the human genome sequence by companies, although notably undertaking such research hardly raises Samad's ire unlike his friends, relatives and co-religionists. Samad mostly responds to the narrowly personal. Only in terms of the historical past does he truly engage with the ideological in another comic layer.

Smith domesticates the exotic, doing so through the comic cruelty of self-knowledge. Much repeated humour derives from Irie's struggle with her size, embarrassed particularly by her rear, and with her hair, especially at puberty, all relating not only to her struggle for identity, but the recognition and coming to terms with her complex genealogy and genetic inheritance. Such ethnic traits are also evoked in an episode when Irie's diverse, multicultural class studies Shakespeare's sonnet to the 'dark lady,' which figure's potential ethnic otherness is only comprehended by Irie and Joshua Chalfen. 'Irie believed she had been dealt the dodgy cards: mountainous curves, buck teeth and thick metal retainer, impossible Afro hair, and to top it off mole-ish eyesight which in turn required bottle-top spectacles in a light shade of pink' (268). These genetic and other multiple doublings reinforce a sense of the uncanny element. If Smith emphasizes inheritance, coincidence and recurrence, their outcome is absurdly banal. This informs episodes such as Irie's struggle at the hairdressers in an attempt to straighten her curls. In another after a marijuana smoking transgression at Glenard Oak School, the children are punished by being sent to study with Jonathan Chalfens at his home. The past is recovered by the narrator. 'Glenard Oak, as any Glenardian worth their salt knew, could be traced back Sir Edmund Flecker (1842–1907), whom the school had decided to remember as their kindly Victorian benefactor' (303). Of course, the reader is informed that Glenard's donation was in fact to a workhouse (euphemized or elided in the politically correct jargon of the PTA booklet) and the Glenard money traceable to Jamaican interests where in Kingston Sir Edmund is impressed by the exuberant religiosity of the black inhabitants, but not their work ethic. He devises a scheme for sending three hundred Jamaicans to work in North London although his interest wanes and the outcome is disastrous. Glenard is a stereotypically English colonial and yet his intellectual obsessions or 'passions' (306) are reminiscent of Samad's. Finally in the 1907 earthquake Glenard is 'crushed to death by a toppled marble Madonna while Irie's grandmother looked on' (306). His legacy is not the desultory fate of the émigrés or migrants, rather ironically for the colonialist his genetic inheritance lives on in Irie (307). This contrasts another more knowing descendant, Samad who is obsessed with his ancestor, Pande, gathering every scrap of historical evidence in order to create a heroic figure of the Indian Mutiny. Whatever the other qualities of this crusade, for the reader its overriding sense remains that of its comic futility, Samad's muddled vision sharing parallels with Glenard's wrong-headed ideas. Samad's passions are more protracted and single-minded than Glenard's intervention with the Jamaicans sent to Britain, but as with the plan to split up his twin sons, they are equally ill-conceived.

The three children's liberally inclined punishment is pivotal, resulting in the two families finding themselves inextricably involved in the lives of the Chalfens, middle-class intellectuals, high achievers who believe in science, therapy, healthy eating, and most importantly themselves. They have been inwardly oriented until this permeation of their family by Irie and the twins, previously proud of their self-sufficiency. 'Under sufferance and on public holidays, they visited Joyce's long-rejected lineage, the Connor clan, *Daily Mail* letter-writers who even now could not disguise their distaste for Joyce's Israelite love-match. Bottom line: the Chalfens didn't need other people' (314). Marcus, the father, is a geneticist and the mother, Joyce, author of several self-help books about gardening.

> They referred to themselves as nouns, verbs, and occasionally adjectives: *It's the Chalfen way, And then he came out with a real Chalfenism, He's Chalfening again, We need to be a bit more Chalfenist about this.* Joyce challenged anyone to show her a happier family, a more Chalfenist family than theirs.
>
> (314)

Such introspection is destined to disintegrate, largely because of Joyce's obsession with the wayward and retrograde Millat which fractures their Chalfenist scientific rationality, but also because of Joshua's incipient sexual drives. As Smith says in 'Love, actually,' 'there are some goods in the world that cannot be purely pursued rationally, we must also feel our way through them.' Smith's parody of middle-class values offers an ironic view of English left-liberal culture. In a startling admission on a major national literary radio programme as later reported by David Sexton in *The Sunday*

Telegraph, in a supposed gaffe by Smith that ironically becomes newsworthy, she reflects on her own inexperience and the novel's moments of patchiness and naiveté.

> As James Naughtie, introducing *Bookclub* (Radio 4, Sunday) put it, her debut novel, *White Teeth*, written when she was just 24, was quickly seen to be 'an epic of our time' and it's already on the syllabuses. But her attitude towards her own book was amazingly brisk.
>
> Asked whether its portrayal of a happily multicultural land was not a little optimistic, she replied, 'I think on one level I was just straight out wrong. I extrapolated from my own experience, as writers do, and I was wrong.'
>
> Challenged about her portrayal of the middle-class couple, the Chalfens, she said, 'Even hearing the name the Chalfens makes me want to writhe. I was so young when I wrote it, and one of the things you rely on is caricature. So when I read it I find slight patches of genuine writing among great swathes of stuff.'

These remarks reveal that Smith remains perhaps her own harshest critic.

As repeatedly stressed elsewhere, Smith, like Magid and Millat (whose uncanny presence renders them more than doubly significant), rejects in oblique Woolfian fashion (echoing Mr Bennett and Mrs Brown) a politically liberal view of an imaginary 'Mr Schmutters and Mr Banajii [...] weaving their way through Happy Multicultural Land' (465). However accepting of each other, her characters are far from 'politically correct.' On the arrival of her family in Willesden, Alsana—comically marked out by her improbably large feet as Samad's equal (64)—has much earlier dismissed his friends, the Joneses, complaining '"Who are they? [...] I don't know them! You fight in an old, forgotten war with some Englishman ... married to a black! Whose friends are they? These are the children my child will grow up around? Their children— half blacky-white?"' (61) before smashing crockery, shredding her clothes and discarding the purloined meat from his restaurant. Certainly, the juxtaposition inherent in each of these manifestations of domestic discord is finely observed, and ironically expressed. It offers an example of Smith's comic subtlety and her timing. Alsana has prejudices regarding Jews, Chinese, blacks but exempts individuals as the narrator reveals. 'Black people are often friendly, thought

Alsana, smiling at Clara, and adding this fact subconsciously to the short "pro" side of the pro and con list she had on the black girl. From every minority she disliked, Alsana liked to single out one specimen for spiritual forgiveness' (65). Samad opines the Westernization and in his terms degeneracy or 'corruption' of the younger second generation of 'migrant' offspring (190), and watching the demolition of the Berlin Wall his conservatism is evident, as Alsana makes clear in mocking tones:

> 'Foolishness. Massive immigration problem to follow,' said Samad to the television, dipping a dumpling in some ketchup. 'You just can't let a million people into a rich country. Recipe for disaster.'
>
> 'And who does he think he is? Mr Churchill-gee?' laughed Alsana scornfully. 'Original whitecliffsdover piesnmash jellyeels royalvarie tybritishbulldog, heh?'
>
> (241)

Given her dubiety concerning Samad's friend with a mixed-race marriage, Alsana's views may be simply regressive (she does later appear more radically enlightened), or part of the paradoxes and contradictions Smith delineates, convey something of the confusion and contradictory nature of individual identity. Smith applies broad satirical brushstrokes. Although Samad's insistence on the monumental significance of the event and its '"enormity"' is humorous, the underlying seriousness of both Smith's aesthetic and her humour might suggest rebalancing one's view of certain elements of the text. Paradoxically, Samad is pompous, overly portentous with his moral panic, and his comments ridiculed. However, he is not only characterized by histrionic knowingness, his rigid insistences, and his egotistical refusal to account for others (much like Glenard). The decisions he takes and the situation in which he finds subsequently himself often *appear* foolish, and *are* misguided and emotional, his remarks contextually inappropriate. However, his commentary on life is acute, making Samad's role confusing. In the novel Smith insists, 'There had always been a manqué preacher in Samad. A know-it-all, a walker-and-a-talker. With a small audience and a lot of fresh air he had always been able to convince himself that all the knowledge in the universe, all the knowledge on walls, was his' (178–9). When he is sent towards the end to attempt to quieten Hortense and the other Jehovah's Witnesses in their noisy protest at the launch of Marcus Chalfen's 'unnatural' biogenetic experiment FutureMouse©, Samad unexpectedly finds himself unwilling to do so, seeing in her spiritual thirst a reflection of his own. 'He knows the dryness. He has felt the thirst you get in a strange land—horrible, persistent—the thirst that lasts your whole life' (530). He is at times both marginal and yet obsessively rational and intellectual, adhering to a traditionalist view that aspires to intellectual credibility, a parody of educated Englishness contrasting his recurrent, yet half-hearted attempts fully retrieve an Islamic identity, one that he hopes his sons will inherit.

McLeod reconsiders his view in 'Revisiting Postcolonial London,' where he concedes that it is within 'the vertiginous consequences of the multicultural city' (41), neglected by the postmodern vision of a plural culture, that Smith foregrounds issues of faith through Millat so as to 'render a distinctly poignant and solemn articulation of the pain of being "different" in London and the dangerous consequences this may create' (42). Significantly, he admits 'in returning to the novel after recent events [the July 2005 London bombings], the millennial optimism which gathered around the novel seems not only sadly misplaced but also dependent upon a misreading of the novel's articulation of London's multicultural vernacular cosmopolitanism' (43).

There is more to *White Teeth* than its intriguing structure, appearing schematic, with four main sections each of five chapters, each one apparently centred around certain named characters, and given the indication of certain years, for them key moments in the past, present and future that would appear to intersect in some ways: 'Archie 1974, 1945'; 'Samad 1984, 1857'; 'Irie 1990, 1907'; and 'Magid, Millat and Marcus 1992, 1999' (ix–x). Closer inspection reveals that although the challenges of the nominated characters are foregrounded in each section, a variety of others interpenetrate their lives, some recurrent, others mentioned in passing, alive textually for a few random moments. The book's intertextuality both extends and transcends its postcolonial perspectives. In 'No More Lonely Londoners' Jan Lowe indicates variously the novel's 'pamphleteering' qualities, its propensity for sketching minor characters, and traces other distinctly neo-Dickensian characteristics:

White Teeth is partly nineteenth century in the inspiration for its form, in the grand manner in which it modulates the inner city London milieu, and its lofty humanism. The Dickensian echoes of the architecture and the atmosphere of north-west London are unmistakable. In a Dickens novel, the individual is knitted into the social fabric of family and society, and has nothing of the extreme autonomy and alienation we get in the modern novel. For all the pressures on them, the characters in *White Teeth* fall short of suffering the alienation we expect them to, though it is evident in the black and Asian mad who walk the streets of Willesden.

(172)

One might usefully extend such comparisons, particularly if one thinks of *Great Expectations, Our Mutual Friend* and *Bleak House* structurally. *White Teeth* shares with them an interrupted chronological trajectory, and within the regressions and recurrences individual histories are set against the backdrop of the city (its monumentality deconstructed and conflicted surely in both writers), but centred almost manically upon a trinity of motifs of family, acquaintance and the local (location), all interrelated episodically. Smith explores the grotesque possibilities inherent in the familiar made uncanny. Furthermore, just as in Dickens the act of work is peripheral and occasional. Archie's clerical drudgery surely echoes that found in her Victorian predecessor. The unconscious model for structuring the bickering family interactions might in part be the Wilfers of Holloway, another quasi-sentimentalized portrait of belonging and under-expressed affection that has a darker side of oppression intermixed with a quotidian delight in the minutiae of ordinary existence. In the confusion of such lives, erratic, oblique and wayward there is also the legacy of Forster, another intertextual influence identified and discussed by Smith in 'Love, actually.' 'His protagonists are not good readers or successful moral agents, but chaotic, irrational human beings.' If Smith's own characters are deficient—and certainly they are—they are Forsterian, evidencing her commitment to an underlying intuitive and moral sense. To her examples of flawed humanity she extends a Forsterian generosity. She refers to

the 'undeveloped heart' that Forster refers to in his letters and diaries and gives to so many of his characters; we can hear in it an antithetical echo of Aristotle's 'educated heart'. The undeveloped heart is the quality, or lack of qualities, that Forster's novels most frequently depict. [. . .] An 'undeveloped heart' makes its owner 'march to their destiny by catchwords', living not by their own feelings but by the received ideas of others.

Apart from the adult, complacent Chalfens (albeit in some ways caricatures, but complex ones) all of Smith's characters draw upon the ideas of others, but not empathically, rather often literally taking the written word at face value as fact, or as a version of history, or a kind of inviolable religious statement. Hence the various fundamentalisms are scarcely debated, simply becoming a matter for outrage or rejection.

In the comic interplays, its set-piece confrontations (in the final set-piece scene the mouse which Marcus reveals may be being chased by history, but it also represents a stock animation creature, of course) there is a cartoonish quality. One can partly understand this limitation by situating it within a Forsterian model of characterization, or at least Smith's particular reading of his aesthetic view. She adds in 'Love, actually' concerning Forster,

> Forsterian characters are in a moral muddle; they don't feel freely; they can't seem to develop. Most comic novelists fear creating one-dimensional characters; Forster bravely made this fear a part of his art. His critical definition of 'flat characters' has been often ridiculed, and Forster was never able to say, analytically, quite what it was he meant by it. He only knew that he recognised one when he saw one, so to speak, and he suspected they had their own particular uses within the ethical universe of his novels. And it is these novels that speak eloquently where his criticism did not. The emotive lesson we gain by reading through them is exactly this: that we lose a vital dimension when we embrace the *esprit des serieux*.

However, citing Wood's notion of Smith's hysterical realism, as a kind of excess, in 'Simulated Optimism: The International Marketing of *White Teeth*' Katarzyna Jakubiak explores the cartoonish sound effects that are interjected in the end scene's description of Mo and which 'are indicators that the world we are observing is virtual; the characters, despite their "real" appearance, never experience pain, no matter how much violence is inflicted on them [. . .]' (207–8). Interestingly, many historical figures—such as Glenard and Mangal Pande—are similarly reduced in personal terms, but still convey pathos. Smith confronts her reader with the difficulty of finding empathy, a limitation shared by her characters, and reminds them that an underlying common humanity persists despite any one-dimensional tendencies.

Migration is about a sense of location that rejects the past in practice, however much that lost location may be idealized. In refuting Bhabha, George points out a contradictory impulse in (re)location:

> One could argue that 'the nation' is precisely that which is not inscribed by writing that is produced at the margins. Perhaps the location sought in these instances ought not to be read in terms of national subjectivity and/or national space. Immigration, one could argue, *unwrites* nation and national projects because it flagrantly displays a rejection of one national space for another more desirable location, albeit with some luggage carried over.
>
> (186)

In responding to what Mirze sees as a doomed attempt 'to triangulate his identity between race, nation, and religion that will be compatible with Britishness' (192), Samad uses religion first to resist, second to mould his sons. Although Samad mourns the loss of his original culture and home from exile, one senses that he enjoys his dissatisfactions, creating the monstrous schism in his family as a result, alienating his wife until the return of Magid, but dividing his sons in perpetuity. Much of this is exemplified in two images used in describing Magid's return to a fundamentally changed country, to the twin so different from him, Magid transformed by the separation. In the interim Samad suffers from a series of illusions, expectations of the efficacy of a return to his homeland in creating a god-fearing, traditional son. Magid refutes these expectations. Ironically, he is left with Millat seemingly member of an extreme fundamentalist group.

> Two sons. One invisible and perfect, frozen at the pleasant age of nine, static in a picture frame while the television underneath him spewed all the shit of the eighties—Irish bombs, English riots, transatlantic stalemates—above which mess the child rose untouchable and unstained, elevated to the status of ever smiling Buddha, imbued with eastern contemplation; capable of anything, a natural leader, a natural; Muslim, a natural chief—in short nothing but an apparition. A ghostly daguerreotype formed from the quicksilver of the father's imagination, preserved by the salt solution of maternal tears.
>
> (216–17)

Opposing any view of the past as static, as an emotional inscription, is the equally illusory dynamism of contemporary mass media, nevertheless conveying the rapidity of events, never fixed, always changing. Hence cultural longings often seem belated, anachronistic. A further irony is that Magid has been subject to various other natural and political disasters, escaping relatively unscathed, but convinced of the virtue of an enlightenment scientific rationality and a peculiarly traditional Englishness. In contrast, Millat in relative Western comfort and security becomes a fundamentalist.

Although in fiction that precedes 9/11 many writers acknowledge disruption and threat, and articulate a loss of universal meaning, prior to this cataclysmic political event the novel was nevertheless nurtured into a relatively stable scene, as one can see from certain elements reflected in *White Teeth*. During this period increasingly American influences appeared culturally and ideologically to be at their zenith. They appeared to represent an almost unchallengeable hegemony, its cultural permeations noted explicitly by a whole range of novelists, including Smith's *White Teeth* in her delineation of a seductive commodified culture that penetrates to the core of the consciousness of the younger Millat in *White Teeth*, and even apparently vies with the skin-deep fundamentalism that he avows under the influence of KEVIN, or the *Keepers of the Eternal and Victorious Islamic Nation*, an Islamic group agitating precisely against such Western influences. Nevertheless as McLeod comments such a contingent affiliation 'segues seamlessly into precisely the kind of fundamentalist ardour which cosmopolitan and multicultural energies are meant, in theory at least, to act as a kind of cultural inoculation' (42). One recognizes a debt Smith owes to Hanif Kureishi's *The Black Album* (1995), although another antecedent for both authors may be found in hostage Brian Keenan's description of his captivity in *An Evil Cradling* (1993). He describes his young Hezbollah kidnappers as paying homage to the self-same Western icon as Millat. 'Emulating Rambo they would conquer the world and simultaneously rid themselves of that inadequacy which they could never admit' (133). Smith's humour related to fundamentalism already seems to derive from a more innocent age, its gestures both awkward and yet telling. Although many academics foreground history as central to the novel, many either downplay the importance or even neglect to consider one overarching historical reality that *White Teeth* reflects on a world prior to '9/11' and the so-called 'War on Terror.' Although such events cannot be regarded as reconfiguring aesthetics or ideology, their impact culturally has been palpable. The issue of Muslim fundamentalism seems different, as have the possibilities and nuances of its aesthetic representation, and critical interpretation. In rereading *White Teeth* post-9/11 one might reconsider the implications of its depictions militancy.

Certainly, despite a status of radical newness conferred by many early critics, Smith's novel looks backwards in a celebratory style, in ways subsequently more difficult after 9/11. In so doing she creates a pastiche of the cultural moods and moments from the mid-1970s that had contributed to the new multicultural Britain. Her satire reflects upon divisions within the self and the body politic, particularly those of the Muslims that are prominent in the narrative. The book's focus is familial and domestic. Nevertheless, and perhaps presciently, the Iqbals are absent from the mock Edenic return to the Caribbean at the narrative's end. Offstage, one infers, continues the conflictual, unresolved dialectic of the partly radicalized Millat, the nostalgic and fissured religiosity of Samad with his rhetorical resistance to the West and assimilation, Alsana's pragmatic yet aggressive conciliations, and the Anglo-Indian tradition upon which Magid draws much to his father's disgust, to create an anglicized Bangladeshi culture. In the final whimsical paradise regained Smith situates Irie, Joshua, Hortense and 'Irie's [unnamed] fatherless little girl [who] writes affectionate postcards to *Bad Uncle Millat* and *Good Uncle Magid* and feels free as Pinocchio, a puppet clipped of paternal wings. . .' (541).[2] Perhaps one is implicitly invited to set this against the despair of Samad at the Western assimilation of his family, particularly that of Alsana's nephews and nieces which induces him to abduct his own son and return him to the homeland and what he imagines is a true religiosity.

> They won't go to mosque, they don't pray, they speak strangely, they dress strangely, they eat all kinds of rubbish, they have intercourse with God knows who. No respect for tradition. People call it assimilation when it is nothing but corruption. Corruption!
>
> Archie tried to look shocked and then tried disgusted, not knowing what to say. He liked people to get on with things, Archie. He kind of felt people should just live together, you know, in peace or harmony or something.

(190)

There is much positivity in Archie's vague idealism, and it stands as much in opposition to the middle-class values of intervening in and shaping culture as it is confused by Samad's paradoxical and self-defeating ersatz traditionalism. Again, Smith's balancing of these contending forces optimistically now reads as very pre-9/11, comically whimsical about fundamentalism, creating a comic motif of Samad's obsession of surviving the last days, and gently satirizing Millat's opposition to his brother, the two contending like children, miming their discontents, their rivalries and their past, confronting the crisis and trauma of their separation.

> Millat uses the filing cabinet as a substitute for another one he despised, fills it with imaginary letters between a scientist Jew and an unbelieving Muslim; Magid puts three chairs together and shines two anglepoise lamps and now there are two brothers in a car, shivering and huddled together until a few minutes later they are separated for ever and a paper plane takes off.
>
> It goes on and on and on.
>
> And it goes to prove what has been said of immigrants many times before now; they are *resourceful*; they make do. They use what they can when they can.
>
> (464–5)

Note that Smith is explicit that Magid and Millat risk a dead end in such ongoing confrontation, the narrator adamant that they cannot manage to weave 'their way through Happy Multicultural Land. [...] They left that neutral room as they had entered it: weighed down, burdened, unable to waver from their course or in any way change their separate, dangerous trajectories' (465). McLeod comments astutely that 'Smith's attention to the less soluble problems of postcolonial London [has] been overlooked – problems of identity crises and divided consciousness have not disappeared in the cheerful polyphony of the city. At the heart of Smith's novel we find a deeply perplexing, disorientating dynamic which is offered as the quintessence of contemporary London life. ...' (40). However attuned to these dynamics Smith proves, she certainly could not be expected to predict real events, although it seems clear that the ending emphasizes the historical (ideological) impasse that Irie's child unknowingly parodies. If one allows that the text's aesthetic emphases have been transformed by subsequent events,

Smith's homilies above must seem partially undermined by the very irresolvable tensions that she charts, especially as ironically they would rupture the public sphere, widening conflicted cultural views, polarizing further divided ideologies.

In his theoretically inclined essay Bentley identifies Smith's critique of multiculturalism as something not antagonistic to Englishness (495), and rather concludes that the novel on one level is 'an attempt to construct a new model of Englishness that is suited to the country's multicultural make-up at the beginning of the twenty-first century' (501). However, he notes that Smith refuses certain essentialisms and 'moves beyond the idea of "hybrid" identities, which again suggests a "mix" of discrete races or ethnicities' (496). Certainly, Smith's characters' lives reflect aspects of a difficult evolution of British culture and identity. Her vision is neither utopian nor essentialist. As Bentley concedes she interrogates the illusory nature of a liberal consensus that aspires to underpin and guarantee our lives. Magid aspires to the latter; both he and Irie specifically see its possibility in the Chalfens. In reality they find life full of remonstration and conflict, both personal and political. The children first learn this when Magid and Irie adopt a silent protest against Samad's objections to celebrating harvest festival. At this time Magid adopts the name Mark Smith as part of what Smith specifies as a larger, 'a far deeper malaise' (151). Magid doesn't just want to be English, simply to assimilate, but aspires to a very specifically middle-class existence, with cats, maternal cello music, pianos, shiny wood floors, biking holidays in France and a father as a doctor. These aspirations he focuses on participation in the Harvest Festival, ironically only to be confronted by the toothless Mr J. P. Hamilton, 'an elderly English bird in Wonderland...' (168), whose rhetoric embraces the past of the '"niggers"' (171) he has killed in wartime Congo, of '"wogs"' (172) when refuting the very possibility of a Pakistani in the English army in the Second World War.

Barbara Korte in 'Blacks and Asians at War for Britain: Reconceptualisations in the Filmic and Literary Field?' focuses entirely on this episode's racism, concluding that Smith's novel 'present[s] the contribution of blacks and Asians in World War II in a positive light and as a marker of a right to belong in Britain' (36). Curiously in a nuance Korte obscures, Hamilton refers to himself as an old 'Queen' or homosexual. Although ultimately he is at least half-mad, obsessed with losing one's teeth, there is a metaphoric significance in this and his initial declaration that he requires less rather than more information. In his final declamation he insists that the third molars or 'wisdom' teeth are a paternal inheritance, his own having been too large for him. In an episode that evokes explicitly the novel's title and its underlying metaphor, he advocates rather their removal and a repeated daily brushing of one's teeth, suggesting metaphorically that some are able to accommodate wisdom, others like himself not. Moreover, only by rejecting the wisdom and inheritance of previous generations may a new wisdom be achieved. Curiously, it is obsessive brushing of teeth that epitomizes Magid when he later returns from an exile in Bangladesh (abducted by his father with Archie's compliance). The children flee this aging dinosaur, 'tripping over themselves, running to get to a green space, to get to one of the lungs of the city, some place where free breathing was possible' (174). Significantly, the literal space of the city offers them nurture, redeeming their presence, despite its many examples of more evident, yet lesser madness. 'These people *announced* their madness—they were better, less scary than Mr J. P. Hamilton—they flaunted their insanity, they weren't half mad and half not, curled around a door frame. They were properly mad in the Shakespearean sense, talking sense when you least expected it' (174). As Smith indicates, here lies some of the wisdom of the city, something not essentially rational. However, as Arthur G. Neal makes evident in *National Trauma and Collective Memory: Extraordinary Events in the American Experience* (2005), 'One of the major assumptions shattered by September 11 was that the end of the cold war had provided ... an increased degree of safety and security' (180), and that it also challenges the trust that supposedly safeguarded people through certain norms found in contemporary urban culture (181), a sharing of values that in *White Teeth* convey a residual sense of familiarity and safety, however illusory, for even the mad in Willesden Green appear relatively beneficent.

Like life, in its ongoing state of irresolution, Smith's narrative is full of myriad curious and paradoxical implications, structured around unresolved contradictions. In one very specific allusion in Chapter Seventeen to Zeno's paradoxes, Smith indicates the impossible task of seeking unity in a world of multiplicity (465–6). Sigrun Meinig in '"Running at a Standstill": The Paradoxes of Time and Trauma in Zadie Smith's *White Teeth*' follows the logic of certain aspects inherent in this episode, suggesting that the central postcolonial condition is one of 'paradox' (241), and that its possibilities are always confounded by an underlying irresolvable quality. However, yet again, Smith's ambitions may be larger, as quite consciously she reads postcolonial subjectivity as part of a universal quest for meaning, for as Meinig indicates, 'The refutation of these paradoxes and their denial of motion and multitude requires considerable intellectual effort as the likes of Plato and Aristotle have shown in their discussions of the Zenonian perspective' (241). Meinig uses the allusion to Zeno to claim that the motionless aspect in Zeno's theory of movement when seen as successive moments refutes everyday experience, using this to suggest Smith embraces paradoxes, using them to 'call into question the various worldviews its characters hold, especially where their conception of motion and time is concerned' (243). Smith's narrator says, 'If you can divide reality inexhaustibly into parts [...] the result is insupportable paradox. You are always still, you move nowhere, there is no progress' (466). There are two obvious implications, no less important for their clarity. First, even metaphysics finds it difficult to account for reality, and one might need one's senses to understand the world. Second, ideology (and the twins are intractable in their positions-taking) and theorizing lead to a similar intellectual intractability. Meinig contrasts Archie's binary aleatory coin-flipping (244–5) to Samad's underlying insistence on an Islamic determinism dependent on God's will (245). For Meinig, Smith finally 'concentrates on openness' (249), the arbitrary (250), and the traumatic belatedness of postcoloniality. Paproth sees rather a postmodern crisis underlying the characters search for meaning while bound by 'various binaries' found in religion, history and 'randomness and predestination' (9). Paproth adds that although Smith rejects any 'absolutes' thematically she writes 'novels [which] are determinedly modernist in their construction' (10) undercutting the underlying message (an observation only marginally reduced by Paproth's later aberrant identification of Samad's migrant destination as 'America' [17]). Yet, as Meinig indicates all such responsive strategies finally represent responses to fate and a submission to history. Smith may indicate simply that migrants (like all subjects) can neither escape their history nor yet perhaps resolve the allure of belonging (implicitly as elusive as Zeno's unitary indivisibility). Like all our lives, their existence is meant to be read as part of a condition of change. Whatever overall one's reading of Smith's oeuvre, perhaps all one can conclude with certainty is that certain broader contexts—aesthetic, social, ideological, theoretical and literary-historical—remain interrelated. The novel's ambitions are to transcend the postcolonial condition without either abandoning or being trapped by its potentially reductive and essentialist dynamics. The above account omits many episodes or incidents (perhaps, even some of your favourites), because a novel of such scope and complexity does not allow a full summary or analysis. Further issues are considered in Chapter 7 which surveys major critical responses.

4

THE AUTOGRAPH MAN

SUBURBAN OBSESSIONS

Great attention was required to produce the British first edition of *The Autograph Man* both in terms of its overall layout as an artefact and also as a narrative. Its design consists of several layered elements, suggesting superimpositions, offering almost a quality of the palimpsest. One has to physically engage with the book beyond normal parameters. First if the book is removed from the dust jacket, one finds printed on the inside of the latter three very short stories described as 'Being No. 1 in an occasional series of Practical and Moral Lifestyle Pamphlets written by the author of the accompanying novel,' entitled 'When You Turn Everything into Symbol, Bad Things Happen or The Same Instinct Runs Through It All' (n.p.). This indicates obliquely one of the ongoing themes of the book, the contemporary preference for the symbolic over the real, image over substance. Opened out further the dust-jacket reveals on the reverse of both these stories and the book's front cover, a whimsically illustrated 'Kabbalah of Alex-Li Tandem' (n.p.), the chart for Smith's protagonist (referred to after the first few pages simply as Alex) who represents 'Presence.' The intricate literal opening required might be taken to indicate symbolically an elaborate opening out, a revelation of sorts. This illustration of the Tree of Life appears to link Alex literally to various famous figures: Muhammad Ali, Bette Davis, Franz Kafka, John Lennon, Jimmy Stewart, Fats Waller, Ludwig Wittgenstein and Virginia Woolf. The drawing relates to a whimsical attempt by Alex's friend Adam, a black Jew, to interest him in Judaism. In the text Alex's autograph appears next to theirs (together with photographs) arranged in the same Cabbalistic formation by Adam on the wall of his flat (127). This is one among a number of shared, masculine private forms of behaviour that cements their close relationship that in the novel is tested by Alex's apparently bizarre behaviour. Both Cabbalistic images highlight the central themes of celebrity, aspiration and fate. The illustrated drawing on the reverse of the cover leads to the *blank* space of the 'Crown' which also is concerned with 'Will,' indicating precisely Alex's deficiency in terms of the latter in the narrative. The novel's many textual illustrations include a similar blank chart labelled 'The Ten Sefirot' (94), or the ten creative forces of the Jewish mystical doctrine of the Kabbalah that intervene between the infinite, unknowable God ('Ein Sof') and the created world, positioned alongside that of the twenty-two letters of the Hebrew alphabet (95). Both are also found on the wall of Adam, who exhibits a penchant for the mystical and for drugs.

Various extra-narrative elements supplement certain of the novel's narrative concerns to establish Judaism and its culture as major themes and contexts of the novel potentially before a word has been read. Smith uses illustrations inside the dust jacket, adding more in the text, and preceding the title page she positions a long quotation taken from *The Essential Lenny Bruce*. In this epigraph, the American comedian categorizes the world in binary fashion, distinguishing as a quality of perspective and behaviour Jewishness from 'goyish.' The latter is a disparaging term for the non-Jew, originally in Yiddish referring to a Jew ignorant of the Jewish religion which very much applies to Alex who is in wilful denial. In the course of the book he ceases to be totally goyish and very reluctantly familiarizes himself with aspects of his Judaic culture, although he abandons his own book based on such binaries, and never becomes truly observant. Moreover, as Frank Kermode says in 'Here She Is' Smith's novel positions 'Judaism as its central religion and [it is] subjected to some teasing: is Judaism "the most goyish of monotheisms"? Paradoxes abound; a father tries to persuade his son not to turn up for his bar mitzvah, and so on.' Precisely the ambivalences of religiosity and belief (including Alex's lack of the latter) abound in the various scenes, not least because Smith locates her narrative in the suburban heartland of Jewish London Mountjoy, where reminders of Judaism are hard to avoid. An otherwise admiring Wendy Smith concedes in 'The Paper Chase' that *The Autograph Man* has faults, principally Smith's shallow depiction of her characters' relationship to Judaism. It's meant to be a major motif—telegraphed by the hilarious epigraph from the late comedian Lenny Bruce—but feels more like a plot premise' (R-5). Andrew Furman in 'The Jewishness of the Contemporary Gentile Writer: Zadie Smith's *The Autograph Man*' argues that the novel's Jewish qualities can be applauded and are sustained despite the non-Jewishness of the author. For him the novel 'marks a welcome return of the Jewish novel actively engaged with the pressing cultural crises of our day, specifically the complexities involved in claiming a viable identity in our increasingly multiethnic, multiracial, and transnational world' (7). As Furman indicates Smith moves Jewishness 'from the periphery to the center,' and the Bruce quotation allows the concept of a Jewish sensibility its own heterogeneity and through it Smith's novel 'defines Jewishness not along inviolate racial or even religious lines, but as a sensibility, both permeable and dynamic' (8). Of course, Smith has already dealt with certain aspects of Jewish life with the Chalfens, but not as centrally so. As Sukhdev Sandhu comments in 'Zadie Smith Bounces Back with Fun and Too Many Facts,' 'Whereas *White Teeth* dwelt on the intellectual world of north London Jews, this one, partly inspired by Leon Wieseltier's excellent memoir, *Kaddish*, focuses more on the devotional and mystical elements of Judaism.' The second novel's more positive Jewish cultural coordinates explain why despite certain accusations of anti-Semitism concerning Smith's first novel, for the second she was awarded the *Jewish Quarterly* Literary Prize for Fiction. Adam Mars-Jones in 'Name of the Prose' concludes, 'All the major characters are Jewish, though their observance ranges from the absolute to the resistant, the would-be non-existent. Jewishness works beautifully in the novel as a source of ideas and symbols. Jewishness is an outsiderdom with a front-row centre seat.'

Despite the Jewish framework, the importance of the theme of celebrity for the book cannot be overemphasized, and it is reinforced when the reader discovers on the cover of the hardback gold lettering which proclaims a well-known line from the theme song written for the movie *Fame* directed by Alan Parker, an immense success when released in 1980 just before Smith's fifth birthday. This reads: ' "Fame! I'm gonna live forever!" ' followed by three gold stars (n.p.), ironic given the fate of Alex's father. While not a recluse, Alex frequently withdraws from the world his relationships threatened by this underlying predilection for solitariness. Alex inhabits obscurity, which with the anonymity of his childhood contrasts the celebrity inherent in his trade. Ironically, such noteworthiness may result famously in withdrawal, as with Kitty Alexander, a film star Alex idolizes. And as Moran points out, there exists 'An uneasiness with the constraints of celebrity [which] often produces a fascination with withdrawal and silence in authors who are not themselves recluses' (74). Beyond establishing certain overall possible contexts, the exact meanings and significance of Smith's additions remain teasingly enigmatic, but still suggestive in many ways. The use of the cover and dust jacket reminds one of the ways in which youth culture expresses itself as part of the culture industry, traditionally the record sleeve and its liner notes which Smith's inclusions resemble more determinedly part of the cultural industry than traditional literary illustrations. This is doubly salient since pop music allusions abound periodically throughout the narrative, as do allusions to movies and their stars, another segment of the cultural industry, as is the spin-off of celebrity autographs and other artefacts that are the primary subject matter of the novel. As noted above Shakespeare suggests that the novel draws upon Smith's friend Adam Andrusier, a real autograph hunter. Even in this bizarre world naturally the reader soon recognizes that the often very public activities involved are subtended by numerous archetypal human interactions and crises.

Despite Smith's elaborations described above and Kermode's favourable view, where he regards the novel as continued evidence of 'the author's exceptional comic skills. She is seriously comic about death, pain, faith,' more generally the novel proved unpopular with many reviewers. Such a general attitude is typified by Alan Cheuse's review, self-evident from his very title, 'Zadie Smith Novel Loses Energy at Midpoint' (2). However, according to Deresiewicz the novel is 'unjustly maligned [...]. By narrowing her scope, she not only created a more thematically coherent and architecturally streamlined work but also got closer to her material' (1); unusually he prefers the second novel, concluding that *White Teeth*, 'while admirable for its ambition, is also a gigantic mess, to which the novel's many divisions and subdivisions (each with its catchy little title) give only the illusion of coherence' (1). Many other critics regard *The Autograph Man* as inferior to Smith's first novel. In Britain the comparison is hardly surprising since although Reynolds says of Smith in 'Britain's Literary Darling Escapes the Hype for an

MA at Harvard' that she rebuffed the hyperbole for *The Autograph Man* (4), the publisher timed its appearance on 26 September 2002 exactly so as to coincide with the mid-point of Channel 4's broadcast of a four-part adaptation of Smith's *White Teeth*, the production of which had cost £3.5 million. Such comparisons were inevitable.

The grounds of the critical comparisons of the two novels are intriguing. Benita Singh in 'Not Quite Signature Piece' initially suggests that Smith in the second novel achieves only 'incoherence,' accusing the author effectively of failing to perform expectedly in her role as a postcolonial author,

> The same ambition that distinguished *White Teeth* is also present in *The Autograph Man*, but this time Smith's drive may have surpassed her abilities. Smith does not pursue the themes of migration and multiculturalism that she handled so deftly in *White Teeth*. Instead, London, and all its diversity, serves as the backdrop, as well as a distraction, to a novel that attempts to confront the banality of modernity by way of celebrities, cinema, and brand names.

Edemariam says, 'The most, some might say the only, really moving section of *The Autograph Man* [...] is the prologue, a simultaneously knockabout and tender portrait of a father and his 12-year-old son.' For James Wood in 'Fundamentally Goyish' Smith's novel is characterized by

> irrelevant intensity. In fiction, information has become the new character, and information is endless. We know the signs of irrelevant intensity: an obsession with pop-culture trivia; a love of the comedy of culture rather than the comedy of character; zany scenes interrupted by essayistic riffs—on hotel minibars, on videophones, on the semiotics of street manners in major European cities, what have you—the riffs always expertly blending the sentimental and the Cultural-Studies-theoretical [...]

Interestingly, Cheuse explicitly refers to a decision not to undertake a comparison of Smith's first two novels, but he does conclude of the second that 'I dragged my way through the book, trying desperately to enjoy Alex but finding that he never really stepped off the page and into my heart. In the second half, I began to appreciate Smith's abilities as a portraitist and cultural analyst, but by then it was too late [. . .]' (2). For Sandhu the novel 'seems too garrulous and random' and remains 'too knowing and can feel like control freakery, circumscribing affect as tightly as Hollywood actors hold on to their image rights. The novel reads like an essay on feeling as much as it is an exercise in one.' However, it is exactly these elements that Furman applauds as 'picaresque' (9), a strategy that potentially frees the novel from both reductive binaries and their essentialisms. Furman says, 'While Bruce's riff allows for a type of post-ethnic identity choice (or "consent," to use Werner Sollor's terminology), Smith, through her protagonist, ultimately rejects the model for its reductiveness' (12) and if Alex has genuinely matured the adolescent cultural and aesthetic determination of his unseen manuscript will prove insufficient. 'The Joke about the Pope and the Chief Rabbi' (142–3) exemplifies the difficulty of a number of relevant issues: culturally divergent interpretations, the threat of oppression and religiosity, the problematic of the non-verbal for joint understanding, and through narrative the compulsive efficaciousness and capacity of humour to both subvert and convey the baffling complexity of human identity.

The prose characterizing the Prologue with which the second novel begins is far more introspective in both its tone and perspective than that of its rambunctious predecessor, mirroring the withdrawn character of twelve-year-old Alex, who is a quiet, almost unobtrusive child on the cusp of adolescence. Nevertheless, a child of a technological age of egotists, Alex presumes first that he has an audience and second that he is the centre of his world. In the Prologue one learns how these characteristics are magnified so as to stunt his empathic and intersubjective possibilities. As the narrative begins Alex's perspective is characterized by a peculiar internalized fantasy, charting his pre-adolescent ability to 'imagine himself as a minor incident in the lives of others' (1). He engages with the cinematic and the performative that typify contemporary self-consciousness. Such an acting out as if one might have an audience is an informing aspect of the narrative throughout. Using an imaginary scenario taken straight from Hollywood, Alex-Li sees himself as a victim of a shark, lifeless, while the lifeguard flirts with the prettiest girl. This is a conscious contraction of his possibilities, a cultural as well as personal withdrawal. Yet in so doing Alex exhibits intense self-awareness verging on narcissism. 'He deals in a shorthand of experience. The TV version. He is one of this generation who watch themselves' (2). These themes recur, suggesting that both authenticity and spontaneity are difficult to achieve in the kind of a secularized world described by Smith, where the obsession for money and fame produce both a sense of tedium and an underlying feeling of crisis that characterize the suburban life of the protagonist. As Furman notes, 'Too many of our actions and reactions today, Tandem recognizes, utterly lack authenticity, owing largely to the ubiquity of media images' (14). Alex's whole consciousness and that of those around him exemplify this quality of diminishment.

Redeploying a motif central to *White Teeth*, the second novel's Prologue introduces a series of flawed fathers seemingly incapable of appropriately articulating their relations with their offspring, exemplified in the oedipal responses of Alex, and Joseph Klein who meet at the Albert Hall while waiting to see the wrestler, Big Daddy. Smith uses the curious, cherubic figure of a real and unlikely celebrity. Christened Shirley Crabtree, Jr, Smith uses him to suggest that manhood is hybrid and mutable, far from what traditionally composes the heroic. Mars-Jones is suspicious, thinking the Jewish element is part of a larger attempt on Smith's behalf (or even directly by her since Mars-Jones' final implication is unclear) to permeate the American market. In his response Mars-Jones neglects the historical resonance of Crabtree and his opponent, Giant Haystacks. Although many in Britain can still recall their frequent appearances on television, Mars-Jones misreads the pair. 'They seem altogether American, in ideology as well as language.' Big Daddy was extremely famous for both his sixty-two inch chest and wearing an infantilizing leotard donned in his expansive middle-age when he returned to wrestling for the second time. Alex's trip—accompanied by Jewish friends Adam and Rubenfine—is suggested by Alex's mother, Sarah, to encourage her son, so devoted to his father, Li-Jin, to broaden his horizons. Ironically, Alex's father guards the secret that he is dying from a brain tumour, but seems equally disturbed at the prospect of his son's forthcoming Bar Mitzvah, extremely hesitant about this Jewish cultural affiliation. The Prologue's sections are divided by the traditional term for God, 'YHWH' or Yahweh, who seems thereby to appear as if in the interstices of the narrative, ever-present yet unknowable. Moreover although the occasion is secular, there is a ritualistic quality, as the fathers and sons arrive from diverse points of origin to pay homage to an incongruous figure. 'Of course Big Daddy will win! How could it be otherwise? Look at him. He wears a red Babygro, he is ruddy-faced, he is white-haired, he is more *famous*' (36).

Clearly, not only does Big Daddy culturally represent the triumph of virtue in a pantomimic, archetypal struggle, for Smith he obliquely exemplifies something of the diverse nature of fame as described by Moran. 'What I have been describing so far is celebrity as a pervasive phenomenon which cuts across cultural boundaries. In theory, then, it has the potential to infiltrate itself into all sorts of spheres not normally associated with celebrity: classical music, jazz, opera, art and other forms of writing [...]' (155). As Moran indicates such structures are inter-fused by 'the logic of the marketplace' (155), an experience Smith encountered herself in terms of the celebrity produced around her first novel (discussed in detail earlier). This very experience and her childhood obsessions are synthesized in the second novel with the contemporary sub-culture of philography (autograph collecting) which is not only highly commodified, but almost cultish. Of course, by focusing on a fixation with one's signature Smith's book thereby indicates thematically larger issues of identity, authentication, and the signification of the individual.

On the day of the bout, Alex finds himself in the company of three boys who will continue to play a part in his life. To each of them Li-Jin, Alex's father, awards what becomes talismanic objects, signed pound notes as part of a bet with them predicting that Big Daddy will lose. Ironically, he knows he is dying, plagued by headaches, and it is in the most surprising elements of popular culture that he finds reminders of his impending mortality rather than those one might anticipate.

Though his death is always there, waiting for him, he can only feel it sometimes, and then incongruously. Not detecting it during the movies *Love Story* or *The Champ*, for example, but in the middle of a tea commercial, in the wild gestures of a ventriloquized chimp [...]. His death is like the soft down on the back of your hand, passing unnoticed in the firmest of handshakes, though the slightest breeze makes every damn one of those tiny hairs stand on end.

(35–6)

Li-Jin endures his illness, of which he refuses to tell his son, failing to prepare him. At the Albert Hall waiting for the wrestling Alex becomes fascinated by Joseph's hobby of autograph collecting, and follows him backstage where they acquire the wrestler's autograph. The double irony is that in so abandoning his father Alex loses him for good, since there out of sight of his son he collapses and dies. As Childs says referring to this key moment in the Prologue and its resolution in the novel's Epilogue, 'This symbolic act of fleeing the real for the artificial characterizes Alex's life until he returns to the memory of his father at the narrative's close' (203). As Childs indicates the first section is referred to as Alex's Kabbalah (203) and the second 'is modelled on the "ten bulls" of Zen Buddhism, representing steps in the realization of Alex's "true nature"' (204). These main sections, positioned between Prologue and Epilogue, are concerned with Alex's life at age twenty-seven, approaching the anniversary of his father's death, gradually accepting that he needs both to deal with his grief and to mature, symbolically announced at the novel's end by his undertaking the ceremony of Kaddish, or the rituals of mourning for his dead parent.

The first chapter opens with a three-day drug-induced amnesia when Alex slowly recalls a hedonistic evening when (with Adam of the Big Daddy trip, brother of Alex's current girlfriend, Esther) he has taken a 'microdot' attempting to uncover spiritual or hidden meaning in life. The episode surely evokes, at least obliquely and partly parodically, Billy Wilder's classic movie, *The Lost Weekend* (1945), starring Ray Milland. When Alex reappears, Smith accentuates his lack of control, using an intertextual echo of the eponymous protagonist of Kinglsey Amis's *Lucky Jim* (1954). Alex's checklist stresses not only his pathos, the particular frailty of youth, but reveals his archetypal male hypochondria and self-obsession:

> He bared his teeth in the mirror. They were yellow. But, on the plus side, they were there. He opened his Accidental eyes (Rubinfine's term: halfway between Oriental and Occidental) wide as they would go and touched the tip of his nose to the cold glass. What was the damage? His eyes worked. Light didn't hurt. Swallowing felt basic, uncomplicated. He was not shivering. He felt no crippling paranoia or muscular tremors. He seized his penis. He squeezed his cheeks. All present and correct.

> (46–7)

Alex recalls various disturbing events in flashes prompted variously by Marvin, his black milk operative, and phone calls and visits from his friends, their badinage still reminiscent of the Big Daddy trip. Akin to the current state of his memory, Alex's life appears fragmentary. Rather than being frenetic, he is withdrawn, quietly undertaking a series of aimless excesses and followed by tentative physical recoveries. Working largely from home, as a result of his lifestyle his rented flat remains unkempt, its disturbing chaos reflecting his world-view. Across the street Marvin points out the wreckage of Alex's vintage sports-car, Greta, jointly owned with Adam, crashed by Alex as a result of the effects of drugs and alcohol, apparently breaking Esther's finger. The reader discovers the coordinates of Alex's life in great part retrospectively, pieced together along with Alex as he recalls memories of various significant events or forms of behaviour either from after his father's death, or from the period of his drug-induced amnesia. A central factor is the claim by his friends and fellow collectors that Alex has faked an autograph of Kitty's which he produced during his time when stoned, so he has no recollection of any culpability in this unethical, if not criminal act. Ignoring the accusation, and maintaining his pattern of obsessive, compulsive behaviour, he begins writing another in a series of unanswered letters to Kitty, his very first meaningful action on recovery.

In adulthood Adam runs a video store, despite films having no interest or attraction for him (135). Perversely, he prefers music and, of course, his esotericism and mysticism, and the consumption of drugs. Joseph has abandoned his hobby, philography, becoming a clerk selling policies by telephone for Heller Insurance. 'In the world of Heller, as Alex understood it, the principles of Heisenberg were dangerously ignored: at Heller, certainty reigned. At Heller, effect was always neatly traced back to cause' (78–9). For Alex his unresolved grief prevails, negating any such sense of order or balance, foregrounding the aleatory, the contingent. In this sense in a minor fashion the novel engages certain belated inflections of the postmodern, like an anachronistic version of Don DeLillo's *White Noise* (1985), attempting to signify the lack of signification, the moral vacuity of the contemporary. Confirming concerning this feature of the novel, Mars-Jones identifies certain aspects of the novel in particular: the removal of names from the landscape. He argues that 'Thematically, this is pointed (the relationship between things and the names for them being a troubled one), but it also frees Smith up stylistically, allowing her prose to explore textures without the neurosis of constant reference'; and calls attention to the name-checking of the famous in unusual ways 'that renders celebrity flat: "the popular singer Madonna Ciccone" tagged equally with "the popular musician Leonard Cohen".' As Mars-Jones indicates in this vein Smith refers obliquely and reverentially to Nabokov by his Russian pseudonym Sirin, and to Larkin by referring to the toad called work, citing him not by name, but simply as Alex's favourite poet. Note that Alex incorporates many of Smith's preferences.

Mark Rubinstine, ironically the bully of the childhood trip, is now a reluctant rabbi who has never spoken to God (201), prompted by his father towards belief and religiosity. He is enthused by the need for an audience (200), his affection for the crowd rather than individuals, his passion for Jewish culture and Mountjoy in particular, contrasting the reclusive tendencies of Adam and Alex. Alex's difficulties and the very mundanity of his and his friends' lives delight Cheuse, who locates the novel very precisely in a Jewish literary tradition. 'Alex comes face to face with problems in business, love and friendship. In the middle of all this, Alex, in a delightfully confused state of mind, thinks to himself in a near-perfect echo of Saul Bellow's character Herzog, "if I am out of my mind . . . it's all right by me."'

Rubinstine encounters the contemporary propensity for celebrity among schoolchildren he encounters during a school visit to explain Purim, a Jewish festival celebrating deliverance, when he asks them for their adult employment ambitions:

> Yes, and in a class of thirty-five, nine wanted to be models, four wanted to be actors, two wanted to be pop stars, ten wanted to be footballers and the remaining ten wanted to be 'entertainers', just 'entertainers'.
>
> (198)

The unrealistic ambitions offer an indication of part of Smith's cultural commentary. They contrast with the seedy world of Alex with its symbiotic relationship with fame, and the mundane quality of Kitty's life that Alex encounters in his transatlantic trip. All of the close group of Alex's friends continue to evoke his father's signed pound note as if the very mention of them were totemic, a symbol binding them together. Although physically and in other senses they appear to have matured, nevertheless an adolescent male perspective subtends both their activities and world-view. This is a characteristic also of many in the autograph traders, including Ian Dove and Lovelear. Each of them appears infantilized, echoing an aspect of the wrestler that brought them together in his overgrown diapers, a cultural refusal of maturity. Although not young, among Alex's contacts is Brian Duchamp, formerly working on the fringes of the star system in films, an ageing, overweight bachelor and occasional forger of autographs who now exists in the nether regions of South London trading oddments and memorabilia. Alex visits him on Thursday mornings, encountering his 'toxic smell' (168), odour of decay (179), 'filthy death-rattle [. . .]' (174). These aspects exacerbate and foreground Alex's sense of the imminence of death and dying. 'He didn't look scared, though. That's the safety net of madness. Duchamp had no goyish fears, thanks to the net. It was only Alex who was feeling a terror grip him. A selfish terror. *How few Thursdays Duchamp has left to him! How many do I have?*' (168). Alex fears Duchamp's physical and mental degeneration which in contrast to his father's secret, private demise, allows anticipation of Duchamp's death. Through Duchamp Alex relives more dramatically the origins of his own fear and self-obsession, the trauma of paternal loss and absence. The episode evokes a motif of morbidity. Even celebrity becomes analogous to deathliness, evident in Smith's grotesque humour when Alex is delayed by an attempted suicide in his travel back to north of the river.

> Somebody at a tube station wanted to be famous. They wanted to be known, all over the city, if only for fifteen minutes. They let their heels cross the white line, they took a deep breath, they leapt into for ever. Thanks to this *passenger action* (a truly majestic new euphemism, emphasizing the inconsideration), it took Alex almost two hours to get from the South to the centre of town.
>
> (175)

As in *White Teeth* Smith introduces variously such elements of a gallows humour, its cryptic, comic inversions of fear still incorporating the secretive and mysterious elements of death identified by Derrida in *The Gift of Death* (19–21), and whose economy for Alex is in Derrida's terms one of both '*incorporation and repression*' (21), of the evidence of death (or its possibility) in each signature, and the effacement of (or turning away from) his father's tragic end leaving his inscription on the pound notes as a memorial.

Only in one way does Alex truly transcend his fears, or set them aside. From age seventeen Alex's letters to Kitty have acquired a life of their own. After initially requesting Kitty's autograph and talking about himself as advised by autograph guides, Alex continues. He has no longer made requests nor offered praise, but rather imaginatively described her responses to the world, actively imagining her otherness, her inner qualities. These are highly significant, for as Moran indicates Hollywood celebrity culture from the 1920s focused on 'the "natural" charisma of the celebrity rather than any exceptional acting talent or technical ability, and which therefore sought to show that the star's on-screen persona and off-screen behaviour were broadly similar' (62). On meeting Kitty, Alex will compulsively look for gestures, signs and nuances that mean the two aspects of her can be conjoined. As Moran makes evident the audience searches for the real in the star, trying to distinguish the 'authentic' and the 'superficial' (62), and often undertakes to appropriate the 'private' (63), which in one sense is exactly what Alex achieves. Nevertheless in so characterizing the then-unknown Kitty in his letters Alex has transcended his interiority, overcoming his solipsistic tendencies. Alex has explored the visceral framework that makes up the self, but has been unable to do so in respect of his own life. In a manner that critiques the postmodern tendencies of late capitalism, however self-conscious Alex becomes, he cannot achieve any real self-awareness. He objectifies his own life and thereby stymies its further development or full participation in the world. In these letters he has exhibited exactly the kind of empathy that has been lacking in the rest of his emotional life, the development of which is not only blocked by the memory of his father's death.

Before his departure to New York, Alex wallows in an abject existential crisis, going through the motions of his trade through which the reader learns of the peculiarities of its devotees or zealots. Checking his emails Alex discovers one from Boot, a 'posh' girl who works as an assistant at Cotterell's Autograph Emporium where Alex is employed periodically for his skill in assessing or authenticating signatures. Boot abjures grammatical niceties, admired by Alex since 'He had little goyish fetishes, one of which was awe for anyone so posh she couldn't be bothered to be embarrassed. Or to *spell* properly' (157). As she draws to his attention, Alex has been avoiding Boot for 3 months, guilty about the affair they have been conducting. From another email he finds also that during his amnesiac period he has booked himself and Esther on flights to America, to visit 'The Autographicana Fair, an annual extravaganza' (157), a series of trade events with celebrities that have included the men who dropped the atom bomb on Hiroshima (157).

In several subsequent phone calls Alex faces various dilemmas concerning his rather perfunctory betrayal of his girlfriend which issue is raised by Esther who notifies him about her forthcoming operation to replace her heart pacemaker. Although troubled Alex has to decide whether to travel to America which clashes with the medical intervention, and interestingly he chooses to do so, a decision that perturbs Adam (178). Drunk and stoned, Alex travels to Cotterell's, clearly in part to see Boot. Interestingly, she is the first woman, who although still marginal like all the others in his life, appears to affect his behaviour, to impress herself tangibly upon him. After he scrutinizes photographs signed by the famous and tries to sell Duchamp's forged signature purporting to be Kitty's to the proprietor, the latter attacking him. Alex's view of these photographs is suggestive in several ways.

> A man could own these photographs and partake (in however minor a way) of the famousness of these people and their remarkable ability to cheat Death of its satisfaction: obscurity. A man wavers between awe and anger at the very famous, as he does the idea of God. This afternoon Alex feels rage. He is having a psychotic interlude.
>
> (182)

Clearly, the implication is that Alex is attracted to his trade as a failed attempt to transcend his father's demise; the latter's passing totally forgotten by those outside Alex's circle. Boot realizes he is suffering a breakdown, and attempts to help him. In this phase Alex seems doubly divorced from reality, drifting through events as if powerless and morally indifferent. This is the lowest ebb in a series of crises, his rock bottom point. He lurches from one to another, refusing medical help apart from Chinese doctors, ironically mirroring choices that perhaps doomed his father, Li-Jin, who had decided not to consult anyone from his own profession except Chinese practitioners. Thus he had left his own diagnosis so late as to be irrelevant in terms of intervention. It is as if Alex unconsciously wills himself a similar fate, but in truth he simply exhibits an excess of neurotic symptoms. On the way to the airport he encounters, as he has severally in the past few days, three rabbis, Rubinfine, Darvick and Green, each time attempting to load heavy, over-large furniture into a small vehicle, reminiscent of various stock images of the cinematic comic tradition and also of the verbal structure of standard joke forms ('Imagine three rabbis . . .').

Crossing the Atlantic transforms the tenor of the narrative, although Alex encounters many he knows from his trade at the convention in his hotel, including some who had only been virtual contacts previously. From this arrival, which seems to so inscribe the curious feeling of a first encounter with North America that one wonders if aspects mirror Smith's own experience, Cheuse feels the novel loses direction. He details this transition:

> The second half of the book [. . .] trades most of the jangly energy of earlier chapters for lip-biting seriousness and a little quest narrative that takes our collector to an autograph-man's convention in New York City and then to Brooklyn, where he confronts the actress of his dreams, both business and pleasure. The polarities of counterfeit and authenticity move into the foreground here, leaving behind the jokey Jewish/goyish motif, as if it were part of an earlier draft rather than the first half of the same novel.

True there is both a change of gear and perspective, although arguably such a change helps one make sense of the overarching narrative, linking the friends' lives, highlighting the celebrity inherent in the act of collecting, and allowing one to finally comprehend the often deceptive signifiers of eminence, of fame. The subsequent episodes allow Smith to further extend her parody of contemporary culture's obsession with identity and celebrity. Given America's dominance from the twentieth century in the new media industries, Smith's second major setting seems appropriate to the whole culture of celebrity and its commercial presence, evoking certain aspects of Martin Amis' *Money* (1984), although Smith's version is less Rabelaisian and frenetic. For Mars-Jones Amis proves to be also Smith's major stylistic influence, her novel permeated by similar attempts to call attention to stylized representations of the demotic and banal.

A more pervasively present absence is Martin Amis, whose hectoringly insightful mannerisms Zadie Smith doesn't always manage to make her own. Withholding a name is part of the novel's strategy in some areas that seem arbitrary and sometimes awkward. Alex turns on not a Mac, laptop or PC, but simply a 'box of tricks'. Instead of the commonest conversational expletive Smith supplies 'ug' and 'ugging', a substitution which seems less coy in the Prologue, when her characters are barely teenagers, than in the body of the book. Running parallel with an extraordinary writerly assurance is a worry about relying on second-hand formulations. This too can be claimed as thematically appropriate (the colonisation of life by representations of itself), but the anxiety seems out of proportion.

Additionally, as Moran points out, Amis also deals with literary celebrity as one of his major themes in The Information (1995) (151–3), which too adopts transatlantic themes and settings, and is self-referential in charting the influence on the imaginative vocabulary of media production. By locating certain episodes in New York and Brooklyn, in her allusions to Amis, Smith compares America's brashness favourably to the greater reserve of the British. She highlights explicitly the odd familiarity of America's landscape to its transatlantic neighbours, mostly victims of the permeation of America's film and television culture, so much so that Lovelear appears indifferent to New York, inciting Alex to explain this familiarity simply by citing numerous filmic, cultural points of reference, to which a waiting taxi driver responds.

'Feel like I've been here before, a bit,' said Ian, levering his eyes open at the moment a cab stopped before them and wound down its window 'Familiar, like from another life or something. That's weird, innit? Considering I——'

'Taxi Driver,' said Alex flatly, removing bags from the trolley. 'Manhattan, Last Exit to Brooklyn, On the Waterfront, Mean Streets, Miracle on 34th Street, West Side Story, On the Town, Serpico, the Sunshine Boys, Sophie's Choice——'

'All about Eve,' broke in the driver, 'King Kong, Wall Street, Moonstruck, The Producers, Plaza Suite, The Out of Towners, original and re-make, the Godfathers parts one and two, Kramer vs Kramer and freakin' Ghostbusters. We can do this all morning, my friend. The meters running.'

(226)

Despite the driver's nonchalance, as strangers their overlapping points of reference allow Smith to stress the characters' transatlantic, yet uncanny cultural coordinates, their ephemeral commonality. And although an underlying transatlantic cultural clash subtends the comedy of many of the episodes located in America, these filmic listings appear as a doubling and redoubling of projections of meaning and location. Fantasy and reality are blurred in the contemporary mind, indistinguishable as points of reference, the city in excess of its reality, a site of repressed and now current longings, all focused for Alex on the quest for Kitty. Lovelear confirms the power of satisfying longings inculcated by images imprinted on the imagination by spurning the taxi and hiring a stretch limousine, culturally so familiar from film, television and the sex industry. Smith thus both establishes the parameters of a generic subset of coordinates of the male psyche and imagination, and simultaneously stresses that Alex is having to confront the ground zero of most of his pre- and post-adolescent fantasies.

This aspect is reinforced when in the convention hotel Alex undertakes prearranged business, meeting a black female dealer, Honey Richardson. Subsequently, he is informed by his fellow autograph men that she is actually Honey Smith a prostitute who has gained her own fame through a professional sexual encounter with a Scottish actor, reminiscent, of course, of services rendered by Divine Brown (originally Estella Marie Thompson) for Hugh Grant in 1995. Honey represents another mode of celebrity (an initial notoriety later capitalized), through circumstances that evince its absence of morality as any part of its particular economy of meaning. She fascinates the juvenile imaginations of fellow traders Lovelear and Dove, who make up the London contingent together with Baguley, another more successful and hated rival. Honey is full of contradictions. She has been a sex worker; she obsessively sanitizes anything she touches; and she has adopted an aggressive and eccentric form of Buddhism. Yet she remains above all practically minded, guiding Alex in his search for Kitty. Despite her public persona, Honey inhabits a world of pragmatic reality.

They encounter Kitty's ex-homosexual husband, Max Krauser, president of Kitty's fan club, but half-mad he refuses them access. Ironically by the simple expediency of following him they find Kitty's apartment. She reveals herself to be a 'fan' of Alex, because of his letters, all hidden by Max. Coincidentally, she discovered them prior to Alex's arrival in New York. She has read them successively, so by accident they obtain the coherence of a longer text. The fragments of Alex's life come together vicariously, through his act of projection in the letters, Kitty reinterpreting their apparently incoherence. She intervenes into Alex's life. As Singh says, 'Alex realizes that unlike his *Jewishness and Goyishness* and Esther's Ph.D. thesis, which were "for no one," in these letters "something he had written had affected someone." So begins Alex's genuine reflection on his life as an "autograph man" and as an author of sorts.' Kitty has other threatening letters that Alex suspects correctly are from Krauser, attesting to his malevolent potential.

In many ways America overwhelms Alex, away from his comfort zone, his narrow world of deferral and avoidance. Honey draws him out of his cocoon. He is aware of being largely disassociated from the present, although phone calls keep him apprised of those left in London. He ends his whimsical entries to the hotel questionnaire (reproduced in full with versions of his handwritten entries) 'Regret everything and always live in the past' (296). Honey rejects his sexual and voyeuristic objectification of a young star they encounter, Shylar, concerning whom Alex admits he 'had once spent three hours staring at pictures of this girl's head attached to the naked bodies of other girls' (300). Pointedly, the cameraman of a documentary team recording Shylar's contrived arrival excitedly notices Honey, who exudes a sense of authenticity. American television also overwhelms Alex. He can neither absorb the plethora of channels nor accept their inanities. Channel switching he chances upon Kitty (302), and impulsively decides to return to see the real woman, as if impelled by something genuine that resides in her. Still drunk and disturbing her in the middle of the night at the home, they watch television which Kitty describes aptly. ' "It is like all the finest food in the world put into a bucket and stirred with a stick" ' (306). It is precisely after this visit, after he has woken innocently next to her, that Alex recites fragments of the 'Kabbalah' in a park in Roebling. Only then might he find courage. He confronts a central truth, which is that he must attempt 'to figure out how to mourn a father dead fifteen years in a dead language' (315).

If there is a transformation in Alex, the ending suggests only a very provisional epiphany. Death haunts the book. Throughout there is an underlying mournful quality, not simply concerning Alex's father, but with a wider cultural significance. As Furman stresses (10) the contents of the box given to Alex by his mother whose very few 'Trinkets and photographs and facts' (78) derive from her family. By their very sparse, lacunary nature these possessions allude to the Holocaust, implicitly rather than explicitly, its only articulation remaining subtle, oblique. In the final section, Alex finally undergoes the Kaddish, a rite of conversing with God (the ultimate patriarch) concerning Alex's by now deceased father, whom one infers is the figure who will be positioned at the Crown of his Kabbalah. Childs believes that the episode indicates Alex's inability previously to engage with his father's 'memory [which] he has neglected in pursuit of signs of fame in a world of transience and artifice. The epilogue is Alex's Kaddish: a Jewish prayer recited in the daily ritual of the synagogue and by mourners [...]' (205–6). In a reciprocity of presence and absence his father permeates the narrative, directly in the Prologue, and indirectly in the Epilogue, both of which are framing episodes. Alex's refusal to mourn subtly and implicitly evokes his father throughout. The final ritual partakes of secret and mystical values that subtend both celebrity and death. Clearly, Alex does sense something beyond the literal, beyond the inscribed, some possibility of further value. This is also inherent in his very trade, but mostly commercialized as if rational, reduced to the possibility of a spectacular monetary transformation. This relation believes in the transcendence of exceptionality, through which it seeks to intimate in fragmentary, often unconscious form something more general, inherent in the belief subtending the exceptional practices of celebrity with their implicit notion of transcendence. They seek what Martin Buber encapsulates in *I and Thou* (1958) when he says 'Every particular *Thou* is a glimpse through to the eternal Thou; by means of every particular Thou the primary word addresses the eternal thou' (75). The significance of Alex's involvement in the final ritual is open, still ambiguous, but he recovers the importance of his father despite his ordinariness, even though the several signatures he has left appear worthless, written ironically on valueless currency subsequently withdrawn.

5

ON BEAUTY

CONCERNING ART AND LIFE

On Beauty views the comedy inherent in university life, a microcosmic world dominated by domestic and professional conflict, its undercurrents, human irresolution and betrayal. Many of the central characters are active or putative intellectuals, and through their lives Smith catalogues the shibboleths and fractures of a contemporary liberal culture in crisis. Beneath the political infighting and family debates lurks Howard's earlier affair with colleague, Claire Malcolm, initially secret and later revealed publicly. Smith cartographizes both parenthood and marital love, through the failings of Howard's marriage investigating concepts of ethics and respect. Howard's emotional inarticulacy is transcended partially only by his belated inner sense of an aesthetic imperative. The novel's humour centres on both the narrator's personal and social observations and the dialogue which is attuned to the misunderstandings of highly intellectualized perspectives and a more common sense view. This animates the various settings intersected by various members of the two central families: the Belsey home, the Kipps homes in both Boston and London, Wellington College's campus, Boston Centre and Common, and the megastore where the youngest Belsey child, Levi, works. Howard and Kiki's conflict, which impacts upon their offspring, allows Smith to explore the tensions of a mixed-race family. However, as the attentive reader soon realizes the fundamental parameters of the disagreements extend beyond issues of ethnicity. As Smith tells Murphy Moo,

> I know it seems improbable, but it really isn't the race thing that I'm
> interested in. I'm just interested in the difference thing. [...] The race

thing is the first thing I reach for, since I was brought up in a biracial family, but I was just as interested in Howard being really skinny and Kiki being really big as in them being of different colors. The race thing is not really their problem.

Nevertheless, another axiomatic (and I would suggest interrelated) problem as Susan Alice Fischer points out in ' "A Glance from God": Zadie Smith's *On Beauty* and Zora Neale Hurston' is that Howard simply cannot understand his children, fearing any conversation about race (286–7). His fear is rooted in his liberally inclined relativism, a residue of 1970s leftist optimisms. The novel explores the humour inherent in the contradictions of the academy, which world is centred on the entrenched and combative relationship of Howard and Monty Kipps, both becoming embattled in institutional politics. White, liberal Howard, career in stasis, opposes the high-profile, arch-conservative Monty. Ironically despite their apparent high-mindedness both fail their families, painfully so. These knowing academics are so confident about the ideological contexts of their interventions, but innocent of or indifferent towards the consequences of their actions. Their conflict becomes by the end secondary to their profound effects on others. They become strangely complicit in their arrogance and deception. As Smith says to Murphy Moo,

> People profess to have certain political positions, but their conservatism or liberalism is really the least interesting thing about them. That's sort of what I wanted to write about. I'm really not interested in whether somebody is a conservative or not. I'm interested in what kind of human being he is when he makes various life choices. Sometimes that can be completely subsumed by politics and ideology, but I was interested in looking at two men who believe that their ideology is king, when actually it doesn't have any impact on their day-to-day decision-making.

In an extended acknowledgement preceding her third novel Smith says: 'It should be obvious from the first line that this is a novel inspired by a love of E. M. Forster, to whom all my fiction is indebted, one way or the other. This time I wanted to repay the debt with *hommage*' (n.p.). Smith's aesthetic provenance and her change of emphasis proved both unsatisfactory and unexpected for many commentators, particularly as Kermode says, 'To take as a model

Howards End, a novel published in 1910, need not be a mere game or stunt, but it does tend to steal the limelight of critical attention. [...] Zadie Smith's real debt may not lie in her echoes of *Howards End*, though she does insist on them.' Various narrative features, including the setting and the practices of the American academy, are clearly drawn directly from Smith's own experiences in 2002–2003 at Harvard, near Boston. She both taught and undertook research for a project tentatively entitled *The Morality of the Novel*, which Suzanne Liola Matus' press release on the institute's website describes as 'a book of essays that explores the novel not only as an analogy of morals, but also as a case for morals.' As Smith explains in 'On the Beginning,' she was responding variously to her rarefied surroundings, her own aesthetic taste and a variety of literary influences that formed the basis of her teaching.

> In the case of *On Beauty*, these books were all old favourites, because I was teaching them at Harvard. Nabokov, Forster, Kafka, Zora Neale Hurston, Paula Fox, John Updike, WG Sebald, to name half the syllabus. I think there are currents that run through *On Beauty* that are profoundly subconscious (I dreamt most of the plot—under the influence of my Forster class), but the greater impulse was certainly 'intended' and fed by the sudden remembrance of how much I loved a certain kind of novel and how I had, in my writing life, suppressed my love for such novels. With a brazen ahistoricism I can't intellectually defend, around February 2003 I indulged myself and sat down to write the big, 'realist' (better to say in the style of Realism), slightly Edwardian novel that I had dreamt of writing as a child. It was the book I couldn't quite manage when I was 20, sitting down to write *White Teeth*.

As David James observes in 'The New Purism,' self-referential postmodern readings reducing comparison to parody remain insufficient to explain 'how writers choose to advance by adhering to what seems past, contemplating their originality through the lens of inheritance' (687).

Fischer contends that 'With the first line of her third novel [...] Smith proclaims *Howards End* as a source,' (285) but as Fischer adds, Hurston inspires Smith's attempt to use an ' "alchemy of pain" [which] turns sorrow into beauty' (286). James concludes that 'Smith consciously attenuates the ebullience of her first two novels to honour Forster's contrapuntal register of satire and dictation.

Without compromising her comedy with the voice of moral gravity, in her latest work Smith rehearses Forster's gnomic use of narratorial intrusion to enunciate her own parable of ethical consequence' (694). For James her narrator is a 'moral commentator' within a broad novelistic tradition while sustaining her satirical view of life (694). Both Smith's intertextuality and the overlapping cultures create an emphatic sense of uncanny doubling, mediating the naturalistic impulse of her prose, Wood's 'hysterical realism.' Smith incorporates something akin to what Henry S. Turner describes in 'Empires of Objects: Accumulation and Entropy in E. M. Forster's *Howards End*' as Forster's propensity for 'delineating a world in which personal objects and places act as repositories for a sentimental "value" that exceeds the vicissitudes of commerce and commodification. The novel articulates an ambivalent fascination with material substances of all types [. . .]' (330). Subtending conflicting world-views, an element shared with *Howards End*, Smith foregrounds the intuitive aspect of people, places and objects, regarding them as existing in excess of any theoretical and intellectual account.

According to Fischer's reading, 'At times, Kiki appears to see herself through the eyes of the white inhabitants of Wellington. She muses about how young white boys see her. [. . .] This double consciousness is also apparent during Kiki's anniversary party [. . .]' (289). While not disagreeing, it is worth noting that this perspective recurs in various episodes where other characters are seen through the perspectives of others, often through the use of free indirect discourse (a classic modernist strategy). Such multiple switching points of view achieve a depth of characterization and enhance the reader's sense a small social as symbolically microcosmic. Smith's world is generally realistically defined and acutely observed. As she explains to Murphy Moo she adopts an essentially 'Forsterian' perspective, re-working his oblique ironies. Despite the knowingness of the liberal arts experts who in many ways centre the novel, literally claiming authority, both the narrative and many of its characters exude a sense of regret and loss, maintaining a melancholic quality despite the constant highlighting of the underlying comedy of campus life. Smith's ironies may echo with Forsterian subtleties, but finally *On Beauty* feels more pessimistic than Forster's work. *On Beauty* mourns the loss of apprehensible meaning signified in the failure to recognize simple truths and celebrate beauty. It focuses on a series of intellectual engagements that for the participants obscure the human pain and distress resulting from their actions. Men betray women; women struggle for respect and status. Several thoughtless yet compulsive infidelities, overlaid with an acute sense of the eventual parting of siblings and lovers, the separation of parents and the effects of divorce, define the mood. Moreover, in Forsterian fashion Smith includes a sudden, unexpected death, shocking enough in itself, but as with Mrs Wilcox in *Howards End* the demise is followed by deceit and manipulation on the Kipps family's part countering of the wishes of the departed wife and mother. Yet any such recurrent negativity is mediated by the novel's avowal throughout of a particular concept of beauty identified by Elaine Scarry in *On Beauty and Being Just* (2000), who notes: 'How one walks through the world, the endless small adjustments of balance is affected by the shifting weight of beautiful things' (15). Unlike Howard, Smith is open to such transcendent ideas.

Responding to Forster's interrogation of what in *Two Cheers for Democracy* (1951) he calls his part in 'the fag-end of Victorian liberalism [. . .]' (41), Smith re-considers her relationship to the propensities of left-liberalism and postmodernism. If the first two novels possess a certain centripetal quality, *On Beauty* is like a gyre whose centre fails to hold, its trajectory the dissolution of the failing marriage, centrifugal. In 'A Touch of Forster,' John Sutherland regards Smith as alluding 'ostentatiously' to Forster although he suspects 'some subtle subversion at work [. . .].' Sutherland stresses *On Beauty*'s debt to a 'post-Forsterian' sub-genre, the campus novel. Of the latter Christine Lanone in 'Mediating Multi-cultural Muddle: E. M. Forster Meets Zadie Smith' in contextualizing the novel's 'farcical sexual scenes' (190) explains that this sub-genre has long been associated with eroticism and compulsive 'seduction [which] provides compensation for professional discontent' (189–90). Smith's transatlantic academic culture allows a sophisticated version of her precursor's notions of class and identity integrated with concepts such as gender, ethnicity and historical change in society. Certain apparent dichotomies are played out in the divergent visions and theories of both aesthetics and life held by Howard and Monty. Howard confronts his nemesis over issues of affirmative action, which Monty finds patronizing and demeaning. Howard's life is turbulent, his views often appearing wayward. Initially Monty appears imperturbable, superior and charismatic, as much a politician as a scholar. However polarized they might seem, their similar failings and vanity see them drawn to young women of great beauty. Their academic dispute over art in general and Rembrandt in particular encapsulates Smith's central theme, the possibility of at least some innate notion of beauty, a transcendent ideal or longing that the post-Marxist, deconstructionist Howard rejects. For Lanone the target is rather 'a politically correct *doxa* which admits no contradiction and bans feelings and personal response [...]' (190). Concerning Monty's opposition much is said of his social and political views, but few details emerge concerning his Rembrandt scholarship.

The novel opens in self-conscious fashion with Howard reading emails from London sent by his son, Jerome, while acting as Monty's intern in London. Of course, the Forsterian allusion indicates perhaps certain universal human qualities prevail. However, as Peter Kemp says undercutting the outcome of Smith's intertextual intentions, '*Howards End*'s studiedly casual opening line, "One may as well begin with Helen's letters to her sister", gets restyled as "One may as well begin with Jerome's e-mails to his father."' Juxtaposed with a typographical layout drawn from an email format, although still implicitly an intensely one-sided perspective, yet with its transatlantic coordinates, and its instantaneity, surely its qualities and implications still differ. There are other crucial differences from Forster. This is an intergenerational missive, not a sisterly one, stressing Howard's baby boomer parenting. Jerome's is the novel's first voice, almost solipsistic, unable to connect with his almost entirely unresponsive father. Jerome recounts his work as an intern for his father's sworn academic enemy into whose home Jerome has moved, only to fall in love with the daughter, Victoria, confirming the Forsterian patterns.

Howard's failure to respond conveys much about his narcissism. Surprisingly, he shares the emotional reserve typical of Forster's more conservative Wilcox men. Smith captures throughout the verbal extremes to which so-called liberal academics are prone, often viewing them from the perspective of others, as in Jerome's second message which reveals the excessive private opinions of his father, particularly concerning Monty. Jerome rejects Howard's 'feud' with Monty (5) and insists of the latter: 'He's not the "self-hating psychotic" you think he is' (6). Ironically in a later message Jerome declares his love for Victoria, Kipps' daughter, but true to his Christian idealism Jerome considers marriage. Parallels abound with *Howards End* Forster, especially Helen Schlegel's letters to her sister, Margaret. Staying with the Wilcox family, Helen precipitously announces her engagement to the younger son, Paul, after a kiss. Smith's couple, one learns retrospectively, copulate, Jerome losing his virginity about which his father has been scornful. Howard is archetypically liberal about sex, discussing the topic candidly with his offspring. However, Jerome's precipitous plan to marry tips Howard into crisis, unable to comprehend Kiki's amusement.

> 'You've got to hand it to Jerome,' she murmured as she read. 'That boy's no fool ... when he needs your attention *he sure knows how to get it*,' she said, looking up at Howard and separating her syllables like a bank teller counting bills. 'Monty Kipps's daughter. Wham, bam. Suddenly you're interested.'
>
> Howard frowned. 'that's your contribution.' [...]
>
> 'Really, Howie. He's *twenty*. He's wanting his daddy's attention – and he's going the right way about it. Even doing this Kipps internship in the first place—there's a million internships he could have gone on. Now he's going to marry Kipps junior? Doesn't take a Freudian. I'm saying, the worst thing we can do is to take this seriously.'
>
> (9–10)

After Smith's *in media res* beginning, this exchange adds provenance and insists on Howard's self-centred nature. Kiki highlights Howard's propensity for intellectualizing, for rendering situations as conflicts, always *in extremis*. Clearly, Howard lacks intuition, worldliness or foresight. She refers to his propensity for stupidity (15), demonstrated in the subsequent episode when visiting the Kipps' London home *en route* for Cambridge. Ironically, Howard knows nothing of Jerome's Forsterian final email retrieved by Kiki, asking Howard to say nothing about the matter, admitting, 'I've made a total fool of myself! I just want to curl up and die' (26). After becoming lost Howard telephones the Kipps' son, Michael, who retrieves their unexpected visitor from Kilburn Underground Station. Howard reveals his son's secret, precipitating a conflict reminiscent of *Howards End*'s second chapter which foregrounds a similar confrontation between the Schlegels' aunt and the Wilcox's eldest son concerning Helen Schlegel's putative engagement with his younger brother, after the aunt has missed

Helen's letter withdrawing her earlier remarks. Later by chance both families become neighbours in London, as do the Kipps and Belseys when Monty is invited as a visiting scholar to teach at Wellington.

Howard's arrival in London is revealing in several ways. First, the narrative offers a glimpse of his destructive childhood and adolescence, and of him smoking near the black cab rank at Paddington, being 'taken aback to hear twice in five minutes the destination "Dalston". Dalston was a filthy East End slum when Howard was born into it, full of filthy people who had tried to destroy him—not least of all his own family' (28). Second, on the tube he reflects on Monty's academic attack upon Howard's scholarship 3 months previously, concerning Howard's mistake over a pedantic yet factual matter, of mixing up self-portraits, mistaking one he had assumed Monty had been referring to in his work. Significantly, Howard fails to recognize the different angle of the head, missing the detail, marginalizing its human qualities. However, there is perhaps an underlying quality to this mistake which is almost an in-joke, a point of reference which can be recovered and highlighted by reference to Smith's background research. As Simon Schama says concerning comparisons of the artist's work in *Rembrandt's Eyes* (1999), 'His early self-portraits, the etchings especially, are strikingly *unlike* each other, the painter handled in drastically different styles. The Gardner Museum portrait was painted in the same year as the raw, freely handled Munich self-portrait, yet it could hardly be more different in its manner [. . .]' (300–1). Smith may be subtly undercutting Howard. The narrative emphasizes the territorial nature of Howard's antipathy. 'Howard had always disliked Monty, as any sensible liberal would dislike a man who had dedicated his life to the perverse politics of right-wing iconoclasm, but he had never *really* hated him until he had heard the news, three years ago, that Kipps too was writing a book about Rembrandt' (29). Howard seems apart both from American life and his family. He avoids questions from Levi, his younger son, whose attempts at street vocabulary represent his search for cultural authenticity. Howard interrogates his son, who advises his father to drop the matter, but Howard concludes, 'If nothing else, the mess in London surely ended the faint whiff of moral superiority that had so far clung to Jerome through his teens' (22–3). Howard finds the American money he hands to Levi unreal, and significantly the trip has allowed an opportunity to renew his *British* passport. Howard remains unassimilated not simply culturally, but more broadly as the narrator stresses by commenting Howard has trouble both 'celebrating or understanding' (22) humanity.

Both the academic setting and the Belsey's home exude tradition and elitism. The Belsey household may inherit the imperfect liberalism of Forster's Schlegels, but Howard's betrayal of Kiki, after 30 years of marriage, subtends every event, each exchange. In Forster a similar revelation by Mr Wilcox to Margaret Schlegel, his second wife, of a pre-marital affair is far less dynamic, perverse and wilful. Howard thereby subverts his deconstructive scepticism, his apparently liberal sense of intellectual entitlement, as Wilcox's admission undermines his conservatism. Sardonic and angry Kiki's striking, violent image suggests breaching patriarchal dominance. 'This nodded at the recent trouble. It was an offer to kick open a door in the mansion of their marriage leading to an ante-chamber of misery' (15). The novel exhibits a Forsterian seriousness, a profoundly moral world-view. As Kermode says, '*On Beauty* is a much less tumultuous novel than *White Teeth*, and a more sober book than *The Autograph Man*.' In *On Beauty* Smith also emphatically creates a visceral register of pain and uncertainty, inflected more sombrely than its predecessors. The domestic sphere becomes a battleground between Forsterian antagonisms. Smith assumes a 'spiritual authority' similar to that identified by Kermode in Forster, Kiki's intuitive sense echoing the pragmatic strand of a Forsterian liberalism.

As Fiona Tolan notes in 'Identifying the Previous in Zadie Smith's *On Beauty*' for many commentators the intertextual relation to *Howards End* obscures Smith's other acknowledged debt to Scarry (130). Drawing on this source allows Smith to frame her didactic critique of intellectualism, and to articulate her concern with the nature of beauty, art and aesthetic representation. Smith also alludes to music and a number of famous paintings and artworks, to aesthetics, perhaps more centrally than Forster. Yet as Lanone points out, such 'pictorial intertextuality becomes Smith's way of reviving Forster's Edwardian meditation on connection and identity' (194), using ekphrasis, retelling with rhetorical vividness the visual as narrative. Lanone interprets Carlene as using Hyppolite's *Maîtrisse Erzulie*, to enjoin Kiki to see what is represented, to see the power of women, a choice between rebelling or simply being passive (195). Zora Neale Hurston in *Voodoo Gods: An Inquiry into Native Myths and Magic in Jamaica and Haiti* (1938) describes her thus:

> To women and their desires she is all but maliciously cruel, for not only does she choose and set aside for herself young and handsome men and thus bar them from marriage, she frequently chooses married men and thrusts herself between the woman and her happiness.
>
> (127–8)

In Smith both the Hyppolite and Rembrandt's *Hendrickje* enact sorceries of inner transformation, both examples of the catalytic effect of art, what Scarry calls 'the ethical alchemy of beauty' through which process of engagement in Scarry's terms, citing Iris Murdoch, one might experience an '"unselfing"' (113) or 'Radical decentring' (114) through which the individual might resist their innate egotism, thus better understanding 'a state of delight in their own lateralness' (114).

Howard's continuing and paradoxical failure to embrace any genuine practice of liberalism towards both his antagonist and others in his family with whom he disagrees subverts Howard's own position, making the reader profoundly doubt his judgement. In an interview with Steve Paulson Smith praises Forster precisely because 'What matters in life is what goes on between two people.' Kiki Simmonds (note that she retains her maiden name) discovers at her thirtieth wedding anniversary party her husband's affair with his colleague who is a guest, Claire Malcolm. Traditionally, this is known as the Pearl Anniversary, and ironically given the revelation of Howard's betrayal as D. W. Robertson, Jr, points out in 'The Pearl as a Symbol' in Christian allegory 'The Pearl [may represent] a symbol of innocence, the possessor of innocence, or the means and reward of salvation. [. . .] The Pearl stands for a gem, the soul, or the kingdom of Heaven' (155–6), it even represents an 'archetype of innocence' (158). One might well interpret Kiki as exhibiting sufficient wisdom and virtue so as to be seen as innocent and possessing such a quality of the soul. As Kermode says Smith's Forsterian impulse extends 'beyond the plot allusions everybody talks about. What lies behind both is an idea of the novel as [. . .] a source of truth and otherworldliness and prophecy.' The only character who exemplifies such judgement, offering these qualities, is Kiki. The revelation of the truth results from one glance, demonstrating Kiki's intuition and long experience of Howard. Ironically, this occurs just as Kiki explains the events of the previous summer concerning Victoria Kipps and Jerome to her husband's former lover, '"Jerome fell in love with the daughter briefly," explained Kiki tersely. "Last year. Her family freaked out a little—Howard made it all a hell of a lot worse than it needed to be. The whole thing was so stupid"' (122–3).

Howard's betrayal reverberates subtly, not just for Kiki, but Claire's third husband, Warren. As the narrator reflects, a year later when Howard attempts to the couple at Wellington,

> Howard scanned the scene for Warren or Claire. The news was that they were still together. [. . .] It was Kiki who had told Warren; the explosion had happened—but no one had died. It was just walking wounded as far as the eye could see. No packed bags, no final door slams, no relocation to different colleges, different towns. They were all going to stay put and suffer. It would be played out over years. The thought was debilitating. Everybody knew about it. [. . .] People don't know what they're talking about. At the water cooler Howard was just another middle-aged professor suffering the expected mid-life crisis.
>
> (143)

This is multiply ironic and suggestive. First, the reader suspects that Howard serves as precisely such an archetype and that Smith undercuts her own use of him in this way, and second, although he may seem a parodic archetype the reader intuits that any such gossip would be entirely correct. Third, these thoughts still represent Howard's own fears. Fourth, Howard's actions however individual for him may seem clichéd, verging on the bathetic, but one realizes no more so than many men of his age and generation. Finally, it reworks the cultural expectations parodied in Malcolm Bradbury's *The History Man* (1975), another clear hypotext, albeit only an implicit one. Such visceral, partial and yet revealing ruminations are part of Smith's forte.

Howard's infidelity continues to haunt the text. In the novel's second phase in a set piece meeting with Jack French, the Dean, Zora uses her father's affair to overturn Claire's rejection of her application to be in the latter's poetry class where the liberal agenda prevails. Certain dynamics of a 'politically correct' ideological agenda are played out in all of the public responses on the campus. Monty disrupts this process, but as Zora explains candidly to French she anticipates eagerly Monty's class after having read a journalistic piece in the local paper:

> 'I'm definitely going to do Monty Kipps's lectures. I read his piece Sunday in the *Herald* about taking the "liberal" out of the Liberal Arts ... you know, so it's like now they're trying to tell us that conservatives are an endangered species—like they need protecting on campuses or something.' Here Zora took time to roll her eyes and shake her head and sigh all at the same time. 'Apparently *everybody* gets special treatment—blacks, gays, liberals, women—everybody except poor white males. It's too crazy. But I *definitely* want to hear what he's got to say. Know thy enemy. That's my motto.'
>
> (148)

Smith's technique of overlaying and multiplying view-points, often refracted by others, is highly effective, adding depth to her perspectives. The ghost of Howard's objections haunts the scene, as does his infidelity. Zora's incipient parochialism and manipulative instinct are poignant, serving to complicate the ironies. Smith's sympathies appear uncertain, the author's position complex, and not simply in terms of her ideological disposition. Like all communities this one is heterogeneous and at times paradoxical. There remains a set of individuals with all of the expected contradictions. Smith confidently presents Monty's conservatism, exploring the potential paradoxes of such an ethnic view of identity, with its rejection of liberal essentialism as incapable of comprehending the world.

In essence by being common and recurrent such overlapping consciousness universalizes her characters, without negating such differences as ethnicity, gender or disposition, and thereby Smith insists on their part of a human condition. In the intellectual debates she also situates the individual self in a broader humanistic tradition, both aesthetically and culturally. This is precisely reason for focusing the text on artistic expression and a cultural notion of beauty. Howard's divorce from reality proliferates throughout. He cannot comprehend or justify his own engagement with the world, resisting the beautiful, and patronizing his wife. He descends into incoherence:

> It's true that men—they respond to beauty ... it doesn't end for them, this ... this *concern* with beauty as a physical actuality in the world—and

that's clearly imprisoning and it infantilizes . . . but it's *true* and . . . I don't
know how else to explain what——

(207)

As an art historian he specializes in Rembrandt, seeking to perfect an interpretative reading that seeks to disavow any notion of
genius and reject the concept of beauty. His readings are based
on deconstruction and materialism, and there is a perversity to
Howard, not only in his scholarship, but in his teaching that
horrifies one of Wellington's youngest students, Katharine (Katie)
Armstrong. Howard is indifferent to her innocent enthusiasm, as
discussed below.

Both Howard and Monty are entrenched, unyielding, both
exposed as hypocrites. The narrative lurches from partial forgiveness after Howard's spurious confession to a one-night stand to the
wider discovery after an argument among the younger generation
of several affairs (two by Howard, and another on the part of Monty
seemingly after many others), resulting in further literal and psychic separations of partners, siblings and friends. The children find
their world subtended by secrets and lies. Fatherhood, a recurrent
Smith theme and motif, is found to be mostly banal and wanting,
yet occasionally profound. The tensions and problems inherent in
both finding a sense of wider *and* individual identity permeate the
scenes concerning the younger generation, which thematically are
largely centred upon certain different kinds of beauty and creativity other than the visual arts that animate Howard and Monty, with
their apparent privileging of the visual.

Zora, Carl and Levi concern themselves variously with poetry
and music (classical and hip-hop). Despite her intentions the former is beyond Zora's creativity. In 'The Aesthetic Turn in "Black"
Literary Studies: Zadie Smith's *On Beauty* and the Case for an Intercultural Narratology' Roy Sommer is entirely correct that the novel
considers 'social and linguistic barriers' (189) and that the Haitian
rappers are rendered incomprehensible (189–90), but this perhaps
neglects the genuine empathy Levi explores even if its outcome is
inconclusive. Sommer adds that although his family find Howard's
attempt to jokingly pretend he can be street or a brother both comic
and excruciating (Sommer 190; Smith 63), the vision of him can be
seen to ironically subvert Levi's own attempts to be cool and political, to ingratiate himself into an identity of political struggle on the

streets, given his failing to surmount the divide between himself and various others. As Sommer concludes, 'it is a social or educational, rather than an ethnic, gap that will always separate Levi from LaShonda, Bailey, or Choo' (190) referring to the less educated, poorer blacks who interact with (or even in some senses are simply foils to) Levi in certain scenes.

The Belseys (apart from Kiki) can be suspicious of the poor as we find during the episode at the classical concert on Boston Common, which both demonstrates the uneasiness of the Belseys together after Howard's admission of an apparent one-night stand, and introduces Carl, a young Black rapper whom Zora takes up almost as a social project, after he has mistakenly taken her Discman, making her doubt him at the time. This echoes Helen's appropriation of the scene Leonard Bast's umbrella in *Howards End*. However, Smith is no naïve copyist of Forster, although such of plot specifics inevitably risks losing certain original nuances. Carl's Discman could never evoke the 'throbbing anxiety' of the 'culturally marginal Bast' that, as Brian May indicates in *The Modernist as Pragmatist: E. M. Forster and the Fate of Liberalism* (1997), derives from and is symbolized by the very shabbiness of his umbrella. In *On Beauty* a number of elements are inverted, including the fact that the young man perpetrates the error rather than the young woman, and unlike Helen, Zora's underlying passion for Carl goes unfulfilled. Later she encounters him at the swimming pool, Carl informing her about his reading concerning the Lacrimosa in Mozart's Requiem, Smith stressing that true intelligence exists in untutored, perhaps unexpected individuals. Despite this when he quizzes Zora about her family, her paranoid response is to intimate a criminal intent, 'imagining all these questions were a kind of verbal grooming that would later lead—by routes she didn't pause to imagine—to her family home and her mother's jewellery and the safe in the basement' (139). Carl's creativity exhibits itself at the Bus Stop venue and Carl is taken up by Claire, joining her poetry class, and is co-opted onto the Black Studies staff as a favour to her so he might continue the class after Monty's attack on discretionary students. Carl becomes a researcher—albeit 'The pay was basic admin wage [. . .]' (372)—cataloguing hip-hop, and is enthused, although he feels Zora patronizes him. Her drunken rage at finding him with Victoria leads to the revelation of the latter's brief sexual encounter with Howard, of Monty's affair with Chantelle and Carl's accusation, ' "People like me are just toys to people like you … I'm just some experiment for you to play with. You people aren't even black any more, man—I don't know *what* you are" ' (418). Ironically when Monty's picture is stolen, he assumes Carl to be the culprit because of his background, rather than Levi, who influenced by his Haitian rapper and activist friends has appropriated the artwork to restore the proceeds to the Haitian people. Their poetic attempts are obliquely inflected by Hurston's *Voodoo Gods*, where she comments, 'The peasants of Haiti were a poetical group. They loved the metaphor and the simile' (194). Ironically, Kiki finds that Carlene Kipps who befriended her has also left her the painting, concealed by the Kipps family after Carlene's death, another Forsterian allusion.

Towards the end Howard is outraged because he sees his wife taking notes at the lecture of his nemesis, Monty. Kiki lambasts her husband: ' "You know, Howard, all you ever do is rip into everybody else. You don't have any beliefs—that's why you're scared of people with beliefs, people who have dedicated themselves to something, to an *idea*" '(392). His defence is to narrow the dispute, to claim liberal virtue in comparison with Monty's conservatism. In response Kiki widens the debate, indicating that Howard subjects everything to his irony, dismissing the ideas of his family that differ from his own as 'clichéd or dull […]' (393) and rejecting his postmodern Baudrillardian account of 9/11, which she admits that she has regarded as lacking, compassion, empathy and any sense of the real (393–4). Through Kiki's view of Howard's empty posturing, Smith parodies and judges postmodernism's separation from aesthetics and any concrete morality. As Ulka Anjaria says in 'On Beauty and Being Postcolonial: Aesthetics and Form in Zadie Smith,' 'he finds himself physically drawn to the most traditional, even clichéd forms of beauty' (46) and 'Victoria's beauty, unlike Kiki and even Carl's, is unflinchingly canonical, and in this way so overpowering, to herself and to others, that it is unable to express itself only in a misguided and undiscriminating sexuality' (47).

As opposed to Kiki who seems transformed by her release from their relationship, Howard seems destined to remain doctrinaire, unless he can question his rational, reductive suspicions of meaning that cannot allow any space for liberalism, any aesthetic sense and in so doing co-opts a deconstructive denial of order, of meaning and of beauty. Domestically Howard ends in an abject condition, unable to navigate either the meanings or patterns of his existence, which is in stark contrast to his intellectual hubris. He realizes his mistake in his final lecture, admitting a sense of art and of Rembrandt that has been anathema to him throughout and that has been evident in his several attractions, not so much Claire but certainly in terms of both Victoria Kipps *and* belatedly his middle-aged wife.

Ironically for a Rembrandt scholar Howard shows little understanding of himself or the human condition, especially as Schama indicates this concept is central to one of the artist's most famous paintings, *The Anatomy Lesson of Dr Nicolaes Tulp, 1632*, which Howard uses in his class,

> is, in the literal sense, from the Greek, an *autopsia*, an act of direct witness or seeing for oneself. [. . .] What Rembrandt has painted, then, is a moment of truth, another instant in which both the immediate and the eternal stand simultaneously illuminated. Both he and Dr. Tulp would have seen the placard held in the bony grip of a skeleton mounted at the back of the Leiden anatomy theater and commanding, *Nosce te ipsum*—Know thyself.
>
> (353)

On a number of occasions—very largely during a reception for Monty, in Howard's two student lectures, and in his final public lecture—the reader encounters Howard's readings of Rembrandt's work and significance. During the reception he argues with Monty, and insults both the curator of a small Boston gallery and a member of the Rembrandt Appreciation Society, the latter incredulous about Howard's title forwarded by his assistant, Smith, for a promised forthcoming lecture series, ' "*Ag'inst* Rembrandt [. . .]" ' and querying the notion of the 'fallacy of the human' (116). Drunkenly Howard dismisses Rembrandt's anthropomorphic centring (117–18). As he prepares the first class he looks at his tattered black and white reproduction of *The Anatomy Lesson of Dr Nicolaes Tulp, 1632*, resisting Smith's admonition in his southern drawl that he ought to use ' "pah-point [PowerPoint]" ' (142), Howard considers the painting,

> that clarion call of an Enlightenment not yet arrived, with its rational apostles gathered around the dead man, their faces uncannily lit by the holy light of science. [. . .] The rigorous scientific pursuance of the

dictum *Nosce te ipsum*, "Know thyself"—Howard had a long shtik about
this painting that never failed to captivate his army of shopping-day
students, their new eyes boring holes into the old photocopy. Howard
had seen it so many times he could no longer see it at all.

(144)

The same reductive familiarity permeates most aspects of his life.
Yet by the end there has been a tentative transformation of his view
of the world obtained through suffering, demanding some empathy. Previously he has resisted any passionate engagement with
art. Suddenly he feels himself drawn into the picture, identifying
with the dead man, feeling as if he were an object of dispassionate
scrutiny. Sommer notes the scene where Howard mentally anticipates and posits art's partiality and complicity with privilege precisely by quoting Howard's thought in *On Beauty* that each year
'he asked his students to imagine prettiness as the mask power
wears. To recast Aesthetics as a rarefied language of exclusion'
(155). Preceding the second class on seventeenth-century art Katie
Armstrong—who is improbably only sixteen (249) and therefore
serves as a symbol of intellectual, unsullied innocence—is quietly
passionate about art, preparing assiduously, making notes of her
close observation, determined to speak to Howard about her ideas.
Alone and unaided in her studies, she is moved particularly by
Seated Nude, noting many of the details Schama explores in terms
of Rembrandt's nudes, more generally (383–99, 551–8) their quality of living bodily presence, for instinctively Katie focuses upon
those qualities that Schama identifies as their very imperfect '*desir-
abilty* [. . .] bodies as palpably, sexually desirable [. . .] vulnerably
exposed, or, in a word, naked' (393), thereby retrieving instinctively a view as if contemporaneous to the painter himself. Thus
I think Sommer is misguided in reducing Katie's interpretations
of Rembrandt's pictures to a narrowly 'subjective' view (185) and
one reason Katie cannot argue with fellow students is precisely
Howard's refusal to see any empathic possibility in exchanging subject responses. For although Katie arrives at her class enthused
by the art and by its ontological vitality, Howard prioritizes the
theoretical. Moreover as Sommer indicates ironically, Howard is
completely insensitive to the implications of his own definition,
allowing the language of exclusion to dominate his own class, effectively silencing his student Katie (184). The episode is seen through

Katie's eyes as her confidence collapses, intimidated by Howard's favoured students, Victoria, Zora and Mike who reminds Howard of his younger self. This trio offers a semiotic, deconstructive reading that excites Howard. He crushes Katie's innocent joy. The scene is telling. Howard is undermined as much by this episode as by his infidelities. Smith uses Howard's conceptual impasse to symbolize one of the central intellectual perversities of a postmodernism embraced both enthusiastically and willfully by many intellectuals. His pivotal difficulty lies in the nature of beauty, in its ephemeral, elusive qualities Scarry describes, and from the fact that as she says if it is reduced to an abstraction unattached to an object, then 'beauty' becomes difficult, almost impossible to define (9). Not only does Howard dismiss art as a Western myth (155), he refuses the 'thinginess' of reality, turns it mostly into symbols and discourse, hence he can neither apprehend nor account for beauty. The final lecture comes after his separation from Kiki; ironically he has ceased coping with the everyday, even putting on weight as a result of quitting smoking. Very late he abandons his car parked five blocks away to avoid the one-way system, in his hurry finding himself before his audience without his lecture notes. This intensity of his comic plight, his adversity echoes that of Jim Dixon with 'Merrie England' drunkenly abandoning his agreed lecture in Amis' *Lucky Jim*. The primary effect of the comic parallel is the sense that both scenes are imbued by the idea of an accidental route to an unexpected epiphany. The focus is on Howard and his mute use of 'pah-point,' while Jack French suggests to his son perhaps the importance of Howard's apparently intentional silence lies is in the order of the images, which serves as a comic undercutting of the kind of obscurity in which he has indulged previously. He sees Kiki in the audience, as if afresh. Suddenly Howard has nothing clever to say, but finally allows the paintings in full colour to speak to his audience, and to himself. Reaching *Hendrickje Bathing, 1654*, he rediscovers the fulsome beauty both in the image and in Kiki, what Katie knew instinctively as an apparently untutored innocent. As Schama comments, 'Rembrandt paints Hendrickje *not* looking at him. He admires her evidently not as a possession but for her self-possession [. . .]' (554). This is Howard's potential epiphany, to recognize the innate element of beauty that ties the object to life, to the act of being and of love. Smith has offered a critique and attack upon the sterile scholasticism of deconstruction and the postmodern age, the divorcing of intellectual engagement from the classical realities, often far more subtle than contemporary commentators can concede and Howard epitomizes that very hubris. Hence his final condition of abjection is essential as his potential demise reinforces the ethical centre of the novel.

PART III
Criticism and Contexts

6

SURVEY OF SELECTED LANDMARK INTERVIEWS

This chapter offers an overview of certain landmark interviews undertaken by Smith, considering key points made by the author, and the commentary and perspective of the interviewers where relevant. It offers an intriguing view of the development of the author in the public domain. The first two interviews are very much inflected by aspects of *White Teeth*'s promotional campaign (and parameters of the myth evoked still persist). Both seem very much of the pre-9/11 period with their optimistic outlook and the underlying postmodern view of scepticism and irony of the interviewers. Stephanie Merritt's interview appeared in *The Observer* on 16 January 2000, preceding Smith's residence at the Institute for Contemporary Arts (ICA) by a month. One senses Smith deferring somewhat to the journalist, Merritt mediates Smith's words and incorporates them into an account which begins 'The hype began in the autumn of 1997,' but initially purveys the line of the publisher's publicity summarizing *White Teeth* as 'a broad, teeming, comic novel of multiracial Britain' citing comparisons with Salman Rushdie and the unusual media attention for a new writer. Merritt describes

Willesden 'caff' where they meet, relating it to Archie and Samad's haunt, according to Merritt 'the book's pivotal relationship.' Merriit describes Smith as both unassuming, but quietly articulate, shy of the interview process, and

> rolling cigarettes with nervous fingers and holding them, unsmoked, like a prop. She is modest, almost dismissive, about the book she has written, as if she genuinely didn't realize how good it really is, and insists that she finds it 'excruciating' to read.

Merritt refers to Smith finding the 'publicity whirl quite daunting' and her large advance scary. Smith's view on prejudice is characterized as optimistic, despite ongoing racism, and Merritt relays Smith's admission that her own desire to overcompensate when faced with prejudice may have permeated her writing in some ways, something of which she disapproves and hopes to scotch. Subsequently, the interview focuses on the facts of the forthcoming American promotion, describing how Smith had been commissioned to contribute a short story for the *New Yorker*'s millennial fiction issue, and was in April about to travel to New York to participate in a literary festival organized by the magazine supporting *White Teeth*'s publication.

Eleven months later another heavily mediated interview, undertaken at the ICA, appeared in *The Observer*. Simon Hattenstone's 'White Knuckle Ride' refers explicitly to Smith's extraordinary year, and that being unknown the previous December *White Teeth* had meant great acclaim and being in spotlight continuously. He ascribes her fame to fortuitousness, as 'she had the fortune, or misfortune, to be the perfect demographic. Young, attractive, black, female—and very talented.' Hattenstone courts controversy by reporting women of his acquaintance commenting on Smith's being 'bitchy, supercilious, smug, cold, a fake, you name it,' followed by his own disappointment at her change of style and looks, referring to her look dismissively as being like 'any number of drained All Saints waltzing around clubland.' He contrasts her zest and liveliness with a morose, resentful self-consciousness when the tape recorder commences. By now Smith articulates her dissatisfaction at her book tour, rejects the role critics have evoked for her as a spokesperson for race, youth, women and multiculturalism. She notes with disdain a recent photo shoot for a magazine as sexist, reducing her to an archetype. She comments that comparisons with Salman Rushdie are essentially 'racist nonsense.' Hattenstone views *White Teeth* as a picture of social fluidity, and comments on Smith's contention that her work is not a statement:

> The trouble is that even when she's rebutting the notion of being a spokesperson ('a white male writer is never asked to be a spokesman for anything; he has complete artistic freedom'), she ends up giving good quote, and keeps the publicity wheel rolling.

Hattenstone responds by alluding to Smith having nurtured a precocious literary ambition and interprets this as spending much of her life preparing for celebrity, citing somewhat improbably writing poems and stories aged five or six when, followed later by Agatha Christie pastiches. Smith admits her studiousness, explaining her choice of Cambridge University because of her academic ambitions, and the fact that 'All the writers I loved went there.' According to Hattenstone her preparation for a literary career was rigorous, at eighteen researching the working methods of favourite authors and purveys the myth of the £250,000 advance for two novels while still a student. He records her sharp criticism of and ambivalence concerning her own work. He records her opinion, 'Novels are not about expressing yourself, they're about something beautiful, funny, clever and organic. Self-expression? Go and ring a bell in a yard if you want to express yourself,' finding her wonderfully haughty. He returns to his reports of her bigheadedness asking her response, evoking her vulnerability and ending with her reflection on the potentially inherent vanity of all writers.

Kathleen O'Grady's interview is significant in that first she knew of Smith's early then unrecognized work from her own role as an editor of the *May Anthology*, and second O'Grady's position as a literary academic. She recalls,

> Smith was already writing opening paragraphs that give readers that goosepimply sensation that starts somewhere at the base of the spine and spreads rapidly to alight the entire body. It was from one of Smith's annual contributions to the *May Anthologies* that a literary agent became interested in her work and the distinguished Andrew Wiley Agency took her on board.

(105)

O'Grady asks Smith about the more complex 'unrootedness' of second generation migrants, to which Smith responded by comparing human history to trauma, especially childhood ones, and the generational transmission of abuse in families (citing her mother's social work experience), and adding that characters are similarly traumatized. She explains that white Western cultured families tend to regard themselves as separate individuals, contrasting the family sensibility of immigrants (105–6).

For Smith, *White Teeth* concerns obsession and the life that results from such compulsions. For her, 'even the worst men in the world and the most evil people consider themselves good and can't really do anything else, and that goes for mass murderers and genocidal maniacs.' In this context she explores self-justifications and their limitations. For Smith, Irie is the centre of a book about others, an exploration in indeterminacy, de-centring. For Nicola Allen in *Marginality in the Contemporary British Novel* (2008), Irie feels excluded and at odds with 1990s Britain because of its culture of 'heroin chic and the super waif, super model' (85). Smith contends,

> I didn't want the community in *White Teeth* to be representative of immigrants in England, that's not my job really, I'm not a politician, and I wouldn't claim such an optimistic vision of other people's experience.

She comments on how enabling Cambridge had been, with its legacy of literary achievement. She reflects, 'role models are another crock and something which limit you. They don't set you free,' and how socially women writers encounter many barriers. She explains her urban settings by reference to her own experience and the alien quality of the countryside. She finds it interesting that new communities are not just place-specific, but organized around other allegiances, but do include 'the old binding ones—the religious communities.' She introduces the focus of *The Autograph Man* on which she was working, 'their lives and their particular obsession. And it's kind of autograph people coming up against Kabbalists—Jewish mystics, and lots of fun ensues.' Clearly, the scene planned for Florida that she refers to was abandoned by the time of submission.

At the PBS interview preceding the broadcast of *White Teeth* in an interview at Harvard University during academic year 2002–2003, overlooking the building where Vladimir Nabokov lived in the 1940s Smith recounts her concept of the first novel being concerned with Archie as a man lives a good life by accident like Jimmy Stewart. The rest of the first novel derives from her reading and life. She views Archie as representing her own simpler side, Samad the intellectual aspects. The two derive much from classic English comedy double acts, like many television comedy routines. For Smith rather than multiracial London being a theme, or even a significant focus, it remains simply a reality, and the postcolonial aspects derive not from first-hand experience, but rather from observation and guesswork. Responding to the idea of September 11, she reinforces the importance of the comic perspective, and the issue of how ideology gets so twisted, assuming such extreme positions of sacrificing both the self and the other for a principle, 'an absurdity.' Concerning the television adaptation Smith regards Phil Davis as physically different from her conception of Archie, but 'When I saw the rushes, I thought he was amazing,' adding a comment regarding Omi Puri as perfect as Samad, and the high quality of the soundtrack.

An intriguing interview, available as a video clip online, took place in Stockholm in 2006 at a literary festival. Smith describes fiction as representing a 'truthful' conception of world, warning that writers should not harangue readers. She cites Iris Murdoch to insist that the greatest obstacles to good are vanity and self-deception which principle also applies to art, evoking Murdoch's case that art offers both a 'case' of and an 'analogy' for morals. Her opinion is that the same flaws, obstacles and personality that apply to a writer appear in their fiction. Interestingly, she places class as an important factor in novels, one she admits preoccupies her, and was a great theme of her own and family's life. She recalls the divide of grammar school in father's generation, relating how her father had passed the entrance exam (the 'eleven-plus') but in a manner now legendary in her family, his mother could not afford the uniform, and consequently he did not attend. Hence his choices were limited and he left school at twelve. Once more the importance of her father in her life emerges. In a postscript she discusses how she tries to avoid the commodification implicit in naming brands in her fiction, despite referring to Nike trainers in *White Teeth*, which she regrets.

On 9 November 2006 Smith was interviewed by Michael Silverblatt for the *Bookworm* programme on KCRW, an American radio station. This considers contexts crucial to understanding Smith's aesthetic commitments. She positions *White Teeth* as incorporating the particular type of traditional English novel that she read from childhood, a tribute to her influences. Smith regards interpreting her work though the concept of self-expression is mistaken, as it fosters a sense of levels of authenticity, and that the constant concern with one's identity is imprisoning, something white people suffer less, enjoying a 'kind of existential freedom' that is assumed and that should be natural for everyone. She suggests that critics misread her work as a search for identity, ignoring her notion of the impossibility of and pointlessness in searching for any coherent identity. Smith continues that culturally people's propensity is to use language as a camouflage, but she does not romanticize 'aporia or silence.' In existentialist or Platonic fashion she holds that certain concepts such as beauty and good are qualities that cannot be articulated, as the idea of beauty cannot be rationalized. This is central to her novel, *On Beauty*. She returns to a radical notion of the good, commenting that her favourite fiction deals with such ideas. She positions good reading as a difficult skill, an art, commenting that many readers respond only to the superficial surface, and that they should not be passive like viewers of television and film regarding the experience as simply entertainment. Rather as Aristotle suggests, now an unfashionable position, literature should engage an education of the emotions, and that good reading is analogous to good living, being about ethical examples and judgment. For Smith good books educate the emotions and the heart, precisely why Elaine Scarry's text guided her writing in *On Beauty* in a novel intended to allow the reader discover its humanity. She argues characters like Monty are not offensive, and for herself she remains ambivalent about any notion of taking offence at other people's views. Again she cites Iris Murdoch, insisting that bad fiction is self-deluding. To conclude, Smith discusses feelings of class and having at university left part of her previous self behind. She comments that the characters in *On Beauty* are confronted with radical divisions of identity and their very search fosters a sense of diminishing authenticity. She concludes that living through other people is the only point of life, and that the leap of empathy to fully understand otherness may be unachievable, but she recommends the attempt, quoting Forster in full: 'Only connect the prose and the passion, and both will be exalted.'

In 'Conversations in the Library: Zadie Smith and Kurt Anderson' the novelist reads a section from *On Beauty* that describes the late preparations and early arrivals for the wedding anniversary party. Subsequently, Smith is interviewed and she answers questions from the audience. Smith accounts for herself as an un-visual person, preferring 'wordy' things. She cites her liking for the extreme artificiality of the film, *Philadelphia Story*, explaining her view that realism and naturalism might appear indulgences, and while writing nineteenth-century style novels is not a strategy she would recommend, it suits her propensities. She admires fiction that inspires an immediacy of response, and incorporates the intuitive. She warns that familiarity and coherence alone do not constitute realism, and writing ought to convey something as close to one's own conception of a 'true world.' According to Smith one is limited often by ability and her early success might have delivered artistic freedom, but also involved enormous responsibility and expectations.

Being of the generation suspicious of popular, mass appreciation and values she finds it strange to have such a wide audience, and that many readers expect to align themselves with similar types of character, a propensity she decries. She believes readers should empathize further 'away from themselves.' She admits to drawing in readers to disturb, as even the possibility of offending or moving them may inspire a profound response. Referring to the scene where Howard visits his father, she relates the feelings to her Cambridge tutors, once 'working class English boys' and now theorists and professors, now with completely different lives, regional and humble origins having disappeared, their pasts lost. She has no religion, but exhibits Protestant mentality in that she is suspicious of things that take her away from her work.

Smith cites Forster's description of one of his characters that she was 'full of consistency and moral enthusiasm,' which is not meant as a compliment—and she thinks of English fiction as sharing a horror of both qualities since it marks them out as 'those [who] are the worst kind of people you could ever come across' adopting rather the very easy default position of cynicism, a postmodern view, fearing those with this kind of moral enthusiasm. Smith quotes favourably David Foster Wallace who comments that you have to find something to worship and live by it, an Aristotelian idea that still pertains. But she expresses a 'horror' of party politics, unable to bear the consistency it implies, following one's side against all common sense, against all evidence. She ruminates on juggling logos, ethos, pathos, thinking over whether writing ought to derive from knowledge, from personhood, whether one is informed by authenticity, the postcolonial, or emotion. She recalls at college given herself to logos—regarding Howard as a personification of that position—but later realized this was at expense of all other parts of life. She argues neither for anti-intellectualism, nor an anti-postmodernism per se, but admits 'there is a certain kind of theory that calcifies and gets stuck, and becomes about careerism.' Nevertheless, she cites Derrida's 'Structure, Sign and Play in the Human Sciences' as extraordinarily beautiful and intellectually sublime. She says,

> I don't see the racial difference as the big difference. Particularly in *On Beauty* I'm really much more interested in the way people behave to each other, their personal ethics [...] of course race is a difference, but it's a small difference. The world is much more split into cruel people and kind people, or generous people and people who hold things back.

Smith admits thinking of herself perhaps in illusory fashion as 'master of negative capability' seeing herself as an observer, although other people's response would indicate otherwise.

7

CRITICAL RECEPTION

This chapter surveys and analyses critical responses to Smith's work, where a blurring, or failure to distinguish one's critical-ideological perspective from the object of criticism is not uncommon, as can be seen below in terms of readings of *White Teeth*. In evaluating her work, Smith's own iconic status is unavoidable, indelibly influencing not only many interviews and profiles, but also the ideological assumptions and presumptions of many academic critics. The latter very often either adopt or take as a starting point the parameters underpinning the 'public,' initially commercially driven discourse which memorialized the meaning of both the first novel and its author in culturally symbolic terms, aspects which were intended by the publicity machine to solicit a feel-good factor among potential readers mostly from the liberal middle classes. Such exaggerated coordinates linger, expressed in a certain critical complicity with a set of apparently progressive neo-liberal signifiers many of which are based on non-textual assumptions or ideological ambitions on the part of the critic.

WHITE TEETH

White Teeth was both reviewed extensively throughout the world, *and* immediately and enthusiastically adopted for courses in universities in Britain, North America and beyond. The rapidity of both processes was truly phenomenal. There were many favourable reviews, including an unexpectedly positive one by A. N. Wilson who in the *Daily Telegraph* is suspicious of the hype, but finally concludes Smith's efforts are praiseworthy.

So hyperbolic were some of the reviews of *White Teeth* that I was pre-pared to suppose it was a dud. I can only say that, from the very first chapter, I knew myself in the presence of a truly remarkable novelist—someone who was writing in the big, broad tradition of comic fiction, with a whole range of characters and situations, a strong (in some ways too strong) plot, many jokes, and an ear for dialogue as good as Kingsley Amis's.

Unlike many others, he implicitly situates her narrative in an English comic tradition, but as can be seen below this is unusual, at least in the initial phase of response.

A year after the novel's first appearance, Squires published her critical guide, *White Teeth: A Reader's Guide*, which although often acute remains in many ways framed by the parameters of the early debates, responding largely in terms of the issues initiated by the promotional campaign. Squires' study outlines most of the novel's major elements, looking particularly at Smith's complex relation-ship to multiculturalism and hybridity, although she considers these notions in terms of Smith reflecting Britain's changing demo-graphics. Squires remains equivocal, for instance she is unwilling to recognize or accede to the broader significance of the essentialist grounds of cultural significations that are identified by critics such as Bhabha, in whose work Dawson finds 'precious little analysis of differentiating social factors such as class, gender, regional prove-nance, and religious affiliation [. . .]' (160). To cite a specific contra-diction which undermines Squires' critique, if the sense of nation as a concept in Bhabha's introduction to *Nation and Narration* (1990) is a haunted ambivalence (1), precisely the kind of equivocation Bhabha describes might equally be applied to the concepts of ethnicity and cultural identity, and it is precisely the latter term's elusive bound-aries, origins and nature that Smith charts and satirizes in her fic-tion. Squires seems eager to situate *White Teeth* through comparison to Rushdie, both in language (16), although surely Smith's linguis-tic referents are more personal, consciously banal, and less elite, and Smith's 'magic realist' plot details (17) despite the obvious fact that coincidence and improbable chance are the stock in trade of the traditional English novel in both the eighteenth and nineteenth centuries, and recurs even with modernist writers such as Woolf in terms of motifs. Squires fluctuates between on the one hand an excellent summary and some sharp observations, and on the other an antagonism exhibited in her implicit suggestion that Smith fails her characters by allowing her comic principle to prevail over their potential authenticity. By expressing this as a negotiation between plot and character, Squires demonstrates that she mistakes the disposition of Smith's writing, subtly insisting that the moral centre of such a fiction ought to be ideologically framed to suit a set of apparently progressive neo-liberal principles. This is curious since explicitly Squires periodically questions such assumptions, noting that 'Smith refuses to preach an anti-racist message [...] preferring instead to turn prejudice into a "nonsense"' (40). Moreover, Squires recognizes levels of complexity, remarking,

> Joyce's smug and spurious assertion of her children's superiority is a parody of the hybridity for which *White Teeth* has been feted. The satirical tone Smith adopts in the extract from Joyce's book offers, then, a warning to any critic wanting to read her multicultural portrayals as simple celebrations.
>
> (35)

Squires fails to remark on a further subtlety, for there is a double irony in that one suspects contextually that despite Smith's narrator's explicit interrogation of the claim that 'the middle classes were the inheritors of the enlightenment [...] and the source of all culture' (435), more locally Joyce's description may well remain largely correct in a narrow educational and intellectual sense, but is ideologically suspect. And tellingly her offspring prove to be emotionally deficient.

Squires misses Smith's disapproval of Samad's excessive notions of guilt either for himself and his host culture, writing from various perspectives (of which Smith has personal experience) so she may precisely capture a larger sense of the contradictions of self-consciousness, identity, subjectivity and their relation to broader narratives both abstract and eventful. Although in her survey of early reviews Squires records that opinions are polarized over 'the question of whether Smith was portraying an actual or an ideal situation' (75), finally Squires relates Smith to a real world zeitgeist (67), particularly in terms of her depictions of immigrant life, narrowing its intellectual, aesthetic and ideological scope. Nevertheless, Squires effectively outlines the issues of history, and its relation to back histories or 'root canals' (45) which metaphor evokes the novel's title. Squires reduces the novel's concept of history to the relativistic (46) despite a narrative whose peregrinations and sufferings insist upon an eventfulness. In truth only the Chalfens have recorded their presence, the successful middle-class. Squires' sense of a historiography derives perhaps from her wish to discover a subversion of meta-narratives, implicitly a postmodernist agenda (66). However, she concludes 'That Smith can treat her characters with empathy while avoiding the sanctimony of political correctness sees her performing one of the most delicate transactions that a novelist can make, and when she succeeds it elevates her novel far above the majority of contemporary fiction' (67). As Squires indicates much early commentary is divided, but a large part frames and interprets the first novel by a sense of its multicultural, millennial optimism. Ironically, as Squire suggests, the novel's satire opposes such views. Smith's humour may use individual foibles as Squires intimates, but does so with a sense of both intellectual exuberance and humility; the narrative informed by existential doubt. Amid the cacophony of life and its conflicts one might find simple truths; hence the importance of the bus journey to the Perret Institute, where Irie and Archie discuss the inconsequentialities of bus tickets, from which Squires deduces 'an appeal for calm and the occasional virtues of quietism' (51).

In an early academic response, Dominic Head's 'Zadie Smith's *White Teeth*: Multiculturalism for the Millennium,' which manages to partly transcend the self-evident, Head interprets cover images of Smith, initially young with 'complexion which betokens mixed-race identity' (106), later after what Head feels is a seductive makeover 'an Asian look, and this demonstrates an indeterminate ethnicity' (106). Head regards such breadth of identity as parallel to that of the novel, its diversity reflective of contemporary Britain. As Smith recognizes in her novel, one lives within a complex and conflicted history, its changing conditions hardly idealistic or optimistic. Head's account of postcolonial identity 'as *process* rather than *arrival* [. . .]' (107) is intriguing, and he tries to contextualize the novel by beginning with his own account of postwar migrant history charting certain cultural and legislative landmarks that are not located in any wider world-view. His decidedly unempirical, non-sociological cartography claims to abjure a sense of nationhood drawing upon Bhabha as if to render all such accounts corrigible, reconfigured by 'cultural difference.' Head identifies problems of assimilation, and his sense of diversity both interrogates and yet later draws upon Rushdie's essentialist view of variously migration, the multicultural and its threat. Head summarizes the major themes of the novel—'part celebration, part cautionary tale [. . .]' (111)—identifying the historical and cultural influences that are not rooted in oppositional views, but a chaotic reality (113). Head ends with the strand of biogenetics that runs from the war to the FutureMouse© event, suggesting implicitly that Smith avows Archie's 'tacit conviction in common humanity' (1140), but perhaps over-determines a notion of the novel's part in a 'quest for multicultural utopia [. . .]' (117). Head draws upon Gilroy's utopian concept which is, as Procter says, part of Gilroy's 'inevitably contradictory, politics of conviviality [. . .]' (119). Gilroy indicates quite a different cultural and ideological zeitgeist, noting an engagement with a more negative re-reading of ideological and critical change in recent years, and as Gilroy explains in *After Empire: Melancholia or Convivial Culture?* (2004):

> Multicultural society seems to have been abandoned at birth. Judged unviable and left to fend for itself, its death by neglect is a being loudly proclaimed on all sides. The corpse is now being laid to rest amid the multiple anxieties of the 'war on terror.' The murderous culprits responsible for its demise are institutional indifference and political resentment. They have been fed by the destruction of welfare states and the evacuation of public good, by privatization and marketization.
>
> (1)

In stark contrast to Head's notion of a 'logic of hybridity [. . .]' (117), the events of July 2005 or the '7/7' bombings noted by McLeod discussed above emphasize a very different sense of London and its communities, after which the aesthetic zeitgeist seems bleak and anxious, rather than convivial or optimistic. Perhaps such events have accentuated the interrogation of the very public profile with which Smith is uncomfortable.

Bruce King in *The Internationalization of English Literature* (2002) describes Smith's work as

> An amusing novel about the new multiracial London that had come about during the past fifty years, it had larger-than-life, cartoonish

characters, large billboard themes, and the caricatured ethnic English and improbable events featured in Salman Rushdie's *Midnight's Children*. [. . .]

While parodying stereotypes Smith's aim was to break down the racial categories and representations of victims and complicities that dominated interpretation of the 'postcolonial.' The novel celebrated a new hybridity, a hybridity that in other ways was the theme of such novelists as Rushdie and such British theorists as Paul Gilroy and Homi Bhabha, and which had been noticed by Stuart Hall.

(289)

The final critical coordinates with their cursory comparisons typify King's agenda, although he concedes Smith's humanistic impulse towards a 'world [which] is governed by chance and personalities rather than the abstractions of science, ideologies, and literary criticism' (290). Despite such passing observations, finally King reduces Smith to an imitator of Rushdie, King's real emphasis being to establish her work's subsidiary relationship to Rushdie's landmark text. In truth Smith exhibits crucial differences, including her Forsterian emphasis on a muddling version of Keats' Negative Capability that in 'Love, actually' she identifies in Forster's fiction. Smith comments that 'Life is easy to chronicle, but bewildering to practice [*sic*],' and also summarizes the vagaries and imprecision of her narrative practice as based upon an aesthetic that is readerly. ' "When we read with fine attention, we find ourselves caring about people who are various, muddled, uncertain and not quite like us (and this is good)." '

Surely although Smith's textual emphases are satiric and she exhibits a certain formal virtuosity, her fiction is fundamentally less muscular, less intrusive, less convinced of their own merits, and finally far more pointillist and less empathic than that of Rushdie whose impulses are cynically Swiftian, if not as acerbic as Céline. Smith's 'hyperbole and far-fetching connections' (186) that Cuder-Domínguez identifies as akin to Rushie are surely inflected in a radically different way, her satire more domestic and positive, her tentative reconciliations at least a partial possibility, her prejudices multiple, racism more casual. Smith's world is less pantomimic, a more familiar, lower-class affair. For Quinn, 'Smith's style is lighter and less fantastical; what's more, there is a quality, a spirit, in her novel that is not to be found in Rushdie's work, and it might be called humility.' Paproth offers a similar distinction finding Smith overly traditional, and more 'leisurely paced, elegantly structured, and written from the perspective of a confident, omniscient narrator' (14). As Kermode says of *White Teeth* in 'Here She Is,'

> Smith began with an encyclopedic novel: it explains the nine acts that invalidate a Muslim fast, describes life in the kitchen of an Indian restaurant, or in Bangladesh, 'God's idea of a *really good wheeze*, his stab at black comedy'; it allows that 'life is a broad church' and situates us outside a narrow church with its 'quivering believers', whence we can look contentedly at 'the smelly bustle of black, white, brown and yellow shuffling up and down the high street'. The subjects of the book are vast and various but its manner is comic, high-spirited, obscene in a long tradition, the multitudinous world as seen by a clear, happy eye. The whole impression is of ribald affection backed by understanding and compassion.

Kermode correctly identifies Smith's commitment to the critically underrated and unfashionable qualities of 'compassion,' an authorial empathy lacking in Rushdie. Hence any common superficial bracketing of the two on that basis alone risks superficiality. Both novelists are reduced by King's notion of their affinity, although to be fair such a comparison is common, but part of an impulse towards the superficial and topographical. Rebecca Dyer identifies in Smith 'her playful, Rushdie-esque writing style' (92). Similarly, Squires identifies the 'linguistic' influence (16) and 'plotting' (17) of Rushdie, although she concedes other stylistic influences including Lewis Carroll. According to Bart Moore-Gilbert in 'Postcolonialism and "the Figure of the Jew: Caryl Phillips and Zadie Smith"' the novel is a 'representation of contemporary intercultural relations, including those between metropolitan minorities of "New Commonwealth" origin and Jews rests on a model of interaction which corresponds closely to Rushdie's celebrated account in *The Satanic Verses* ...' (107–8), although he does add importantly that 'Smith's vision of cultural hybridity is not one of unalloyed celebration' (108), and that her 'brand of comic realism, her predominant narrative mode, belongs to a long-established mode of British fiction, represented pre-eminently, for Smith, by E. M. Forster' (109). Lowe admits that despite its postcolonial credentials 'Enigmatically, it is also a deeply English novel [...]' (166).

Many postcolonial critics project onto Smith's work a neo-liberal, multicultural positivism, the very perspective her novel parodies and subverts. Paradoxically, such readings negate Smith's often ironic view of hybridity and migration, compressing the interpretative range of coordinates. Tabuteau sees Smith as revisiting her predecessor and succeeded with the literati with 'her hybrid literary style hinging on various voices and tones, and by her description of a modern multicultural city from an immigrant's perspective [...]' (82). He does perceive the oddity of a precision of detail which nevertheless lacks specificity (83–4) and which he explains by an 'impressionist' quality shared with Selvon (84). Interestingly, he sees in both an inflection of tradition, including Dickens with the latter's view of London as both seductive and enmeshing (87). Ultimately, Tabuteau regards the novel as primarily celebratory. While closely reading the historical consciousness of Smith's first novel Dyer is determined to also foreground certain intertextual elements despite acknowledging these may actually derive from elements commonly located in novels concerned with London (83). She also prioritizes Smith's ethnicity in a particular manner, adjuring the difference between initial migrants and their offspring, largely denying Smith any interrelation with her father's inheritance. 'On one level, all the fictional works by the postwar migrant generation owe their existence and subject matter to a violent history, specifically to Britain's colonization of other regions and peoples. [...] As [...] White Teeth reveal[s], the legacy of British Imperialism is a long-lasting and far-reaching one' (97).

One can trace in certain responses an often unconscious critical predilection to discover in Smith essentialist forms of identity. Lassner focuses on the second generation. Although she regards the novel as part of a 'construction of a multivocal civilization' (194), Smith is constructed in opposition to certain forces that define her identity and aesthetic vision. 'Situated in a Britain bounded by the historically verified racist origins and remains of colonialism, Zadie Smith dramatizes a kind of fundamentalist agency that allows her young characters to free themselves from those post-colonial lessons that reify victimhood' (195). This restrictive reading allows Lassner to characterize Smith as 'Britain's most celebrated postcolonial prodigy' (193) and negate the influence of traditional aesthetic forms. Lassner finds neither humour nor subtlety, simply evidence of 'the oppressively racist history and conditions of either colonialism or postcolonial Britain' (194). Peter Childs correctly identifies Smith's satirical mode (201), and interprets Smith setting thus: 'Irie's birth year is not that of a nation: it is the year of the proclaimed end of the world, inserted in a spectrum of other key dates: 1857, 1907, 1945, and 1999. 1975 is put forward as a post-colonial year zero for Britain, when the apocalyptic pronouncements [. . .] are coming true, but a new London is in the process of being born' (202). Childs recognizes Smith's satirical treatment of multiculturalism, but using statistics from a 2000 newspaper article rather dramatically he claims that 'the novel disseminates a multi-ethnic view of London, where currently over forty per cent of children are born to at least one black parent' (209), a figure referred to by Laura Moss in 'The Politics of Everyday Hybridity: Zadie Smith's *White Teeth*' citing a range of secondary sources rewriting official statistics (11). Both ignore overall figures from the most recent National Statistics survey, *Resident Population: by Ethnic Group, 2001: Regional Trends [Dataset RT380307]*, that tabulates those of mixed race origin in London as representing 3.15 per cent of the population (the national average in 2001 being 1.15 per cent) which suggest something askew with their claims. While not rejecting such readings outright, the novel surely requires a more nuanced, better informed, less singularly ideological reading for a credible understanding of Smith's subtleties and her aesthetic ambitions.

Jesse Matz summarizes the initial responses to Smith in *The Modern Novel: A Short Introduction* (2004) which position her as globalizing 'the postcolonial postmodernism of Salman Rushdie. Like Rushdie, Smith has chosen to make the absurdities of cultural diversity a comic way to explore and explode myths of identity' (177–8). Such readings (which are rooted primarily in unflattering comparisons to Rushdie and in part stem from the initial media promotion of her image) risk superficiality, but once established prove persistent. Brian W. Shaffer reflects in *Reading the Novel in English 1950–2000* (2006) that 'Smith's wildly popular *White Teeth*, a novel at once Dickensian and Rushdiesque, deserves special mention because it has come to be seen by many as the quintessential "black British" novel, one that probes what Caryl Phillips calls the "helpless heterogeneity" of Britain's present multiracial reality' (29). As Benita Singh concludes in 'Not Quite Signature Piece,' 'To Smith, the comparison is well-intentioned, but "racial nonsense" nonetheless.' Aijaz

Ahmad's critical characterizations of Rushdie's early work precisely illustrate the profound differences between Rushdie and Smith and thereby suggest ways in which the latter's work can be situated more generously (and less dismissively). Ahmad—who regards Rushdie as a 'self-exile' (131) rather than a migrant—demonstrates how Rushdie's notion of 'migrancy' derives from and reformulates modernism (128) and is predicated upon 'the individual's freedom, absolute and mythic, that is derived from the fact that he belongs nowhere because he belongs everywhere [. . .]' (127) which position is not comparable to the dilemma of Smith's migrant characters, nor does it inform her sense of London and second-generation belongingness explored so radically and insistently in *White Teeth*. Moreover, for Smith, history is both materially as well as ideologically inscribed, responsive to intervention; inflected differently to that of Rushdie who, according to Ahmad, perceives a 'History [which], in other words, is not open to change, only to narrativization' (131). Moreover, Smith's use of dislocation, in Ahmad's terms her 'handling of ambivalences and conditionalities' (134), is more to do with a dynamic sense of the real than is the case in Rushdie's fiction. In Smith one finds concrete histories as opposed to Rushdie's anti-universalism and provisionalities concerning which Ahmad says there is an 'Irony of "I tell myself", which is so clearly intended to suggest that what follows is mere self-persuasion, not the truth but a hallucination of the truth [. . .]' (134). Moreover, if one uses Ahmad's analysis of Rushdie as yardstick for comparison, immediately one perceives in Smith crucial and obvious differences in terms of geographic and class origin, gender, mode of writings, and the opposite of what Ahmad calls 'Rushdie's aesthetic of despair' (155).

In *Postcolonial London* (2004) John McLeod draws variously upon Peter Brooker's notion of the novel's positivist trajectory, Yasmin Alibhai-Brown's journalistic and reductively rhetorical vision of a vibrant 'magic carpet of multiple cultures in London' (Alibhai-Brown 36; McLeod 160), and Caryl Phillips' reading of its celebration a hegemonic heterogeneity so as to position Smith as quintessentially part of a multicultural '"millennial optimism"' (160), where 'Smith's novel offers a version of London in which the depressingly familiar social conflicts of previous decades are no longer determining the formation of character and fortunes of plot' (161). Alibhai-Brown attempts to co-opt Smith by nominating her as 'Your archetypal Londoner [. . .]' and does so in prose so partial and ill-judged in its convictions that when it suits her she elides the multiplicity of cultural difference and its problematic realities (32). According to such accounts Smith's literary narrative offers (historically) an image of culturally relative harmony, a comic rendition of a new, adaptive real-life Britain. Moss identifies instead 'A multiplicity of identities [. . .]' (12).

After the orthodoxies of heterogeneity and hybridity expressed by the first wave of 'postcolonial' critics enthusing about Smith, often in interpretations that render her as variously rejecting the past, as being naïvely optimistic about multiculturalism, as a sub-Rushdiesque proponent of an essentialist postcolonial aesthetic, or as being propagandist for a postracial society, subsequently other critical parameters have highlighted a more nuanced and perhaps less assumptive view. In changing historical conditions, such readings have often become interrogative, divergent, perhaps more sophisticated. Although Dawson feels that 'the success of the novel attests to the enduring fascination with racial mixing and hybridity that characterizes our supposedly "postracial" era' (152), for him the novel's emphasis 'offers a salutary reminder of the intractable character of racial inequality by tracing the homologies that link the experience of different generations of black and Asian Britons. This flies in the face of accounts of our "postracial" moment' (153). Dawson subsequently points out that Smith herself satirizes genetic and 'biodeterminism' (25, 151–2, 159), subaltern studies (158), 'Samad's belief in cultural determinism as well as his dogmatic pride in his lineage' (164), middle-class multiculturalism (166–7), and several forms of fundamentalism expressed in animal rights campaigns and by the young Muslims of KEVIN (171). Exacerbated by the glib essentialism of certain responses which Dawson describes as undermined by 'ethnic primordialism [. . .]' (160), he comments,

Although theories of hybridity are intended to challenge exclusionary models of belonging, they suffer from their own forms of determinism as a result of their programmatic assertion of diasporic cosmopolitanism. All too often, this analysis simply inverts the dominant tropes of colonial discourse by representing diasporic populations as inherently progressive.

(160)

Dawson's reading focuses on how *White Teeth* relates to the dogmatic master narrative of 'biological determinism' (150) Dawson sees in the racialized possibilities of DNA and the Human Genome Project, finding parallels between the latter's public launch at the White House and the novel's final scene (152). In this reading both the Chalfens, with Joyce's notions of hybridity which term's origins Dawson situates in racist classifications, and Marcus' biogenetic experimentation, and the interconnection with the wartime scenes stress the complicity of the West in prejudicial views. However, Dawson rejects Gilroy's utopian flirtations with bio-determinism (153–4), insists that Smith both parodies subaltern studies (153) and rejects Samad's 'essentialist cultural identity' (162). Importantly for Dawson the title of the chapter where Magid and Millat are separated is scientific term 'Mitosis,' ironic since in spite of their genetic indivisibility culture and history render two quite separate identities despite an underlying uncanny synchronicity that Dawson elides. Finally, he regards Smith as rejecting neo-liberalism and fundamentalism, and says of any final equivocation, 'While *White Teeth* can warn us facile liberal models of multiculturalism by highlighting the disturbing return of an age of eugenics, it cannot predict the outcome of this return' (172).

According to David Sexton's account of Smith's confessional radio interview, she resists any such shift towards any literary 'ghettoization,' either critically or culturally, that can be seen to subtend many postcolonial readings, not wanting to be regarded narrowly as simply a black or postcolonial writer. Additionally, Smith insists she is not to be limited in terms of influence. Sexton reports,

> [S]he delivered a tremendous tirade against the idea of role models, having herself been held up as one for young black women wanting to write: 'Role models are useless. If I can only respond to role models who are going to be like me, then I can't like Virginia Woolf or Nabokov. What you need is black children and Asian children feeling that anything within a culture that they're interested in, they can respond to. Not that to read Shakespeare is being white or to read Nabokov is anti-black. It's a mistake.'

Sell claims *White Teeth*'s famous epigraph from Shakespeare's *The Tempest* indicates several things. First, 'the effect of this quotation is, I think, to indicate the novel's rupture with what might be considered conventional postcolonial hang-ups' (29). Smith not only breaks with that notion of the past, moreover she abjures history's usual logic and teleology, opting for something entirely more random and arbitrary, where the relationship 'may be simply coincidental, rather than necessarily causal [. . .]. Obviously the past is there, but it has lost the crushing weight so manifest in postcolonial fiction' (29). According to Sell's account, this is subtended by her use of a broad, comedic tradition which helps situate the absurdist quality several episodes are set in 1945 detailing the wartime experiences of Archie and Samad in a tank regiment engaged in mine clearance rather than combat (this rather incorporates Harvey Smith's far more heroic wartime experience who while serving in the 6th Assault Regiment Royal Engineers as part of the 79th Armoured Division was sent on 5 June 1944 to invade Normandy). Marooned in Bulgaria, leaderless after their officers have been killed, the pair are unaware the war in Europe is over. As elsewhere Smith's perspective is the complex morality of the experiential despite the comic inflection, for as Sell insists, 'Even if *White Teeth* was still stalked by some denizens of Rushdie's fabulous world, such as Mo Hussein-Ishmael, by and large hyperbolic hybridity was cut down to quotidian, human size' (33).

As Sell indicates the wartime experiences makes sense when in an episode towards the end of the novel, a French doctor and collaborator with the Germans, Dr Marc-Pierre Perret or Dr Sick as the locals call him, reappears even though Archie had supposedly executed him at Samad's insistence. Perret suffers from diabetic retinopathy and it is from his bloodied tears that they both recognize the true identity of Marcus Chalfen's mentor, aiding the genetic engineering and thereby linking it thematically with Perret's work in the death camps. The episode works because the meaning of the past is re-rendered, mysterious, surprising and mutative. Despite Sell's reading, which is topographically correct, Smith's novel is inflected by a logic of meaningful recurrence, an emphatic but variable doubling, akin to the folding Maurice Merleau-Ponty describes in the working notes that conclude *The Visible and the Invisible* (1997) where 'there is not identity, nor non-identity, or non-coincidence, there is inside and outside turning about one another——' (264). This shifting is not a lack of meaning, but its surplus.

Tobias A. Wachinger in *Posing In-between: Postcolonial English-ness and the Commodification of Hybridity* (2003) doubts specifi-cally whether Smith really offers a radical or fresh perspective, saying,

> But a look at the way Smith has been publicised and mediatised as 'young, black, British' writer sensation (*The Observer*) indicates the machinery of the market recuperation of a certain type of 'in-between' fiction is well lubricated. This fashioning by the metropolitan cultural industries that have turned *White Teeth* into the latest 'hot' commodity from multicultural London (complete with Rushdie's appraisal on the cover blurb), however, would not have been possible without Smith's novel's own stressing of its undeniably multicultural sweep.
>
> (194–5)

Wachinger clearly situates Smith's work as implicated in the glob-alized marketing of fiction, part product, part celebrity culture. Also initially he sees her work as akin to Rushdie's in the limited sense of purveying a notion of 'in-betweenness' that Wachinger finds unconvincing. Further, he attacks the very notion of hybridity including by implication Bhabha's as 'predicated on the Manichean binarism of the categories it seeks to overcome' (193) and also Gilroy's concept of a Black Atlantic for an essentialism underly-ing any concept of a generic 'black' experience (197). Referring to Smith's own allusion to her novel being like watching old British sit-coms, where a repetitious trauma underlies migration, Wachinger allows that in an unspectacular way:

> the whole novel sums up the different problems [. . .] with regard to the negotiation(s) of subject-positions that inhabit cultural spaces in-between. And Smith seems to know all too well that the 'in-between' position is likely to prove a condition of (comic) entrapment and (self-parodic) repetition.
>
> (195)

Wachinger perhaps underestimates both the strength of Smith's textual ironies *and* the hard-nosed and concise parodic world-view that underlies her narrative of the contemporary in its often hubristic relation with the past. These positions variously inform what Dawson describes as her 'acid' commentary 'on the contradictions in contemporary middle-class discourses of multiculturalism through its [*White Teeth*'s] portrait of the molecular biologist Marcus Chalfen and his wife Joyce. [. . .] Smith focuses her critique on the far more subtle bias of bourgeois white Britons such as the Chalfens' (166).

Clearly, though, Smith's acidity applies its dyspeptic critique far wider than the Chalfens. McLeod reconsiders his view of Smith in 'Revisiting Postcolonial London,' where he concedes that it is within 'the vertiginous consequences of the multicultural city' (41), neglected by the postmodern vision of a plural culture that Smith foregrounds issues of faith through Millat so as 'render a distinctly poignant and solemn articulation of the pain of being "different" in London and the dangerous consequences this may create' (42). Significantly he admits 'in returning to the novel after recent events [the 7/7 bombings], the millennial optimism which gathered around the novel seems not only sadly misplaced but also dependent upon a misreading of the novel's articulation of London's multicultural vernacular cosmopolitanism' (43). Such recent events so relevant to certain of Smith's themes suggest one might reconsider the first novel's dynamics. At least tacitly McLeod recognizes that *White Teeth* was never naïve enough to convey an unproblematic vision of urban utopian conviviality, simply many critics, himself included, wanted to so situate and read this text because of their particular agendas.

Wood in *The Irresponsible Self: On Laughter and the Novel* might concede that *White Teeth* is a 'large, inventive book' (171), but he describes it as part of a self-generating 'hysterical realism' (168) (a term also used previously in his journalistic exchanges with Smith in the pages of the *Guardian*). According to Wood in such contemporary novels, there is 'an excess of storytelling' (171) the narrative borrowing from and overloading realism while evading reality or the problems of representation, thereby producing 'inhuman stories' (180). Hence the interconnection of characters fails precisely because such characters 'are not fully alive, not fully human, their connectedness can only be insisted on; indeed the reader begins to think that it is being insisted upon precisely because they do not really exist' (171). Such an approach amounts to an exaggeration of the real in which the narrative nevertheless remains rooted.

Wood's criticism of the novel is partly, as Daniel Lea explores in 'Aesthetics and Anaesthetics: Anglo-American Writers' Responses to September 11,' a reaction to the over-clever knowingness, to what Wood terms particular '"things"' of contemporary novelists, who have 'abandoned their historical roots in social commentary in favour either of ostentatious displays of arcane and localised knowledge or the directly personal and domestic, ascribable only to the private consciousness' (9). A similar objection lies at the heart of Berlinski's critique of Smith and *White Teeth* already discussed in terms of Smith's alleged misrepresentation of experience in a multicultural, yet racist city. In 'Ethnic Cartographies of London in Bernardine Evaristo and Zadie Smith,' Pilar Cuder-Domínguez considers the tensions of Englishness, its adaptations, and sees Smith's novel as 'polyvocal,' concerned with hybridity as a hidden history of colonization (183), and also notes the historically interlinked nature of experience, adding 'the pursuit of purity (biological or psychological) haunts many of the characters in Smith's novels, particularly first-generation immigrants' (184). For Cuder-Domínguez, Smith exposes the myths and prejudices of White Englishness, and although she concedes that 'Smith displays a certain tenderness in her handling of [. . .]' Archie (185), she directs the reader to the novel's condemnation of the warlike and imperial Dickinson-Smith (185) and of Joyce Chalfen and Poppy Burt-Jones' exotic objectifications of Millat and Samad (186). Although Cuder-Domínguez notes the excess of irony in the novel, overall she diminishes the effect of the broad sweep of Smith's comic mode and her strong sense of pathos, of history as a force largely although not entirely beyond individual conscious volition. Hence Archie defies its peculiar logic with his own, the aleatory nature of random chance. Her conclusion that Smith 'strike[s] at the very heart of the middle-class, heterosexual, patriarchal values that have persisted to this day in the English identity [. . .]' (188) seems both grossly exaggerated and gratuitous. More interestingly, Bentley argues in 'Re-writing Englishness: Imagining the Nation in Julian Barnes's *England, England* and Zadie Smith's *White Teeth*' that the 'imagined community' of nationhood is 'unfixed [. . .] open to varying interpretations and claims' (485) but constructed in a Lacanian 'fantasy space' (486) where signification defies referentiality and adapting what Slajov Zizek regards as 'multiculturalism as a manifestation of postcolonial guilt (The Real)' (487). Moss allows that this is 'not an outright celebration of hybridity, but nor is it a denunciation of the processes that have led to the existence of such hybridity' (11). She notes the increasing ordinariness, and mundane contexts of cultural and racial hybridities which she reads as a mark of 'assimilation and multiplicity' (12) to the point that the textual dynamic is not an interrogation of the cultural interstices, more a broadly based existential query of the human condition in certain contexts (13) and it is in Moss' view the older generation typified by Samad and Hortense that 'is most upset by the very ordinariness of the children's integration into a multiplicitous landscape' (14). Moss understands Smith's passing description of a youth intent on racist violence from its juxtaposition 'with the farcical description of the thinly-veiled racism of Joyce Chalfen, the middle-class-white-liberal-intellectual-feminist author of *The Inner-Life of House Plants* and condescending patron of Millat and Irie' (15), ignoring that through Joyce's book and her opinions Smith parodies her character without vilifying her, a woman rejected as the narrator specifies by her own family for her 'Israelite love-match' (314). Joyce focuses upon Millat hoping once more to be the centre of things, as she was with her family, to dissipate a sense of the present where 'the boredom was palpable' (314).

Towards the novel's end a very stoned Millat rejects his father as a failure, finally perceiving history as a battle of contending forces, as if engaged in a bout, each determined to be inscribed, often by acting murderously much like Havelock who executed Millat's ancestor, Pande, during the mutiny (506). Yet, as Smith insists, intentionality does not primarily shape history. The world and events are aleatory, and in this context Millat engages with the unpredictable causality of the world unconsciously having an effect upon certain outcomes apparent in his attempt to assassinate Perret which allows Archie to liberate the Futuremouse© (540–2), an action possibly symbolically indicative of a natural impulse towards freedom which reasserts itself in the face of dogmas underpinned by prejudices, an occurrence that rejects the logic of essentialisms and fundamentalisms.

The aleatory, accidentalism and an interrogation of concepts of history inform Fred Botting's reading of *White Teeth* in 'From Excess to the New World Order' which essay appears in a collection concerned with British fiction in the 1990s, so its focus is Smith's reflection of that period and its development. Botting refers to the Freudian *fort-da* game of oedipal opposition played out between Samad and his sons with its implications of loss and trauma as the context of Samad's choice to divide his sons, and which act renders Samad complicit with Archie's trust in the haphazard randomness of fate. Botting highlights the theme of the apocalyptic, either banalized for popular consumption (as with coverage of the destruction of the Berlin Wall) or variously reduced to the comic especially in terms of the 'excessive intensity of fundamentalism [. . .]' (25). He reads Marcus Chalfen and Magid's rational scientificity as implicated in a different apocalyptic order or threat with its roots in the Nazi past. Through an iterative, recursive narration of the historical Botting suggests Smith nevertheless conveys a sense of immobility, 'eternal recurrence' (30) and the collapse of historical certainties in a commodified society (31). Botting interprets the endless hours in O'Connell's as configuring a presumably symbolic or subliminal resistance to the logic of exchange that defined the public discourse of the era, and rather expressing an exchange 'beyond the circuits of economic calculation and reason' (29). Botting's sense is that the final scene cannot transcend the everyday that Archie and the mouse represent (34), rather it interconnects the various doubling that recurs in the novel, and represents 'the novel's celebration of the last days of paternal order [. . .]' (34). The implicit claim that the ambivalence of the ending might retrospectively breach, however, tacitly the contradictions of modernity is a grandiose claim for a novel, which like the escaping mouse is never totally 'beyond chance and nature' (35). Subverting Botting's notion is the fact that although its longevity is pre-programmed, the genetic coding determines very little else.

AUTOGRAPH MAN

Alex Clark in 'Signs and Wanders' in *The Guardian* considers *The Autograph Man* to be darker and subtler than the first novel, its paraphernalia to be distracting, although he finds it 'Full of the same easy humour and ironic flourishes, the tongue-in-cheek smart-aleckry and generous, tossed-off characterisation [. . .]. At times, one feels that the cleverness, the wilful irreverence, the attitude, are getting in the way of something more substantial [. . .].' Adams Mars-Jones in 'Name of the Prose' recognizes that anonymity is a major theme, deciding that a significant 'absence is Martin Amis, whose hectoringly insightful mannerisms Zadie Smith doesn't always manage to make her own. Withholding a name is part of the novel's strategy in some areas that seem arbitrary and sometimes awkward. Alex turns on not a Mac, laptop or PC, but simply a "box of tricks".' Mars-Jones finds the novel at times unconvincing, pedestrian, and decidedly uncharismatic, adding 'Jewishness works beautifully in the novel as a source of ideas and symbols. Jewishness is an outsiderdom with a front-row centre seat. It's also a shrewd way for a British novelist to excite an American market, without needing to relinquish domestic subjects.' In 'Here She Is,' Kermode concludes the novel exhibits comic virtuosity. 'She is seriously comic about death, pain, faith.'

Such responses typify the positive responses among the mixed reviews Smith's second novel received, which when favourable were often only partly so. Others were more hostile, often alluding to the compromise of Smith's initial success by the second novel's long, elaborate and at times irrelevant inventory of contemporary life. In 'An Elusive, Whimsical Autograph' in the *New York Times* Michiko Kakutani judges it as lacking authentic precision; he adds that its plot is 'simultaneously schematic and messy [...].' Generally he feels the structure insufficient for the weighty themes considered, of death, mourning, loss, and confusions of identity in a world of commodity and fame. He judges Smith to have created archetypal and symbolic characters 'rather than multifarious individuals,' and concludes the novel represents 'a pokey, pallid successor and a poor testament to its author's copious talents.' James Wood finds *The Autograph Man* better written technically than the first novel, but returning to certain interpretative themes expressed in the critical debate between Smith and Wood, the latter in reviewing *The Autograph Man* in 'Fundamentally Goyish' situates Smith among the contemporary novelists that Wood finds are 'in love with what might be called irrelevant intensity. In fiction, information has become the new character, and information is endless,' who he finds are obsessed with 'the signs of irrelevant intensity [...],' of the trivial ephemera of culture in 'their gross mimetic appetite.' In contrasting Smith's second novel with *White Teeth*, he admits the latter's 'cartoonish energy' and 'perpetual mobility' are offset by the strength of the central narrative of the two main families. In contrast, for Wood, *The Autograph Man* fails to be either serious or faithful to the literary culture from which it emerges, since it 'bears the impress of American writers like Dave Eggers and David Foster Wallace, clever, nervy exhibitionists, [...] writers with a gift for speedy cultural analysis, whose prose is choppy with interruption.'

For Wood, Smith's protagonist is 'an empty centre entirely filled by his pop-culture devotions. Around him swirls a text incapable of ever stiffening into sobriety, a flailing, noisy hash of jokes, cool cultural references, pull-quotes, lists and roaring italics.'

Wood reads Smith's second novel as full of empty complications, dismissing as irrelevant the whimsical digest with which each chapter begins. For Wood the very intensity of the novel's preoccupation with Jewishness remains both surprising and problematic, the debates undertaken by the main characters concerning Alex's oppositional categorization of everything into Jewish and goyish not convincing, failing to express a believable or authentic Jewish perspective. Wood seems unwilling to admit such a cultural obsession might be intended to verge on the pathological, rendering most aspects of the victim's life as distorted by what Wood describes as 'the shallow binarisms of Lenny Bruce' precisely as a technique of avoidance. Alex's existence seems unreal because he avoids depth, commitment and maturity. His preoccupations are rooted as extensions of those of adolescence, a well-recognized contemporary cultural dynamic. Wood interprets a certain weakness in the relationship between the scheme of the book and its intentions:

> And should a serious novel—if this is what *The Autograph Man* is—proceed from, and then only lazily confirm, the shallow binarisms of Lenny Bruce? Despite its Judaic theological literacy, the novel's Jewishness is so dominated by Bruce's taxonomic vulgarity that it often seems no more than crude externality.

For Wood finally Smith over-identifies with Alex, creating insufficient ironic or other distance, and 'Fatally, she can't decide about the extent of his corruption by popular culture.' Wood claims that Smith fails to create sufficient 'sincerity' so that the fiction lacks a definite moral centre, apart from a sense that media images precede every thought or action, reducing human actions to banalities. Wood concludes that Smith's attempts to subvert the cleverness of narrative are inflected overly by a reflexivity that fails to distance itself from the flaws of such irony, for

> Paradoxically, for all that this kind of self-consciousness about our unoriginality seeks to tear through the veil of representation, it is

itself a highly aesthetic gesture, for it is a self-consciousness about self-consciousness.

Wood regards Smith in her structural relation to the society of the spectacle, at least covertly either enamoured or complicit. Nevertheless, Wood approves of the idea of the final redemption overturning a life spent shallowly worshipping dead celebrity, and finally, 'The man who trades in false signs is finally led into synagogue to do business with the great transcendental signified Himself.' As Wood indicates, Alex—in the detritus of his fractured but banal existence—is buried by the weight of intertextual reference, comparing himself to Job, appropriating the title of a Primo Levi book, and rephrasing Saul Bellow's first line of *Herzog*. Despite what Wood evidences as Smith's ear for the varieties of speech and the momentary power of her descriptive prose, according to Wood among the 'anarchy of styles, amid the cartoonishness and excess, the misplaced ironies and grinning complicities' Alex remains a 'nullity' or 'absence', finally lacking pathos.

Other reviewers identify merits both in Smith's structure and her central themes; Aida Edemariam in 'Learning Curve' argues:

> The ideas that strike us as disjointed in *The Autograph Man*—cultural identity and modernity—perhaps need not be connected at all in order for *The Autograph Man* to gain lucidity. And the racial descriptions that seem cumbersome and disconnected from plot are simply a function of Smith's realism. To read them otherwise is, as Smith would say, 'racial nonsense.' Once we accept the multiculturalism that is a 'fact of life,' *The Autograph Man* redeems itself. As we express our disappointment with Zadie Smith, we should also realize that she too has written a critique of us as readers.

Unlike Wood who dismisses the central Jewishness, Furman applauds its presence, situating Smith in a mainly American tradition of the Jewish novel, regarding her text as both redeeming and extending the possibilities of this genre with its Jewishness consciousness in a multicultural world. Citing Cynthia Ozick he charts her call for a revision of the post-immigrant generation whose ethnic coordinates became clichéd, calling rather for what in Ozick's terminology is a more '"liturgical"' (6) vision. So Furman analyses Smith's novel in terms of 'gentile writer' (8) sensitively demonstrating the 'welcome return of the Jewish novel actively engaged with the pressing cultural crises of our day, specifically the complexities involved in claiming a viable identity in our increasingly multiethnic, multiracial, and transnational world' (7). Furman sees Smith as subverting Alex's overwhelming categorization in his almost mythic and encyclopaedic work that only appears in fragments, displaced by significant symbols of Jewish culture (8–9), by allusions to classic Jewish novels (9). Furman compares the 'picaresque quality' (9) to Bellow, citing positively the allusion to *Herzog*'s first line. Furman interprets Alex's world as evoking 'A post-ethnic construct of identity [...] [and] a growing multiracial and multiethic citizenry [...]' (10) that challenges the purity or relative stasis inherent in traditionalist views of ethnicity, both reactionary and progressive. Alex's desire for substance and presence can in this context find its true expression 'in Judaic terms, [in] this covenanted existence' (12). For Furman by drawing on Leon Wieseltier's *Kaddish* (1998) Smith explores and mediates upon bereavement and loss (13), through a protagonist struggling with mortality, attempting to domesticize and sentimentalize the world through everyday paraphernalia until finally he can at least go through the motions of mourning. In the final ceremony Alex undertakes 'an act of will, if not faith, that transcends the realm of cliché to which so many of our daily actions have been reduced' (14).

Using *The Autograph Man* together with *White Teeth* to demonstrate his own ideological template concerning postcolonial identity, Moore-Gilbert situates Smith's use of Jewish figures as part of her Rushdiesque vision of cultural hybridity (107–8). He interprets this as part of desire to transcend racism and anti-Semitism in 'a desirable dialectical process in which different traditions, cultures and identities merge to create a new, superior, unified third term' (108). Her mixed race characters evince for Moore-Gilbert a refutation of tradition where Jewishness becomes implicitly radical, an 'integral part of contemporary metropolitan life' (109), its relation to 'New Commonwealth' minorities 'symphonic' in Said's terminology according to Moore-Gilbert, since it effects a harmonious overlapping. For Moore-Gilbert even the Holocaust does not preoccupy the second novel's protagonist or central characters, although Moore-Gilbert manages to stretch a single sentence reference to the predominance of Hitler on Alex's hotel television's history channel. In the text this reflects one fragment in the random, passing thoughts of Alex when drunk. Moore-Gilbert reads this somewhat improbably as offering a parallel to 'Smith's treatment of slavery and colonialism in *White Teeth*' (110). Moore-Gilbert sees the apportioning of Jewishness according to the Lenny Bruce inspired categorization of Judaic identity as postmodern (114), co-opting its peculiarities so they might indicate that 'Smith rejects any kind of racial or cultural exceptionalism including, by implication, Jewish exceptionalism' (114). Finally, this critique reveals itself as explicitly and determinedly political, since by noting Smith's failure to incorporate mention of Palestine (114) Moore-Gilbert renders this apparent deficiency of Smith's cultural politics to accord with his version of a historical agenda concerned with Palestine, whose treatment he finally evinces as a major factor in 'Islamic Fundamentalism' (115). One might finally object that surely the potential historical parameters of the relationship of Jews, Israel, Muslims, Palestine and various 'New Commonwealth' identities simply cannot be so marshalled to support an aesthetic analysis in this way, that is tangentially to imply a larger critique with so little historical context.

Childs interprets the International Gestures that are a motif in *The Autograph Man* as akin to the shorthand of emotions and experience in which Alex both seeks refuge from and diminishes the real, which of course is the motivating force behind the autograph hunting (203). The latter is part of a 'lucrative economy of images [. . .]' (204) where authenticity is in question, and as Childs specifies the novel seems indirect, with experiences and emotions mediated (205). Nevertheless, unlike many critics Childs feels Alex develops empathy, for Childs lacking in *White Teeth*, evidenced in Alex's donation of his commission to the dying, Brian Duchamp, and in Alex at last participating in the final Kaddish. Yet Childs concedes that throughout the characterizations are mediated by a narrator intent on both making general cultural observations, but evoking the vicarious quality of a generation raised on televisual and cinematic representations of life, clearly a major theme of Smith's novel.

Sell's essay considers the second novel in its relation to the first and both in terms of a world of chance where through a series of gestures individuals attempt 'pragmatic self-representations' (27). Interestingly, Sell is uninterested in hybridity of character since 'any such assessment would rely on an essentialist view of identity which Smith's novels quite plainly reject' (28), rather seeking a philosophy underpinning multicultural identities. According to

Sell's account although *The Autograph Man* exhibits 'a realist model of identity' (34), Book One indicates by its chapter names the possibilities of the Kabbalistic *sefirot*, Book Two a Zen Buddhist schema. However, 'neither cultural scheme is adequate to circumscribe Alex-Li's identity. [...] For Alex-Li, and for Zadie Smith, identity is too myriad and adventitious to be reduced to a single cultural essence' (34). Sell highlights the metaphysic of chance, a world where identity cannot be maintained and Alex's phenomenological categorizations collapse. This is emphasized by the ephemeral, chameleon qualities of celebrity. In Smith's fiction Sell finds the logic of identity incompatible with a fixed 'historically-determined self' (36), and the implications of the final scene are only gestural and temporary. Cultural and divisions of identity for Sell threaten disintegration by being cacophonous. He refutes Wood's reading of Alex's 'nullity' by fusing a gestural temporality which is 'accidental and in constant flux' (40) with a pragmatic performativity within cultural constraints (using as his exemplar the joke of the miscommunication between the Pope and the Chief Rabbi). Although not finally resolving the paradoxes of identity, Sell's scheme is underpinned by synthesizing theoretical models that avoid simplistic assertions. He implies the novel's overall scheme is essentially comedic, necessarily humanistic and offers epiphany through laughter. According to his account any resolution is tentative, the perspective local and domestic.

ON BEAUTY

By the time of this novel's publication Smith seemed irritated by stereotypical views of her work, annoyed by the anticipation on the part of readers and critics alike that she ought to produce something in the vein of the two preceding novels. Such assumptions underpin Deresiewicz's unenthusiastic response:

> Instead of building on the strengths of *The Autograph Man*, Smith has fallen back into the weaknesses of *White Teeth*, but without recovering its particular strengths. The satirical eye is still there—Smith is unfailingly great at rendering the texture of social and especially family life, its moment-by-moment play of habit and hypocrisy, self-dramatization and self-pity—though without generating the same humor as before.

Fiona Tolan in 'Identifying the Previous in Zadie Smith's *On Beauty*' regards the third novel as reworking *White Teeth* in terms of its multicultural dimension, its domestic setting and the fact that it is 'founded on the interconnecting relationships of two families [. . .]' (128). Peter Kemp reviews the novel dismissively in the *Sunday Times*, finding Smith's Forsterian comparisons unconvincing. Kemp adds that its comprehensive quality is evidence of Smith's strategy of 'cannibalising' common features found in her previous novels. Murphy Moo contends that Forster's intertextual presence recurs in Smith's fiction more generally. Among critics, interviewers and reviewers the compulsion for comparison, an insistent retrieval of continuities tends to limit readings of Smith's work.

Murphy Moo prefaces her interview with a description of the main elements of *The Autograph Man*, which she summarizes as 'a sprawling Edwardian novel set in a fictional Massachusetts college town, which casts a struggling marriage against the backdrop of the racial and cultural questions of today.' She stresses that following an Aristotelian model of literature, Smith regards the novel form as a space to hypothesize or 'experiment with possible courses of action,' and in this particular case the central concern is the possibilities of moral choice. In a more substantial and influential review, Kermode analyses both the difficulties and significance of Smith's *homage* in *On Beauty* to Forster, first considering the fact of Forster's historical specificity, and though Kermode outlines the parallels with *Howards End* in Smith including a 'preemptoriness of manner,' finally he situates her debt more subtly. He identifies the 'magic' in both novels, considers specifically the unaffectedly moral qualities of Kiki and details qualities Forster considered essential to an effective novel (precisely those lacking in James), including the philosophical, the prophetic and the transcendent ('the superhuman'). As Kermode concludes, 'The main resemblance between the two books goes beyond the plot allusions everybody talks about.' He insists that the two worlds are radically different, using Forster's non-sexual use of the word 'relationship' as his litmus test. Kermode positions Smith's reworking of a famous Forsterian passage, which facetiously trivializes some admittedly glib, intellectualizing interpretations of a performance of Beethoven's Fifth Symphony, as a strategy leading her into a similar aesthetic misjudgement when Smith describes the Belsey family listening to Mozart's *Requiem* on Boston Common. Kermode's discrimination may seem arcane to many. Otherwise he finds the narrative deft, particularly endorses both Smith's use of rap as a contemporary poetry, and finally he sees in Smith a similar moral seriousness. However, Kermode concludes her ethical understanding of relations to be less rich in implications because in the contemporary world the nuances of all such relations between individuals have become too suffused with sexual possibilities. Nevertheless, this is offset by Smith's exuberance and the subtlety of positioning Kiki rather than anyone from the intellectual sphere as the moral compass of the book.

In 'None but the Fair' Sophie Ratcliffe gestures to the Forsterian parameters, Smith's turning away from the 'hysterical realism' levelled at the author and her ongoing stylistic virtuosity supporting her commitment to a comic mode very much *en passant*, but with care and detail Ratcliffe takes time to elucidate Scarry's influence, Smith's reintroduction of 'the occult category of beauty into academic discussion [...]' (10), the concept that beauty demands attention and as a catalyst for social justice (10). Ratcliffe concludes *On Beauty* proficiently and wittily incorporates these elements into a text modelled on the classic campus novels of the 1980s. As Ratcliffe indicates the philosophical concerns are played out more in the minutiae of academic life than the set-piece intellectual exchanges stymied or tortured by Howard's deconstructive semiotics. Personal beauty in Ratcliffe's account is rapturous and a cause for suffering, but much of the focus is centred upon imperfection, among the '*jolie-laide*' (10) such as Zora whose imperfection (like her mother's) exudes that of Rembrandt's women. And as Ratcliffe adds, 'The differences, and similarities, between male and female desire, central to *Howards End*, dominate this book' (10–11), which is full of 'Forsterian reticence' (11). Smith in this reading attempts, as Forster did, to interrelate the aesthetic and political, to see if 'the idea of "fairness" can be translated from art to life' (11). For Ratcliffe the final paragraph which describes the scene of Howard confronting both his fate and a sense of aesthetic and literal beauty provides not only an example of an economy of complexity and cultural reference, but her narrative's apotheosis.

Walters' collection, like the proverbial curate's egg, is good in parts (even including a contribution without a bibliography). Maeve Tynan in '"Only Connect": Intertextuality and Identity in Zadie Smith's *On Beauty*' regards the novel as firmly 'within a postcolonial paradigm,' but rather than 'adversarial "writing back" [...] instead the more diffident aim of establishing links' (73), adding that 'her explicit literariness leaves her vulnerable to accusations of elitism' (74). Tynan positions Smith's 'rewriting' as failing to fully radical-ize its origins in the hypotext, but allows its addition of ethnicity to Forster's issues of class. Tynan explores the intertextual param-eters of Smith's characterizations in terms of their metropolitan identities, including different versions of blackness, Kiki limited by stereotypes, Levi seeking a black authenticity that can only be con-tingent. 'Identity, then, is a matter of *positioning* as well as simply being. [. . .] Existence resides *in* the chaos of a constant becom-ing' (86). Walters in 'Still Mammies and Hos: Stereotypical Images of Black Women in Zadie Smith's Novels' considers Smith's use of such stereotypes in relation to three prejudicial images dili-gently resisted by other black women writers, 'the mammy, the jezebel, and the matriarch' (123). Walters asserts historical impli-cations rooted as they are in slavery, and implicit in pervasive 'derogatory' language about black women in black culture (124). She notes Smith's 'difficulty creating female characters (both black and white) that are more than one-dimensional character types' (125). However, Walters concedes Smith can transcend such lim-itation, particularly with Kiki whose portrayal problematizes the mammy. Walters sees her as initially submissive and domestic, dis-connected from her 'cultural heritage' and silence by Howard (131). For Walters, first, Kiki is marginalized by her body, Smith alluding specifically to her great-great-grandmother, a house-slave. Second, Kiki is only redeemed by removing herself from the white world (132). Walters reads Hortense Bowden in *White Teeth* as a matri-arch (133), and Honey Richardson as a jezebel becoming in part a mammy in *The Autograph Man*. Although dogged by her prosti-tute past, she is finally inscribed as 'loyal, intelligent, and vulnerable' (135). Walters identifies the jezebel in *On Beauty*'s Victoria Kipps, and although she concedes a certain humour in Victoria's sexual obsessions, Walters diminishes the power of Smith's critique of a contemporary culture of commodified orthodoxies in the pri-vate imagination of the young by concluding that Victoria does not evolve, 'another black woman who is defined by her sexuality' (137) evidenced by the emails to Howard which 'reinforce sexual deviancy and the representation of black women as deviants' (136).

James Lasdun in 'Howard's Folly' applauds the adaptability of Smith's style, with what he regards as its profoundly more

interior characterization than Smith's previous novel. He notes
the 'vividness' of mimetic description and cultural observations of
the narrative, its plethora life's significant minutiae. He views the
're-engineering' of the Forsterian plot as 'ingenious,' adding that
Forster's own influences allow Smith to vicariously incorporate 'the
epigrammatic polish of Jane Austen [...] [with] the looser, more
discursive amplitude [...] of contemporary prose' (9). Lasdun has
reservations about the narrative's beginning, the Forsterian residue
in the novel's style and the use of what he considers an unconvincing level of coincidence. He contends that *On Beauty* extends
the modest frame of the campus comedy genre precisely because
unlike most contemporary fiction the novel embraces both the
grandeur and seriousness of the Forsterian themes: friendship, marriage, social tension and the function of art. Perceptively, Lasdun
situates 'liminality' as central to the narrative, the interrelation of
characters inhabiting very different lives so divided conceptually,
by age, experience and identity that they fail to fully comprehend
each other. Lasdun notes first the underlying 'psychological violence' in the interrelation of the characters, and second how the
profound and unexpected effect upon Howard of Mozart's *Ave
Verum* at the London funeral leads to his sentimentalism followed
by 'ancient antagonisms' with his estranged father. This confrontation leads to the seduction scene that undermines the fragility of
his relationship with Kiki. Lasdun feels the latter's characterization
limited by the requirement that she represents an archetype that
challenges 'Howard's hyper-intellectuality but never quite comes
out from behind the enormous bosom with which her creator has
a little too symbolically endowed her' (9). The implication is that
as much as Kiki is intended to undermine certain traditional ethnic stereotypes that she rails against in the text, she is still within
their penumbra. Lasdun concludes that *On Beauty* is a novel of great
intelligence, its other characterizations engaging and acute, such as
Carl, Claire Malcolm and Howard 'whose limitless capacity for folly
keeps deepening and strangely sweetening his character' (9).

Tolan sees the novel as structured around the challenge to the
two central families by the infidelity of the father (128), where initially beauty is regarded as a commodity to be protected (129).
Tolan notes Forster's influence as a factor common to all of Smith's
novels, and that Smith appears to be responding to Scarry's observation that beauty is not considered or discussed in the modern

humanities (131), and that through the section from Scarry used as an epigraph Smith foregrounds its 'precious' qualities. The pairing of Monty and Howard epitomizes the liberal and conservative viewpoints, and 'The text sets up an opposition between a transcendent and culturally situated understanding of art and beauty' (131). As Tolan explains Monty's view is closer to that of Scarry as any historically inflected notion of beauty incorporating transcendence is 'inimical to Howard's beliefs' (131), capable as he is according to Smith's narrative of reducing Rembrandt to competence and of seeing aesthetics as exclusionary. Tolan outlines how both Victoria and Jerome critique the limitations of Howard's view (131–2). The perspicacity of this essay's analysis is most acute in terms of the abstract painting beneath which Howard and Kiki fight, identifying its artificial binary quality which 'interrogates connections between movement and stasis, between the artificial and the real' (132–3). Among the parallelism is that of the wives, and the relationship between Carlene and Kiki which, as Tolan says, highlights the importance of the Haitian painting, the legacy. According to Tolan the Belseys tend to determine everything by economic value (which is at the heart of Zora's suspicions of Carl) and Carlene shows Kiki a more transcendent, spiritual economy contradicting 'Kiki [in her] attempts to appropriate Howard's language in compensation for what fears to be her critical competence [...]' (133) thus dispelling his influence. As Tolan specifies the theme of the transcendence of art derives equally from Forster. Nevertheless, Carlene's reading cannot account for the complexity of the socio-politics of Haiti. Tolan points to the painting's figure of the goddess as a focal point for a gamut of interpretations, from the maid's superstitious fear, Monty's mission to preserve black art to Kiki's identification with its vengeful quality and the painting's economic value, all indicating its contextual, historical significance (134–5). According to Tolan art from Rembrandt to rap is discussed throughout the novel, 'But where Howard dismisses the concept of genius as an attempt to reify the liberal humanist self, Carl seeks to democratize genius' (135). Moreover, Smith sees that 'the connected principles of art, beauty and genius participate in more than aesthetic pleasure [...]' as it can indicate the good (136). Tolan cites Smith's reflections on Forster as meaning that the novel develops a training of feeling, but Smith also incorporates Forster's refusal of absolutism (136), and in a world of contention following Scarry's concept of the priority of beauty leads even Howard to authentic feeling, prompting a radical change (137).

Fischer's '"A Glance from God": Zadie Smith's *On Beauty* and Zora Neale Hurston' considers both Forster and Hurston as influences, but reads the novel very much in terms of a number of issues that determine the nature of inter-racial politics in the United States, particularly affirmative action (positive discrimination according to some accounts) and the legacy of slavery. Both are certainly important themes, but Fischer positions the Belsey house as 'symbolic of race relations in the United States and emblematic of who "belongs"' (286). One can take a position as to whether she over-determines Smith's decision to have the house built during the year the Supreme Court in the Dred Scott case affirmed slaves as property (287), but it is an interesting point. As Fischer's title indicates her intention is to broaden the range of Smith's influence from Forster and Scarry to include Hurston, to whom as Fischer points out Smith strategically alludes in certain details set out by Fischer (290), who argues that the companion with her predecessor allows Smith to challenge stereotypes of Black women, acquiring a vocabulary that includes the central reference to the Voodoo Goddess described in Hurston's anthropological-ethnic study, *Mules and Men* (1935). In Fischer's reading allusions to Voodoo allow an alternative view of 'Kiki who is associated both with Hurston's Janie and with the Voodoo goddess Erzulie, can be read less as a stereotypical black earth mother, as white Wellinton sees her, and more as a woman who is defining her own reality away from the paradigms of racist and sexist America' (291). Worrying that Victoria represents 'another iteration of the stereotype of the hyper-sexualised black woman' (291), Fischer emphatically makes the case that Vee (Fischer relates her abbreviated name to Voodoo) follows Hurston's heroine as an image of the celebration of female sexuality and in showing Howard her genitals, repeatedly sending him pictures of them, and in dressing for an assignation to exude raw sexuality, as a spirit of Erzulie Victoria embodies transformation (291). Elaborate as her reading might be, Fischer worries 'Yet the problem remains that she can still be read—perhaps more easily—as exploited, confused or indeed as the usual stereotype of aberrant black female sexuality' (292). Fischer might remember Victoria's British cultural roots (shared with Smith) and situate her as one of a new generation of women, more sexually forward, exhibiting nevertheless confusion and vulnerability. Like all characters she has multiple functions, and may be read variously as a result. Nevertheless, many of Fischer's observations are acute. As she says of Zora, 'Like her father, she believes in nothing' (294). Despite this initial state of mind, like all of the younger generation she undergoes a metamorphosis (294–5), that is she progresses emotionally. And finally the central work of art does indicate and symbolize the transformations in Kiki, the realization of otherness apart from the penumbra of Howard, but it takes Rembrandt to teach Howard to open his eyes.

8

OTHER WRITINGS

In order to extend comprehension and contextualize certain features of Smith's aesthetic development, and potentially add to the illumination of aspects of her longer prose works, this chapter examines in detail Smith's shorter fiction, the majority appearing in the *New Yorker*. Although Smith's output of such writing is hardly prolific, their qualities and focus are perhaps unexpectedly diverse, and readers familiar with her novels may find certain of their perspectives surprising. A large proportion of these stories are not readily available. Hence the following close analysis may prove particularly useful in comprehending the full range of Smith's themes, settings, characterizations and stylistic characteristics.

SMITH'S EARLY PHASE: *THE MAY ANTHOLOGY* STORIES

Smith's very first published prose was 'Mirrored Box,' a story written as an undergraduate, featured in *The May Anthology of Oxford and Cambridge Short Stories* (1995), a collection selected and edited by John Holloway. Intriguingly, none of the Cambridge contributors has an entry in the section for biographical details, hinting at some deficiency on the part of whoever collected these stories at Cambridge, and leaving no early glimpse of the young undergraduate Smith (160), apart from the story. Smith prefaces her contribution with a quotation from Hurston, concerning the very different hopes and notions of truth of men and women, suggesting the latter exist according to the demands of dreams. Smith's writing is sophisticated, already compressing a great deal of information, found in minutiae, descriptive details and dialogue. The initial third person narrative describes a middle-aged woman, 'reflecting on herself. What is called faded beauty: aristocratic, elegant, with scruffy, unkempt edges—brown dress, brown hair, breasts weary, hips not quite right, thickening around the middle, the faded watercolour version of a once vibrant pastel' (126). The tone evokes poignancy, a certain sense of irony, but is not primarily comic, but certainly exhibits knowingness.

The narrative shifts to the perspective of Philippa, the woman, her thoughts reported first person, her reflections slightly paranoid. She ruminates on the deficiency of the inattentive Alicia, an agency cleaner half Philippa's age. The coupons Alicia neglects to use for food suggest the 1940s. Chiding Alicia concerning finger-marks on mirrors elicits an accusation of barren middle-age with Alicia touching Philippa's belly, articulating words which Philippa has to look up. The ringing of the telephone and her answer are revealing. Smith secretes much information among apparently casual references, including that Philippa is married—'Hello? Yes, this is Mrs Randall—(128)—and yet lacks her husband's address. She has to compete with Alicia's suggestive singing, concerning love and longing. Philippa has been betrayed by her husband in his affair with a younger woman—a secretary half his age (131)—a recurrent theme in Smith's later work. The call concerns five suits of her husband, Max, a politician, at Carter's drycleaners. Philippa is haunted, anticipating the journey to collect them, imagining the assistant and owner gossiping excruciatingly about Max's departure overseas with lover or 'Whore' (130). She feels the locals' likely criticism of Max derives from envy.

Threaded into her crisis is Philippa's abandonment of her identity to satisfy Max's domestic demands. Philippa watches Alicia in a beam of sunlight, shamelessly naked, both alluring and angering for Philippa, imagining Alicia a witch. Recalling the dunking of witches intended to save them, Philippa thinks of drowning herself in the lake. Philippa recalls 'Max's old Parliamentary knick-knacks [...]' (134) which her husband had swapped for Spanish lessons from Alicia, but the servant is no longer interested in the photograph Philippa offers, since Alicia has split from her sweetheart, its intended recipient. The suggestion she might prefer Philippa's photograph confirms the underlying sexual tension, and the next scene describes their first erotic encounter. Later the two cultivate vegetables in the garden. Philippa senses enormity of the house, unable to abandon it, yet feeling stuck.

> One morning, news of Max winds it's [sic] way through the breakfast room, from the radio Alicia switched on to hear the weather forecast. His past had come back to him like a faithful dog, his money transactions are being looked into, the sum he owes is thought to be large, it has been rumoured he's having an affair. Bitter-sweet news, thinks Philippa, the house will probably be taken.
>
> (139)

The two collect together Philippa's meagre belongings, and leave, stopping perversely to see Lisa, Max's new woman, on their way to the seaside, 'A small, tasteless English hotel with plastic plants and a plastic landlady' (140). Overcoming her pain and Max's triumphs over her, at the beach she is reborn, cleansed and symbolically baptized into her new identity by the seawater, 'she watched the sky, the sluggish clouds, the erratic seagulls, and finally her gaze rested thankfully on Alicia. The seawater framing her face, the sand mingling with her hair' (141).

Smith's second published story, 'The Newspaper Man,' appears in *The May Anthology of Oxford and Cambridge Short Stories* (1996), which collection boasts the very first tentative, cursory interpretation of Smith. Penelope Fitzgerald in her introduction says that this story 'is particularly interesting because the subject seems to be Ruth's father "a paternal enigma, a white man with a black daughter, dying in a foreign land" both as she remembers him and as she's tried to paint him. But Ruth's deepest relationship is with her friend, Liz' (n.p.), her oldest friend, a rebel with whom Ruth has experienced the various styles, movements and fashions of the contemporary period, including feminism. The opening scene is a childhood one, of Ruth Mackintrye and her brother, Mickey, pondering over fathers, thinking of them as fantastical, distant beings. In the next at fifty she reflects on her life and a wish to leave England, listing pros and cons in two columns, allowing Smith to reflect on contemporary British culture from the 1970s and on being mixed race, detailing mostly reservations. 'I place my pen on the second column and underline two words in green felt-tip. English men' (11). In the third scene Ruth attends a parents' evening with Liz, reflecting on how the 'liberal' upbringing of Caspian by Liz might prove damaging, deriving as it does from 'that unconditional love for her child non-parents find inconceivable' (12). Throughout the story scenes from Ruth's past intersect those from the present. Ruth recalls her own successes and isolation at school, her father embarrassing her with her English teacher at parents' evening, and realizing, 'He is working class and I am educated. But as of yet I do not know the words. There is a feeling in the school, in the belly of the school in the recess beyond language, that I am smart because I am half-white' (13–14). She recalls her fascination with a group of black girls, against whom she defines the details of her difference.

Relocated in Tuscany, accompanied in a visit to Florence's San Croce church by her agent, Phillipo, Ruth watches a confrontation between a local security guard and two women, an argument over the latter kissing each other being regarded as an insult. Ruth has decided to sell at a discount price her largest, most personal painting which has made her name, 'The Newspaper Man,' to an ex-boyfriend, Jake, so he and his new wife will be faced with the realities of Ruth's life daily, and also perhaps because the canvas charts her feelings for her father, suggesting at least an underlying oedipal quality to her relationships with men. The picture 'stands, a paternal enigma, a white man with a black daughter, dying in a foreign land' (24). Her thoughts of Mickey, her brother, lead to a specific recollection of the surprising, initial visit of a half-sister, Laura, whom the younger siblings think of as the White Witch, beautiful and uncanny. Their first encounter with their father's white daughter from his first marriage evokes an unknown past. As with the Hanwell stories, such details constitute some of Smith's most revealing moments autobiographically. Subsequently, Ruth recollects the drive for her day at university as a radicalized young woman with her father and his employer, Mike Bravo (remarkably similar to Archie's boss in White Teeth, Mr Hero), realizing she has since abandoned her radicality. Smith's dynamic involves inferences, of the effects of past on the present, and the shifting perspectives of the individual. The story ends with lunch with Laura in Florence, and Ruth's realization that not only is her half-sister a lesbian, but that they share a similar physiognomy, and that their apparently dying father will survive. 'This crisis is passing, the old bugger, despite twenty cigarettes a day for twice as many years, has pulled through again. I puff on a Malboro in tribute to him' (32). She watches Italian fathers and daughters promenading, ambivalent about the suggestion that she might do so with her own, but recalling a school Religious Education lesson that indicates variously the lineage, love and conflict inherent in patriarchy (33) and Ruth's own unresolved sexual inclinations.

The May Anthology of Oxford and Cambridge Short Stories (1997) published two more Smith stories, the first 'Mrs. Begum's Son and the Private Tutor' which represents retrospectively early drafts of episodes and ideas that would contribute in revised form to *White Teeth*. Similar characters include a combative Bengali wife based in Willesden near Gladstone Park, Alsana Begum, who is cutting and opinionated, dismissive of others. She seeks a tutor for her supposedly genius son, Magid, who requires an English education because '"he must, one day, save his people"' (92). Narrator, Alex Pemrose, recalls being hired and meeting Alsana, young daughter Geeni, elder son who refers to himself as Mark (anticipating the actions of *White Teeth*'s Magid), and the unnamed, elusive father seen only in the garden, passing an occasional comment in Bengali. Alex recollects Alsana applauding outwardly the borough's liberalism, while privately voicing certain underlying doubts (91–2). Among Alex's numerous pupils is Hindu Parjev, whose family is the subject of Alsana's invective (93–4).

On subsequent Tuesday mornings on bus journeys from Cricklewood, Alex encounters each time at the back 'The Communist candidate for Brent East [who] lived in Cricklewood [...]. We both got the bus that packed twice the regulation passenger allowance on it and hurtled down the hill, narrowly missing the lamp posts on its way to Willesden Green Station' (95). This figure is clearly modelled on Ken Livingstone, former Labour Leader of the Greater London Council (GLC) from 1981 until its abolition in 1986, subsequently Member of Parliament from 1987 for Brent East, celebrated for media appearances, controversial gestures, commuting by public transport and his left-wing views, known popularly as 'Red Ken.' Alex describes the GLC in its struggle with an unnamed Thatcher, the candidate apparently crushed by the onslaught. Smith introduces incidental figures to convey a sense of the multicultural setting, two geriatric Jamaican men who in appropriate dialect criticize the bus driver, clearly precursors of Clarence and Denzil who haunt O'Connells alongside Archie and Samad.

On arrival Alex is accosted by Mark, sending him to the park to meet Alsana and Magid. The latter responds by inverting everything spoken to him and is knocked out by a boomerang after many unsuccessful throws. Subsequently, Magid appears precocious and obsessive, turning every topic into a metaphysical, spiritual query. The planned lessons abandoned Alex is re-employed 'as a kind of baby-sitter' (100) reading articles from newspapers to Magid. On the next bus journey the Brent candidate is picketed by 'The Asian Women's Community action Group' (9101) seeking an old bingo-hall as a centre for their communities, but as reported in the *Willesden and Brent Chronicle* the plan has been rejected. Alex responds to Magid's dismissal of Britain as a bad country, his reluctance to see it as his own.

> Magid, had, as a child (and did later, as a man) the unnerving ability of being so familiar with strangers (his eyes, his touches) that you felt you'd missed something. That he knew something about you that you didn't. Prophets have this.
>
> (103)

Reading about the rejection persuades Magid to become involved, much to his over-protective mother's consternation, who only agrees to him attending a political meeting at Willesden Library if accompanied by Mark. The latter is drawn to young men distributing leaflets about an ideal Muslim state, and Magid interrupts the Brent candidate to speak in Bengali, creating frenzy in the crowd, changing the minds of various councillors after the speech is translated. The meeting echoes one in Hanif Kureishi's *The Black Album*, where similarly white patronizing liberalism is one of the targets of the satire. The press and Brian, and the Brent candidate, are ensconced in Alsana's home. Alex and his girlfriend, Alison, arrive. Magid is mocked by Mark using a Uriah Heep voice and actions (much as Shiva parodies Samad in *White Teeth*), and Magid admits his speech amounted to very little. The irony throughout is the emphasis on the boy and his quasi-spiritual authority that leads Mark to parody him by calling him a 'Guru.' Mark draws attention to the fact that a bag of excrement has been thrown into their garden by a dog-walker. He indicates the limits of freedom of his father trapped as a waiter for 15 years, and the inadequacy of gestures such as the centre (110). Alex feels a sense of estrangement, heightened by his final recollection of Magid's next inconsequential speech in English at the opening. The streets are still haunted by gangs of youths. In a postscript Alex meets an older Magid, who ironically has changed his name to Matthew. The underlying tone exudes a more explicit disquiet than *White Teeth*, a more precise critique of a failing liberalism. Alex expresses his doubts saying that 'after so many years of being certain, sure of where I stood on English ground, I felt like a stranger. But it was momentary. This is my only story: it's just a moment when I didn't know what and I wasn't sure where and I needed a Guru' (111).

The title of the second 1997 story, 'Picnic, Lightning,' refers to the cause of death of the mother of Humbert Humbert, protagonist of Valdimir Nabokov's *Lolita*, which text's influence on Smith is further credited by her parenthetical epigraph '(*Apologies to Nabokov*)' (115). The narrative concerns thirty-eight-year-old Mrs Clara Carshalton who improbably commutes daily to Paris to work in the Embassy, unwilling to forego an English education for her children. She lunches daily in the same brasserie, the *Café Pic-nic*, with a colleague, Elaine Kopfker, drawn despite its youthful crowd living a hustler's life because they can smoke. One discovers that the narrative is related by Alexi, jealous of 'The Boy,' a young Persian or Iranian to whom he notices Clara's gaze is drawn. 'I was not, at first, interested in Clara. I had, at first, only faint suspicions. So when the chapter and verse of it, the face and the bottom of it, the dirty little gun, the lover, the corner, accomplices and grubby francs in Juliette's palm—when it all came out in that smudge of local newspaper print—I was somewhat surprised' (116). Alexi in a detached tone tells of the attraction between Clara and The Boy, and how Juliette, his former girlfriend, first blackmails Clara, second is paid by her blackmail victim to kill The Boy, and third how she succumbs to his passion, lastly setting him up when she kills Clara in front of the embassy disguised 'in Patras' familiar duffel-coat and then let the prints do the rest' (122). Juliette finally retains the money and disappears. Ironically, Alexi's prime emotion is jealousy of The Boy, even envying his final notoriety, since 'insolent school-girls would cut him out like a movie-magazine idol and stick him to their lunch-boxes on sunny days' (122). This foray into unfamiliar contexts, settings and themes is only partially successful, with too many assumptions and loose ends. Moreover, the cold indifference of such a narrator is not quite convincing, but the concept of his overriding vanity is an intriguing insight for such a young writer.

THE MID PHASE: MILLENNIAL FICTIONS

In May 1997 *Granta* published 'The Waiter's Wife' where Smith adapts aspects of the protagonist of an earlier story, 'Mrs. Begum's Son and the Private Tutor', adapting Alsana Begum and adding different emphases to create the character of Samad's wife. Smith describes the arrival of Samad and Alsana Iqbal in spring 1975—they arrived in 1973 *White Teeth* (12)—met by Archie and Clara Jones, whereas in the novel Samad nostalgically seeks out Archie after his arrival and before his marriage (12). Two shorter sections—one introductory and another concerning Alsana's prejudices and exemptions taken from the novel (65)—preface two longer episodes that are almost synonymous with those that will appear in the first section of *White Teeth*, the first being the Iqbals struggle to move from Whitechapel to Willesden High Road and two scenes in the restaurant where Samad works (*White Teeth*, 55–64, 74–81). In the first a young waiter, Shiva, resents the older waiters not contributing as many tips to the 'Piss-Pot,' singling out Samad for his particular venom. Subsequently, Samad attempts to obtain a raise from his cousin, the owner. In the second scene Alsana, Clara and the Niece of Shame sit together in the park discussing Alsana's odd logic concerning marriages being better with less knowledge of each other. One significant difference between the two versions is that in *White Teeth* Sol Jozefowicz, a paid park keeper in earlier version (140), more comically in the novel becomes 'the old guy who back then took it upon himself to police the park (though his job as park keeper had long since been swept away in council cuts) [...]' (79).

Set in north-west London Smith's first *New Yorker* story was 'Stuart.' It concerns an incident, the dynamics of a momentary, almost inconsequential event, marked by a concern for exactitude in inflecting the quotidian. Despite its shifting perspectives, it offers an unashamedly universal narrative voice, purveying a knowing cartography of the minutiae of a minor incident. Its tone is partially ironic. 'This is the truth, whichever way you look at it.' The surface is not the focus, but the unpredictable causalities concerning human interactions in the public domain that appear banal. Smith describes two Greeks, one big and melon-faced, both organized, efficiently running their hot-dog stall. Smith may be a humanist, but indulges in minor cruelties. 'It is clear that this guy has a hard time with clothes in general; buying them, getting into them, getting out of them. Nothing quite fits' (609). Three pubescent spindly white boys, fashionable in differently coloured shirts and baggy jeans, arrive followed by a gaggle of pre-pubescent girls, discouraged by the subjects of their attentions. An unexpected escalation follows in a banal confrontation between the big Greek and the boys concerning a beer can dropped by the boy in the pink shirt which has soaked the trousers of a passer-by. The latter insults the big Greek on his phone:

> Loud enough for the big Greek to hear how he is being described to somebody he will never meet. Maybe it is a woman. A white woman. Maybe she is beautiful, with long blond hair and teeth like in the ads. The big Greek, he's not cruel; he's not cruel like some guys in the city; but somebody's to blame for this latest humiliation, small but painful.
>
> (64)

The narrative switches from the outer to the inner world, from one view point to another. Smith emphasizes the imagination, miscommunication, differing perspectives, chance, resentments and prejudices that subtend the life and dialogue on the streets. After the big Greek demands his money in his anger, he hits the pink-shirted boy, and in an ensuing chase Stuart, a tremendously fat McDonalds employee, is knocked over by the mean Greek in the pursuit, and this inelegant and large man 'lands, badly, horribly, as only a fat man can land' (66). His right leg is broken badly, its angle grotesque, his pain palpable. The story focuses on moments that become public spectacle and narrative in such a city, first the balletic leap by the blue shirt over three-foot railings outside McDonalds 'landing as firm as a Russian gymnast [. . .]' (66) and Stuart becoming

> the center of the city, the median coordinate, a dubious honor he never hoped for nor expected to receive. He is in enough pain for the entire city. Everybody watches him begin to hyperventilate and dig his fingers into his stomach, searching for where it hurts, for where the hurt begins.
>
> (67)

The shock overwhelms the bystanders, diffuses the conflict instantaneously. In the common response are moments of empathy. In his inversion, the victim of the unexpected, his limb distorted, Stuart becomes a symbol for the city, as is the oddly causal series of events that become increasingly heightened and confrontational. It is a cautionary tale, a parable of sorts.

'I, the Only One' is set in America. Jono, a fourteen-year-old boy, in first person responds to the return home of his brighter, artistic sister, Kelly, a film director who had a 'fling with some pretty boy in the film industry' (89), destroying her relationship with Irish boyfriend, Aidan, of whom Jono approved. The latter is displaced from his room where he does weights, having to disperse them around the house because Kelly needs her own room as a study. He positions his bar for chin-ups so he can see people passing their home, and invites in Cole, an immensely tall black teenager, of the same age and who had been in 'this new school for my retakes. [...] Cole was retaking practically everything too' (92). The essence underlying the story is the unspoken rivalry of the family, Kelly is preferred by their Canadian mother. Jono attempts both to impress his sister and to negate her presence, refuting their mother's favouritism in this household of women (the father and brother having left for different reasons). Kelly constantly replays *The Philadelphia Story*, significantly about the sudden arrival of a former husband (Cary Grant) who forgives his former wife (Katherine Hepburn) about to marry another man and remarries her, although she is drawn to both and the young newspaperman covering the wedding. Ironically, even as a viewer Kelly also vacillates,

> 'Now, you see Jimmy Stewart? There was a man. There was a tall handsome man.' Or if the other guy was on the screen, she'd be like 'That's how a man should wear her suit. Can you see the cut of that suit?' I didn't give a shit about the film or anybody in it. Kelly was always telling me about stuff I didn't give a shit about.

> (94)

Jono remains unimpressed by her intellectual, artistic vagaries or ambiguities. Despite the apparent chasm between their worldviews, as siblings they are fundamentally well-disposed towards each other, and a resolution of their topographical conflicts is mediated when Kelly is impressed for a passing moment by Cole, part of Jono's adolescent world. Jono admits that the look on his sister's face reminded him of the surprise of those seeing the first film by the Lumière brothers (85). His sister turns their conversation back to herself, returning to replay her film, and yet Jono recognizes an ephemeral transition. The story concludes enigmatically, 'I think Cole did me a great service that day. But every time I try to pin it down, all I have is the image of his long, sleek calves in front of me as I climbed the stairs, his massive hand on the bannister' (97). Smith captures the unspoken element in life, a sense of interaction and mutuality in among the many nuanced conflicts of family life.

'The Wrestling Match,' which appeared in *The New Yorker*, is similar essentially to the the first section of the *Autograph Man* describing the father and son's last time together, the fateful trip to watch wrestling at the Albert Hall, although additional passages are added in the novel, as are the section headings of 'YWWH.' Otherwise there are minor variants in the story, including: 'intersection' (89) is preferred to the later 'junction' (8); in the story the boys discuss 'the black woman painted green with two trunks coming out of the top of her head, who played Oola in "Return of the Jedi"' (122), whereas in the novel the reference is to 'the alien Kolig in the film' (15); the 'opening' (122) of the Albert Hall becomes its 'inauguration' (19); and Joseph's second film star reference to '"Ethel Merman" later becomes "Betty Grable"' (30).

Also published in *The New Yorker* in December 2002 'The Trials of Finch' is complex, telling of the friendship of Finch, a stuttering, eccentric, guileless, awkward middle-aged woman with her 'three friends: Claire, Karen, and Jemima. These were tall, lucky, professional Enlglishwomen in their early forties [. . .]' (116). Each adopts Finch as if a charitable contribution to the world. Finch, living on a legacy and occasional substitute teaching, has Rubenesque proportions. The unattractive Finch is the ideal foil for the three stylish women who assume superiority compared to her, although curiously when their composure is fractured by various marriage crises, Finch is suddenly less attractive as a supposedly inferior being and is abandoned for several months. Finally Claire visits, delivering news of the end of her marriage to Geoff. She offers Finch the fox-fur intended for Geoff's lover, and which subsequently Finch is encouraged to wear by her supposed friends specifically to gall Geoff. Finch's only other contact is her mother, who resents her partner whom Finch has never met, upset by her mother's deletion of the man in her biweekly, telephone monologues. 'Though it was true that Mr. Frost was a bore, was a bully, Finch believed in the sovereignty of other people' (87). In its first phase the story's theme seems limited to the nature of relationships, their manipulative, patronizing, mercurial qualities, and their paradoxical centrality. The catalyst in changing both the trajectory of the story and of Finch's life is a letter informing her she has jury service, for which as the narrator says 'Finch was not eligible for jury duty. Not eligible. Not at all!' (118). This assertion remains enigmatic while Finch obsesses over her role, running through the journey, and obsessing over the trial.

The second section outlines an event that occurred when Finch was eleven, when 'Her name, her real name, was Rosalind Jane Gordon' (119), staying on holiday in Padstow, Cornwall with her parents. She befriended two attractive children, Beth and Andrew, siblings younger than Finch, and on impulse, in a shocking moment, pushed them over a cliff. The reader learns retrospectively of their deaths, of Finch's ten years in care, undergoing therapy, abused and raped, patchily educated, and prone to simplistic ethical judgements. She has awaited punishment or retribution, dreaming of a trial and jury. She lacks a sense of atonement or forgiveness; justice takes on a sexual, almost penetrative meaning. 'She fell in love with the idea of a judge the way other girls envision their princes. Finch wanted to feel the law' (120). However, she is released, later voluntarily readmitting herself into an adult-care facility, Hollingsworth in Holloway under her new name, where she is raped. It is as if Finch's emotional possibilities have been suppressed by her guilt, her sense of requiring justice, and the narrative declares 'Finch had no emotional vocabulary' (121). After acquiring a degree in pure and applied maths, after 20 years and the facility's closure, she moves into a flat near Hampstead Heath bought by her mother. Smith is perceptive in conveying just how external forces can shape certain people, as their lives drift. Finch's notoriety haunts her, the tabloids periodically searching for her since 'she was one of very exclusive and notorious band of Englishwomen whose curling passport photos inspired extraordinary repulsion, vengeance. People wanted to burn her in Hell. People thought hanging was too good for her' (121). As Smith says to Ben Greenman in 'Dreaming up Finch,' although the story derives from an actual case, it was difficult to structure:

I had to keep changing the order of how the story was told (putting the murder up front, in the middle, at the end) to try to reduce the melodrama. I did think very specifically of Mary Bell, who was given a new identity upon her release, rather than the Bulger case. But I thought of her mainly as my defence, rather than my inspiration. To the accusation 'Things like this never happen!,' I can say, 'But they do . . . see here, yes, they do.'

Obsessed by the beauty of the law and the trial process, Finch ignores anything beyond the bare facts, but worries that Danista, who has stabbed her boyfriend, Paul, might escape retribution. Isolated by her determined view, and frustrated by the other jurors' deliberations which focus largely on Danista's victimhood, overnight in a stay at a hotel Finch decides to write a letter to the others, citing her past crime as grounds for her authority on guilt. They shun her. The media descend, hounding her. Smith explains to Greenman, 'Four years ago, when Mary Bell's identity was revealed, she was chased down the street by journalists and spat on as she walked down the street with her daughter. I put a spitting scene like that in "Finch" and then took it out, because of the melodrama. And yet these things happen—very extreme things happen in people's lives.' Successive friends offer support on her answering machine. Paradoxically, 'Finch feels she is taking on the dimensions of a character' (123), as if reborn, her innocence renewed, no longer culpable. As Smith suggests to Greenman the story concerns the incredible moral piety that surrounds childhood in the Anglo-American cultures, where 'The child is now the impregnable symbol of good,' and Smith concludes of Finch that 'She is guilty of an act. But it has a sort of randomness that escapes the idea of justice.' Despite her crime Finch is a portrait in human endurance, one that hints at inner redemption. Smith attempts a Nabokovian sense of comic seriousness, where guilt or blame are complex issues with a catalogue of contextual nuances. The story celebrates the possibilities of epiphany, of overcoming trauma.

VISIONS OF AMERICA AND RECOLLECTING THE HANWELLS

'Martha, Martha' appeared in *Granta 81: Best of Young British Novelists 2003* and was reprinted in *Martha and Hanwell* (2005). Set in Massachusetts in winter, the third-person narrative describes the eventual arrival of the eponymous young Black English woman,

Miss Martha Penk, at a real estate office run by Pam Roberts who while singing to the opening of Mozart's *Requiem* watches Martha confused by 'the higgledy-piggledy arrangement of the ground floor—a busy bookshop and a swing-doored optician obscured the sign that told you of the dentist, the insurers, the accountant and Pam's own dinky realty business at the top of the building; also the antique elevator that would take you to them' (325). As the 'Lacrimosa' section begins a Middle-Eastern arrives, to be joined by two others, thinking Martha's office is the temping agency which is actually above another branch of Milliner's books, where Martha has gone by mistake. Both circumstances stress their shared quality, that of the alien, the outsider. Essential to the story is a sense of the most significant events preceding the narrative, of journeys and their causality. The paradoxes of Martha's responses have an anterior, unfathomable genealogy. The everyday minutiae are charged with implicit meanings. Some are self-evident, others more inscrutable. Pam's pleasantries have an agenda, a commercial one. Her conversation with Pam demonstrates the cultural differences between an English perspective and a New England one, but also the divergence of their view of Martha's potential rental, Pam attempting to edge Martha higher, the latter resisting. Martha climbs the stairs, the coincidence of the music suggesting something of her mental state, since although ignorant of classical music it appeals to her.

> Usually Pam would use these minutes in the office to ascertain something about likely wealth, class, all very gently—what kind of house, what kind of taste, what kind of price—but she had been wrong about English accents before, not knowing which were high class, which not. Or whether high class meant money at *all*—if you watched PBS as Pam did you soon found out that in England it could, often did, mean the exact opposite.
>
> (327)

Martha ignores the realtor's attempts to convey her version of the logic of rental prices. After dismissing Martha's idea that there are few black students Pam attempts to uncover the source of Martha's surname, intimating a divorce or separation. They tour two houses, the first Professor Perrin's, Pam trying to sell the idea of an association with privilege and the previous occupant's university connections, ignoring Martha's insistence about her price limit. On the way to the final viewing they encounter as part of an underlying synchronicity the three Middle-Eastern men building a snowman. Although Martha finds them foolish, childish, Pam transforms the encounters into an anecdote for owners, Yousef and Pam, appropriating the men's narratives. A family context with a young daughter and Amelia's pressure unsettle Martha. She retreats to the bathroom, tearfully studying a photograph of a man and boy inscribed to her. She leaves mumbling about a one-bedroom rental, signifying the irrevocability of a loss suddenly realized. As with much of Carver the underlying structure emphasizes the difficulty of communication, events overlaid by the business of dealing with a commodified world, a system inimical to openness and feeling.

'Hanwell in Hell' appeared in the *New Yorker* in September 2004, narrated by Clive Black, a passing acquaintance of Hanwell, responding to a small ad request posted by the latter's estranged daughter, Claire, that prefaces the story, seeking information concerning her father's life between 1970 and 1973 in Bristol (a city where Harvey Smith had spent time post-war). Sharon Raynor in 'From the Dispossesed to the Decolonized: From Samuel Selvon's *The Lonely Londoners* to Zadie Smith's "Hanwell in Hell"' seems confused, situating the meeting of the two men in London (142), using this as part of her framing comparison based largely on the shared environment, regarding both men as racial and cultural outsiders.[1] However, Raynor later identifies the daughter's search for information as centring on Bristol (147). Black recalls that 'We had both suffered dramatic reversals of fortune and recognized immediately that we had failure in common—a rare example of masculine intuition.' His reply details their sole encounter, initially meeting in the restaurant of Barry Franks, later a celebrity chef, 'It is easy to forget now that Barry Franks was not born on the BBC holding a glass of red in one hand and his own cookery book in another' (1). Smith's model for Franks is Keith Floyd, a once famous English celebrity chef celebrated for his on-screen drinking, in the 1970s owner of three restaurants in Bristol.

Black is drawn by the local jazz band for a late night visit, among the local crooks that frequented Franks' establishment. Its proprietor too drunk to cook, dishwasher Hanwell produces delicious French crêpes. Black invites him over to join him and his female companion, with whom Hanwell flirts. 'Her name is lost to me, but the outline of her chest is not—huge, carefully wrapped and can-tilevered, like a present on the shelf which she had not yet decided to give away. She was thirty years my junior and also a diluted Ital-ian, though she was still taking her Catholicism neat' (1). The two men discover common experience: origins in East Anglia and army service on D-day, oblique allusions again to Smith's father, to whom she referred with pride as having 'stormed the beaches at Nor-mandy' while mentioning his first family in the 1950s (see Diane Rehm interview). Central to the story is its Carveresque qualities: an unexpected encounter; the narrator's fluctuating view of other-ness; intimate revelations to a stranger; a strong sense of alienated loss; unlikely parallels; incongruity in the characters' actions; and a glimmering of hope against the odds. Also there is recognition of human dignity in someone socially, economically and personally dispossessed. Typically English, Black admits, 'In all my probing, I could not get from him what I wanted: a clear sense of his class' (3). After Black's date disappears—which Raynor over-determines as sacrificial (149), as the 'unobtainable object of the male gaze' (150)—Hanwell describes such beautiful women as a sign of hope. After closing-time Black persuades Hanwell to share a nightcap, a tentative intimacy among strangers.

The story's transition is two-fold. First, Smith includes an odd image of vulnerability, a helpless fox found in a local square, des-perate and anguished like the two men, which to suppress its agony Hanwell kills. Black vomits and recollects falling: 'I had the keen sense that this was the lowest moment of my decline, that there would be nothing beneath this. Time has proved that instinct cor-rect' (5). Second, after Black peruses a photograph of 'three appeal-ing dark-haired teen-age girls sitting on a bench,' when Hanwell admits rather than being in London, his wife has committed suicide and he found her hanging body (7). As Raynor comments, 'Poignant to the narrative is the insinuation that Hanwell feels responsible for ending the suffering of his family, or at least his wife' (150). For Black, Hanwell represents something quintessentially English and reassuring, imagining him as the type found in the burial mound at Sutton Hoo, in the Anglo-Saxon kingdom of East Anglia. In this he seems akin to Archie in *White Teeth*, and one wonders if in these affable, flawed white Englishmen one glimpses aspects of Smith's own father, with some sense of his culture and tradi-tion. After drowsing Black joins Hanwell in painting a room for his daughters, Black recognizing Hanwell's plans are fanciful but sincere. He contextualizes the man closely.

> I held my counsel. More and more, I suspect the men of our generation were not to be lived with. We made people unhappy because we our-selves were made unhappy in irrevocable ways [. . .] These days, every-one passes blame backward—but we couldn't do that. We kept blame close, we held it tight. I'm sorry your father made you so unhappy. [. . .] When I saw your request in the paper my first thought was of a man likable enough to remember—this is no small feat. Almost everyone I met back then I'd rather forget. Even writing this I feel happy at the thought of Hanwell's prawn-and-mushroom crêpes and the care with which he touched up the skirting board. I think you are too hard on him. And I think you were wrong to think that he knew all the time you and your sisters wouldn't come, or that he didn't want you to. Hanwell had a beautiful way of hoping. Not many men can hope red yellow.
>
> (7)

Hanwell's colour blindness has led him to misrecognize the colour, guided erroneously by the paint's label, 'Deepest Sun.' Black attempts to redeem the absent neglectful father for the daugh-ter, inspired by his sense of Hanwell's charm and innocence. He reminds her, 'These days, everyone passes the blame backward—but we couldn't do that. We kept blame close, we held it tight.' Underlying these observations is a sense of common decencies and humanity, an explicitly Carveresque notion that in adversity odd, undervalued gestures and actions can represent or epitomize positive values, imbuing with symbolic and literal meaning.

Illogical and disruptive passion are the central themes of 'The Girl with Bangs,' an enigmatic story submitted as part of a larger project, *Timothy McSweeney's Quarterly Concern* (2006) where in the sixth issue edited by Dave Eggers (a writer Smith admires greatly) various writers and graphic artists respond in narrative to 'tracks' on a CD by various artists, but mostly by the band, They Might Be Giants. 'Bangs' is a song apparently concerning an attraction but actually about the murder of a girl perhaps paid for sex.[2] Smith's contribution takes the theme of sexual availability. With gender ini-tially unspecified, Smith's first person narrator recalls being drawn by a compulsive desire into initiating an affair with a fellow student, Charlotte, who lives across the hall in college, a slovenly and self-centred individual exuding the sexual. The latter's bangs emphasize her girlish attractiveness, indicating a putative innocence, but representing something behind which she hides obscuring her true nature. Its punning reference may be to the term's double meaning of having sex (inherent in the song) signifying her libidinous proclivities. After the departure of Charlotte's Belgian boyfriend, Maurice, for a TV job in Thailand an affair commences. The narrator reflects on her own previous radical naiveté and her irrational, later counter-intuitive attraction:

> I believed Charlotte Greaves and her bangs to be good news. But Charlotte was emphatically bad news, requiring only eight months to take me entirely apart [...]. I'd never dated a girl before, and she was bad news the way boys can never be, because with boys it's always possible to draw up a list of pros and cons, and see the matter rationally, from either side. But you could make a list of cons on Charlotte stretching to Azerbaijan, and her 'bangs' sitting solitary in the pros column would outweigh all objections.
>
> (65)

A visual metaphor runs through the story, the concept that the emotions impelling such an affair are comparable to instinctively reaching for a precious item thrown out of an upper window during a conflagration. The narrator recollects Charlotte's squalid room, her disorganization and her bemusement at Maurice's reappearance offering Charlotte marriage, the Belgian realizing the new affair, calmly discussing the possibilities and his proposal. The narrator has an epiphany, a discovery of her own vulnerability, her recognition that Charlotte only seems so. 'I thought of this girl he wanted back, who had taken me apart piece by piece, causing me nothing but trouble, with her bangs and her anti-social behaviour. I was all (un)done, I realised. I sort of marvelled at the devotion he felt for her' (69). Her sense of Charlotte is confirmed when she and Maurice find her in bed with another man, a four-month affair, despite which Maurice abandons his fellow news anchor, Annepa, and marries Charlotte despite her shaving her head to spite them all. In many ways this story complicates in gender terms *The Philadelphia Story*.

'Hanwell Senior,' first published in the *New Yorker* in May 2007, is reprinted in *The Book of Other People* (2007), a collection edited by Smith. Another third person narrative, its focus is oedipal, describing the unreliability of Hanwell's father, a huge man who 'came to Hanwell like a comet, at long intervals' (1) only to disappear. The story recuperates a lost past, full of wartime and postwar period detail, recollecting an Englishness recoverable from memory. One senses the narrator's fascination and distance from her heritage, emphasized by the implied racial hybridity of her origins. Hanwell Senior's life is finally 'recorded here by a descendant of Hanwell Snr of whom he could have had no notion, being as unreal to him as broadband or goblins' (1). In the 1920s after his womanizing he vanishes. He reappears briefly pretending to be an Irishman during Hanwell's military service, popular with his young comrades-in-arms. 'It was eerie to witness. Words held no security with Hanwell Snr, served as no anchor, bore no relation to the things of the world. A darker shade of this same tendency is called "psychopathy"' (1). In 1956 summoned unexpectedly by his father Hanwell takes a bicycle trip to Kent, where they discuss Hanwell's wife's hysteria, and the father criticizes his son for failing to choose or see things accurately, as they watch a pair of attractive young women. The narrative moves to 1986 when (cooking as in Bristol in the earlier story) Hanwell is interrupted in making homemade pizza for his second family by a call, announcing that 'his father had died, a sentence that required us—my mother, my brother, and me—to invent a whole human in one second and kill him off the next' (4) and reveals he had known of the imminent death weeks earlier, talking of ' "the end of the road [. . .]" ' (4) for his father, which Hanwell's family interpret literally as Brighton pier. The narrator reveals her dream of being laid out Jewish-style on Brighton beach body covered in stones, part of the Hanwell legacy, an image of the weight of inheritance and the past.

NOTES

1 INTRODUCTION: SMITH AS CULTURAL ICON OR PRODUCTION?

1. Mountjoy might be regarded as synthesizing elements of three areas in London with significant Jewish populations: Finchley, Golders Hill and Stamford Hill.
2. Walters insists nevertheless on recovering the novel as celebrating hybridity, claiming 'Smith achieves a fusion of British and Black British, reforming both literatures and proving the two to be mutually exclusive' (321).

2 A BIOGRAPHICAL READING

1. Rushdie's Italian translator, Ettore Capriolo, was stabbed on 3 July 1991 in his apartment in Milan and seriously wounded. He survived, but Rushdie's Japanese translator, Hitoshi Igarashi, was murdered on 11 or 12 July 1991 in the hallway outside his office at Tsukuba University. Also in 1993, Rushdie's Norwegian publisher William Nygaard was shot and severely injured outside his house in Oslo. Thirty-seven guests died when their hotel in Sivas, Turkey, was burnt down by locals protesting against Aziz Nesin, Rushdie's Turkish translator. Many political and artistic figures prevaricated over the affair, many seemingly uncertain about being regarded as politically incorrect if they criticized Muslim leaders and communities who were inciting murders.
2. See, for instance, Anon. 'Author Smith Raps English Culture.'

3 WHITE TEETH

1. The boyfriend was Jimmi Rahman upon whom Millat is based and to whom the book is dedicated.
2. Pinocchio might seem a bizarre image, as in the original story he is a victim of forces beyond his control, his idleness condemning him to undergo several transformations and only finally after many vicissitudes and learning the value of work and charity does he become a human boy.

8 *OTHER WRITINGS*

1. Hanwell, a west London suburb, is not well known for its bombing victims as Raynor claims, but there is a mass grave for central London victims of the Blitz, including 'Al' Bowlly a popular singer during the 1930s (148).
2. Bangs in Britain is referred to as a 'fringe.'

BIBLIOGRAPHY

Where relevant details of the year of publication of the first edition of a book has been added below in square brackets next to the edition consulted, the original being unavailable.

SECTION ONE: SELECTED WORKS BY OR FEATURING ZADIE SMITH

NOVELS

White Teeth (London: Penguin, 2000 [2001]).
The Autograph Man (London: Hamish Hamilton, 2002).
On Beauty (London: Hamish Hamilton, 2005).

SHORT FICTION

'Mirrored Box.' *The May Anthology of Oxford and Cambridge Short Stories.* John Holloway, Ruth Scurr and Chris Taylor (eds) (Oxford and Cambridge: Varsity and Cherwell, 1995): 125–41.

'The Newspaper Man.' *The May Anthology of Oxford and Cambridge Short Stories.* Nick Laird, Toby Smith and Penelope Fitzgerald (eds) (Oxford: Varsity/Cherwell, 1996): 7–33.

'Mrs. Begum's Son and the Private Tutor.' *The May Anthology of Oxford and Cambridge Short Stories.* Martha Kelly and Jill Paton Walsh (eds) (Oxford: Varsity/Cherwell, 1997): 89–113.

'Picnic, Lightning.' *The May Anthology of Oxford and Cambridge Short Stories.* Martha Kelly and Jill Paton Walsh (eds) (Oxford: Varsity/Cherwell, 1997): 115–22.

'The Waiter's Wife.' *Granta.* 67 (May 1999): 127–42.

'Stuart.' *New Yorker.* Winter Fiction Issue. (17–24 December 1999): 60–7.

'I, the Only One.' *Speaking with the Angel.* Nick Hornby (ed.) (New York: Riverhead Books, 2000): 87–97.

'The Wrestling Match.' *New Yorker* (17–24 June 2002): 116–29.

'The Trials of Finch.' *The New Yorker.* Winter Fiction Issue. (23; 30) (December 2002): 116–23; http://zadiesmithnews.wordpress.com/2002/05/27/the-trials-of-finch/; accessed 24 December 2008.

'Martha, Martha.' *Granta* 81: *Best of Young British Novelists 2003*. 81 (2003): 323–39; also *Martha and Hanwell* (London: Penguin, 2005): 1–24.

'Hanwell in Hell.' *The New Yorker* (27 September 2004): n.p. http:// www.newyorker.com/archive/2004/09/27/040927fi_fiction; accessed 16 June 2008; also *Martha and Hanwell* (London: Penguin, 2005): 25–49.

'The Girl with Bangs,' *Timothy McSweeney's Quarterly Concern: We Now Know Who Edition*. Dave Eggers (ed) (2006): 65–71.

'Hanwell Senior,' *The New Yorker* (14 May 2007): n.p. http://zadiesmithnews. wordpress.com/2002/05/27/the-trials-of-finch/; accessed 18 June 2008; also Zadie Smith (ed.) *The Book of Other People* (London: Hamish Hamilton, 2007): 61–71.

COLLECTED SHORT STORIES

Martha and Hanwell (London: Penguin, 2005).

ESSAYS, JOURNALISM AND OTHER WRITING

'Piece of Flesh: Introduction to this Book.' *Piece of Flesh* (London: Institute of Contemporary Arts, 2001): 6–14.

'This is How it Feels to Me.' *The Guardian* (13 October 2001): http://www.guardian.co.uk/books/2001/oct/13/fiction.afghanistan; accessed 24 December 2008.

'You are in Paradise.' *New Yorker* (17–24 June 2002): n.p. http:// www.newyorker.com/archive/2004/06/14/040614fa_fact3; accessed 14 June 2008.

'If a Man Picks Up a Microphone, That's it, You See? It's Not a Gun.' *The Daily Telegraph* (13 January 2003): 16.

'Love, actually.' *The Guardian* (1 November 2003): n.p. http://books. guardian.co.uk/review/story/0,12084,1074217,00.html; accessed 17:15, 10 September 2005 [from 'E. M. Forster's Ethical Style: Love, Failure and the Good in Fiction,' 2003 Orange Word Lecture].

'On the Beginning.' *The Guardian* (15 July 2006): n.p. http://www. guardian.co.uk/books/2006/jul/15/zadiesmith; accessed 4 January 2008.

'What does soulful mean?' *The Guardian* (1 September 2007): n.p. http://books.guardian.co.uk/departments/biography/story/ 0,,2160075,00.html; accessed 4 January 2008.

'Breaking News: Short Story Competition Result 2008.' *The Willesden Herald* (6 February 2008): n.p. http://willesdenherald. blogspot.com/2008/02/breaking-news-short-story-competition.html; accessed 15 June 2008.

'Dead Man Laughing.' *The New Yorker* (22 December 2008): n.p. http://www.newyorker.com/reporting/2008/12/22/081222fa_fact_smith; accessed 24 December 2008.

COLLECTIONS EDITED BY SMITH

(With Adrian Ellis, Hannah Wozniah, Benjamin Hewitt, and Thomas Hill). *May Anthologies 2001: Short Stories* (Cambridge: Varsity/Cherwell, 2001).
Piece of Flesh (London: Institute of Contemporary Arts, 2001).
The Book of Other People (London: Hamish Hamilton, 2007).

TELEVISION ADAPTATION

Jarrold, Julian (dir.); screenplay Simon Burke. *White Teeth* (Company Pictures, 2002) broadcast as four one-hour episodes by Channel 4 (subsequently as two episodes in United States in May 2003 on PBS *Masterpiece Theater*).

INTERVIEWS AND PROFILES

Anon. 'An interview with Zadie Smith.' *Masterpiece Theatre, PBS website* n.p. http://www.pbs.org/wgbh/masterpiece/teeth/ei_smith_int.html. 20093; accessed 5 December 2006.
Axelsson, Jonas. 'Zadie Smith Interview: Stockholm Literary Festival 2006.' *You Tube* (Summer 2006): n.p. http://www.youtube.com/watch?v=2PAmXET6hT8; accessed 1 July 2008. [Download available].
Barton, Laura and Zadie Smith, 'Friday Review: We Are Family,' *Guardian, Review Section,* 4 March 2005, 8.
Edemariam, Aida. 'Learning Curve.' *The Observer* (3 September 2006): n.p. http://www.guardian.co.uk/books/2005/sep/03/fiction.zadiesmith; accessed 4 January 2008.
Greenman, Ben. 'Q & A: Dreaming Up Finch.' *The New Yorker* (23 and 30 December 2002): n.p. http://www.newyorker.com/online/content/articles/021223on_onlineonly03; accessed 10 September 2007.
Hattenstone, Simon. 'White Knuckle Ride.' *The Guardian* (11 December 2000): n.p. http://books.guardian.co.uk/whitbread2000/story/0,6194,417437,00.html; accessed 5 December 2006.
Kearney, Martha. 'Interview: Zadie Smith.' *Woman's Hour: BBC Radio 4* (9 September 2005): n.p. http://www.bbc.co.uk/radio4/womanshour/2005_36_fri_01.shtml; accessed 14 June 2008.
Lyall, Sarah. 'A Good Start.' *The New York Times* (30 April 2000): n.p. http://www.nytimes.com/books/00/04/30/reviews/000430.30lyallt.html; accessed 4 January 2008.

Mahoney, Kevin Patrick (ed) 'Authortrek: Zadie Smith'. Undated: n.p. http://www.authortrek.com/zadiesmithpage.html; accessed 10 September 2005.

Merritt, Stephanie. 'She's Young, Black, British – and the First Publishing Sensation of the Millennium.' *The Observer* (16 January 2000): n.p. http://books.guardian.co.uk/departments/generalfiction/story/0,, 122817,00.html; accessed 18 January 2008.

Moo, Jessica Murphy. 'Zadie, Take Three.' *The New Atlantic: TheAtlantic.Com* (16 September 2005): n.p. http://www.theatlantic.com/ doc/200509u/zadie-smith-interview; accessed 3 March 2008.

O'Grady, Kathleen. '*White Teeth*: A Conversation with Author Zadie Smith.' *Atlantis: A Women's Studies Journal*. 27 (1) (Fall 2002), 105–111.

Paulson, Steve. 'To the Best of Our Knowledge: Interview with Zadie Smith.' *Wisconsin Public Radio* (16 April 2006): n.p. http://www. wpr.org/book/060416b.html; accessed 5 January 2009.

Rehm, Diane. 'Zadie Smith *On Beauty*.' *The Diane Rehm Show*. WAMU 88.5, *American University Radio* (29 December 2005): n.p. http://wamu.org/ programs/dr/05/12/29.php; accessed 15 June 2008. [Download available].

Russo, Maria. 'Girl Wonder.' *Salon.com* (28 April 2000): n.p. http:// archive.salon.com/books/feature/2000/04/28/zadie_profile/index.html; accessed 10 September 2007.

Silverblatt, Michael. 'Zadie Smith.' *Bookworm: KCRW Radio* (9 November 2006): n.p. http://www.kcrw.com/etc/programs/bw/bw061109zadie_ smith; accessed 27 December 2008.

SECTION TWO: OTHER WORKS CITED

Anjaria, Ulka. 'On Beauty and Being Postcolonial: Aesthetics and Form in Zadie Smith.' *Zadie Smith: Critical Essays*. Tracey L. Walters (ed) (New York: Peter Lang, 2008): 123–39.

Ahmad, Aijaz. *In Theory: Classes, Nations, Literature* (London and New York: Verso, 2008).

Alibhai-Brown, Yasmin. 'A Magic Carpet of Cultures in London.' *New York Times* (23 June 2000): 1, 30–1.

Allen, Nicola. *Marginality in the Contemporary British Novel* (London: Continuum, 2008).

Amis, Kinglsey. *Lucky Jim* (Harmondsworth: Penguin 1961 [1954]).

Amis, Martin. *Money* (London: Cape, 1984).

——. *The Information* (London: Flamingo, 1995).

Anon. 'Author Smith Raps English Culture.' *BBC Online News Channel* (9 September 2005): n.p. http://news.bbc.co.uk/1/hi/entertainment/arts/ 4228840.stm.

———. 'National Statistics Survey.' *Resident Population: By Ethnic Group, 2001: Regional Trends [Dataset RT380307]*: n.p. http://www. statistics.gov.uk/STATBASE/ssdataset.asp?vlnk=7666; accessed June 2008.

Bataille, Georges. *The Unfinished System of Nonknowledge*. Trans. Stuart Kendall and Michelle Kendall (University of Minnesota Press: Minneapolis, MN, 2001).

Bentley, Nick. 'Re-writing Englishness: Imagining the Nation in Julian Barnes's *England, England* and Zadie Smith's *White Teeth*.' *Textual Practice*. 21 (3) (September 2007): 483–504.

Berlinski, Claire. *Menace in Europe: Why the Continent's Crisis is America's Too*. (New York: Crown Forum, 2006).

Bhabha, Homi K. 'Introduction.' *Nation and Narration*. Homi K. Bhabha (ed) (London and New York: Routledge, 1990): 1–7.

Botting, Fred. 'From Excess to the New World Order.' *British Fiction of the 1990s*. Nick Bentley (ed) (London: Routledge; 2005): 21–41.

Bourdieu, Pierre. *The Field of Cultural Production: Essays on Art and Literature*. (Cambridge: Polity, 1993).

Bradbury, Malcolm. *The History Man* (London: Secker & Warburg, 1975).

Buber, Martin. *I and Thou*. 2nd ed. (Edinburgh: T & T Clark, 1958).

Buonaiuto, Claudia, and Maria Castella. 'A Western/Eastern Map of London.' *Cross-Cultural Encounters: Literary Perspectives*. Silvia Albertazzi and Claudia Pelliconi (eds) (Rome: Officina Edizioni, 2005).

Capra, Frank (dir.); screenplay Lewis R. Foster. *Mr. Smith Goes to Washington* (1939); starring James Stewart.

Carpenter, Louise. 'Mr and Mrs Smith.' *The Sunday Telegraph* (24 July 2005): 1. http://www.telegraph.co.uk/culture/donotmigrate/3645356/ Mr-and-Mrs-Smith.html.

Cheuse, Alan. 'Zadie Smith Novel Loses Energy at Midpoint.' *Chicago Tribune: Books Section* (29 September 2002): 2.

Childs, Peter. *Contemporary Novelists: British Fiction Since 1970* (Basingstoke: Palgrave Macmillan, 2005).

Chittenden, Maurice 'Zadie Didn't Tell the Real Race Story.' *The Sunday Times*. (19 February 2006): n.p. http://www.timesonline. co.uk/tol/news/uk/article732529.ece: accessed 11 February 2008.

Clark, Alex. 'Signs and Wanders.' *The Guardian* (14 September 2002): n.p. http://www.guardian.co.uk/books/2002/sep/14/shopping.fiction1; accessed 15 June 2008.

Cuder-Domínguez, Pilar. 'Ethnic Cartographies of London in Bernardine Evaristo and Zadie Smith.' *European Journal of English Studies*. 8 (2) (2004): 173–88.

Cukor, George (dir.); screenplay Donald Ogden. *The Philadelphia Story* (1940); starring Cary Grant, Katherine Hepburn and James Stewart.

Dalleo, Raphael in 'Colonization in Reverse: *White Teeth* as Caribbean Novel.' *Zadie Smith: Critical Essays*. Tracey L. Walters (ed.) (New York: Peter Lang, 2008): 91–104.

Dawson, Ashley. *Mongrel Nation: Diasporic Culture and the Making of Postcolonial Britain* (Ann Arbor: University of Michigan Press, 2007).

DeLillo, Don. *White Noise* (London: Picador, 1985).

Deresiewicz, William. 'Zadie Smith's Indecision.' *The Nation* (15 September 2005): n.p. http://www.thenation.com/doc/20051003/deresiewicz; accessed 15 June 2008.

Derrida, Jacques. *The Gift of Death*. Trans. David Wills (Chicago and London: University of Chicago Press, 1995).

Dyer, Rebecca. 'Generations of Black Londoners: Echoes of 1950s Caribbean Migrants Voices in Victor Headley's *Yardie* and Zadie Smith's *White Teeth*.' *Obsidian III: Literature in the African Diaspora*. 5 (2) (2004): 81–102.

Fischer, Susan Alice. ' "A Glance from God": Zadie Smith's *On Beauty* and Zora Neale Hurston.' *Changing English: Studies in Culture and Education*. 14 (3) (December 2007): 285–98.

Fitzgerald, Penelope. 'Introduction.' *The May Anthology of Oxford and Cambridge Short Stories*. Nick Laird, Toby Smith and Penelope Fitzgerald (eds) (Oxford: Varsity/Cherwell, 1996): n.p.

Forster. E. M. *Howards End* (London: Penguin, 1989 [1910]).

——. *Two Cheers for Democracy* (London: Edward Arnold, 1951).

Frey, Jennifer. 'Zadie Smith, Putting Herself into Her Work.' *The Washington Post* (14 November 2005): C01. http://www.washingtonpost.com/wp-dyn/content/article/2005/11/13/AR2005111301299.html; accessed 12 December 2005.

——. 'Providing a Piece of Her Young Life.' *Los Angeles Times* (25 November 2005): E-26.

Furman, Andrew. 'The Jewishness of the Contemporary Gentile Writer: Zadie Smith's *The Autograph Man*.' *Melus*. 30 (1) (Spring 2005): 3–17.

George, Rosemary Marangoly. *The Politics of Home: Postcolonial Relocations and Twentieth-Century Fiction* (Cambridge and New York: Cambridge University Press, 1996).

Ghafoor, Bilal. 'Last Word on the Competition Result 2008.' *The Willesden Herald* (6 February 2008): n.p. http://willesdenherald.blogspot.com/2008/02/last-word-on-competition-result-2008.html; accessed 10 September 2008.

Gilroy, Paul. *After Empire: Melancholia or Convivial Culture?* (London: Routledge, 2004).

Gritten, David. 'An Everyday Story of Willesden Folk: *White Teeth*, Zadie Smith's Cross-cultural Novel Set in North-west London, is Coming to Our TV Screens.' *The Daily Telegraph* (31 August 2002): 11.

Hallward, Peter. *Absolutely Postcolonial: Writing Between the Singular and the Specific* (Manchester: Manchester UP, 2002).

Head, Dominic. 'Zadie Smith's White Teeth: Multiculturalism for the Millennium.' *Contemporary British Fiction*. Richard Lane, Rod Mengham and Philip Tew (eds) (Cambridge: Polity, 2003): 106–119.

Hurston, Zora Neale. *Mules and Men* (Philadelphia: J. B. Lippincott, 1935).

——. *Their Eyes Were Watching God* (Philadelphia: J. B. Lippincott, 1937).

——. *Voodoo Gods: An Inquiry into Native Myths and Magic in Jamaica and Haiti* (Philadelphia: J. B. Lippincott, 1938).

Jakubiak, Katarzyna. 'Simulated Optimism: The International Marketing of *White Teeth*.' *Zadie Smith: Critical Essays*. Tracey L. Walters (ed) (New York: Peter Lang, 2008): 201–18.

James, David. 'The New Purism.' *Textual Practice*. 21 (4) (December 2007): 687–714.

Johnson, B. S. *Aren't You Rather Young to be Writing Your Memoirs?* (London: Hutchison, 1973).

Kakutani, Michiko. 'An Elusive, Whimsical Autograph.' *The New York Times*. (25 September 2002).

Keenan, Brian. *An Evil Cradling*. (London: Vintage, 1993).

Kemp, Peter. '*On Beauty* by Zadie Smith.' *The Sunday Times* (4 September 2005): n.p. http://entertainment.timesonline.co.uk/tol/arts_and_entertainment/books/article560815.ece; accessed 10 August 2008.

Kermode, Frank. 'Here She Is.' *London Review of Books* (6 October 2005): n.p. http://www.lrb.co.uk/v27/n19/kerm01_.html: accessed 11 August 2008.

King, Bruce. *The Internationalization of English Literature* Vol. 13, *The Oxford English Literary History*. Jonathan Bate (ed) (Oxford: Oxford University Press, 2002).

Korte, Barbara. 'Blacks and Asians at War for Britain. Reconceptualisations in the Filmic and Literary Field?' *Journal for the Study of British Cultures*. 1 (1) (2007): 29–40.

Kureishi, Hanif. *The Black Album*. (London: Faber and Faber, 1995).

Laird, Nick. 'On Beauty.' *In to a Fault* (London: Faber and Faber, 2005): 43.

——. *Utterly Monkey* (London: Fourth Estate, 2005).

Lanone, Christine. 'Mediating Multi-Cultural Muddle: E. M. Forster Meets Zadie Smith.' *Études Anglaises: The Contemporary Novel: 1996–2007*. 60 (2) (April–June 2007): 185–97.

Lasdun, James. 'Howard's Folly.' *The Guardian* (10 September 2005): 9; http://www.guardian.co.uk/books/2005/sep/10/fiction.zadiesmith: n.p.

Lassner, Phyllis. *Colonial Strangers: Women Writing the End of the British Empire* (New Brunswick, NJ and London: Rutgers UP, 2004).

Lea, Daniel. 'Aesthetics and Anaesthetics: Anglo-American Writers' Responses to September 11.' *Symbiosis*. 11 (2) (2007): 3–26.

Lefebvre, Henri. *Everyday Life in the Modern World*. Trans. Sacha Rabinovitch (New Brunswick and London: Transaction, 1999).

Lowe, Jan. 'No More Lonely Londoners.' *Small Axe: A Caribbean Journal of Criticism*. 9 (March 2001): 166–80.

McAlpin, Heller. 'Howards End, Her Beginning.' *Los Angeles Times: Book Review Section*. (September 25, 2005): R-8.

McLeod, John. *Postcolonial London: Rewriting the Metropolis* (London and New York: Routledge, 2004).

———. 'Revisiting Postcolonial London.' *The European English Messenger*. 14 (2) (Autumn 2005): 39–46.

Matus, Suzanne Liola. 'Press Release: Zadie Smith to Present Dean's Lecture: Award-winning Novelist to Discuss the Morality of the Novel.' http://www.radcliffe.edu/about/news/press_releases_03zsmith. aspx; accessed 24 December 2008.

Mars-Jones, Adam. 'Name of the Prose.' *The Observer* (8 September 2002): n.p. http://ww.guardian.co.uk/books/2002/sep/08/fiction.zadiesmith; accessed 24 December 2008.

Matz, Jesse. *The Modern Novel: A Short Introduction* (Oxford: Blackwell, 2004).

May, Brian. *The Modernist as Pragmatist: E. M. Forster and the Fate of Liberalism* (Columbia and London: University of Missouri Press, 1997).

Meinig, Sigrun. '"Running at a Standstill": The Paradoxes of Time and Trauma in Zadie Smith's *White Teeth*.' *Beyond Extremes: Repräsentation und Reflexion von Modernisierungsprozessen im zeitgenössischen britischen Roman*. Stefan Glomb and Stefan Horlacher (eds) (Tübingen, Germany: Gunter Narr Verlag, 2004): 241–257.

Merleau-Ponty, Maurice. *The Visible and the Invisible* (Evanston: Northwestern UP, 1997).

Mirze, Z. Esra. 'Fundamental Differences in Zadie Smith's *White Teeth*.' *Zadie Smith: Critical Essays*. Tracey L. Walters (ed) (New York: Peter Lang, 2008): 187–200.

Moore-Gilbert, Bart. 'Postcolonialism and "the Figure of the Jew": Caryl Phillips and Zadie Smith.' *The Contemporary British Novel Since 1980*. James Acheson, and Sarah Ross (eds) (New York: Palgrave Macmillan, 2005): 106–17.

Moran, Joe. *Star Authors: Literary Celebrity in America* (London: Pluto Press, 2000).

Moss, Laura, 'The Politics of Everyday Hybridity: Zadie Smith's *White Teeth*.' *Wasafiri*, 18 (39) (Summer 2003): 11–17.

Neal, Arthur G. *National Trauma and Collective Memory: Extraordinary Events in the American Experience* (Armonk, NY: M.E. Sharpe, 2005).

Paproth, Matthew. 'The Flipping Coin: The Modernist and Postmodernist Zadie Smith.' *Zadie Smith: Critical Essays.* Tracey L. Walters (ed) (New York: Peter Lang, 2008): 9–29.

Phillips, Caryl. '*White Teeth* by Zadie Smith.' *A New World Order* (London: Secker & Warburg, 2001): 283–87.

Procter, James. 'New Ethnicities, the Novel and the Burdens of Representation.' *A Concise Companion to Contemporary British Fiction* James F. English (ed) (Malden, MA: Blackwell, 2006): 101–20.

Pynchon, Thomas. *Gravity's Rainbow* (London: Cape, 1973).

Quinn, Anthony. 'The New England.' *The New York Times* (30 April 2000): n.p. http://www.nytimes.com/books/00/04/30/reviews/000430.30quinnt.html; accessed 10 June 2008.

Rastogi, Nina Shen. *Zadie Smith's White Teeth* (New York: Barnes & Noble/Spark, 2003).

Ratcliffe, Sophie. 'None but the Fair.' *Times Literary Supplement.* 5344 (2 September 2005): 10–11.

Reynolds, Nigel. 'Britain's Literary Darling Escapes the Hype for an MA at Harvard.' *The Telegraph* (5 September 2002): n.p. http://www.telegraph.co.uk/news/uknews/1406331/Britains-literary-darlin-escapes-the-hype-for-an-MA-at-Harvard.html; accessed 10 June 2008.

Robertson, Jr., D. W. 'The Pearl as a Symbol.' *Modern Language Notes.* 65 (3) (March 1950): 155–61.

Sandhu, Sukhdev. 'Zadie Smith Bounces Back with Fun and Too Many Facts.' *The Daily Telegraph* (5 September 2002).

Scarry, Elaine. *On Beauty and Being Just* (London: Gerald Duckworth, 2000).

Schama, Simon. *Rembrandt's Eyes* (London: Allen Lane, 1999).

Sell, Jonathan P. A. 'Chance and Gesture in Zadie Smith's *White Teeth* and *The Autograph Man*: A Model for Multicultural Identity?' *The Journal of Commonwealth Literature.* 41 (3) (2006): 27–44.

Sexton, David. 'Zadie's Mistake Radio.' *The Sunday Telegraph.* Review Section (9 January 2005): 7.

Shaffer, Brian W. *Reading the Novel in English 1950–2000* (Oxford: Blackwell, 2006).

Shakespeare, Sebastian. 'Showbiz News: The Secret Life of Zadie Smith.' *Evening Standard London Lite* (5 September 2002): n.p. http://www.thisislondon.co.uk/showbiz/article-1257109-details/The+secret+life+of+Zadie+Smith/article.do; accessed 19 December 2007.

Simpson, Janice C. 'Zadie Smith.' *Time Magazine* (30 April 2006): n.p. http://www.time.com/time/magazine/article/0,9171,1187314,00.html; accessed 19 December 2007.

Simpson, Richard. 'Zadie Gets in a Whirl over Flat Noise.' *Evening Standard* (22 April 2004): n.p. http://www.thisislondon.co.uk/news/article-10370501-details/Zadie+gets+in+a+whirl+over+flat+noise/article.do; accessed 19 December 2007.

Singh, Benita. 'Not Quite Signature Piece.' *The Yale Review of Books.* 7 (2) (Spring 2004): n.p. http://www.yalereviewofbooks.com/archive/spring03/review13.shtml.htm; accessed 19 December 2007.

Smith, Wendy. 'The Paper Chase.' *Los Angeles Times* (29 September 2002): R-5.

Sommer, Roy 'The Aesthetic Turn in "Black" Literary Studies: Zadie Smith's *On Beauty* and the Case for an Intercultural Narratology.' *'Black' British Aesthetics Today.* R. Victoria Arana (ed) (Newcastle: Cambridge Scholars, 2007): 176–92.

Squires, Claire. *Zadie Smith's* White Teeth: *A Reader's Guide.* (London: Continuum, 2002).

Stanley, Alessandra. 'TV Weekend; Lovable Eccentrics in Multicultural London.' *The New York Times* (9 May 2003): n.p. http://query.nytimes.com/gst/fullpage.html?res=9F00E7D8163FF93AA35756C0A9659C8B63: accessed 20 June 2008.

Sutherland, John. 'A Touch of Forster.' *New Statesman* (12 September 2005): n.p. http://www.newstatesman.com/200509120043; accessed 19 December 2007.

Tabuteau, Éric. 'Marginally Correct: Zadie Smith's *White Teeth* and Sam Selvon's *The Lonely Londoners.' Cities on the Margin; on the Margin of Citie: Representations of Urban Space in Contemporary Irish and British Fiction.* Philippe Laplace and Éric Tabuteau (eds) (Besançon: Presses Universitaires Franc-Comtoises, 2003): 81–96.

Thompson, Molly. '"Happy Multicultural Land"? The Implications of an "excess of belonging" in Zadie Smith's *White Teeth.' Write Black, Write British: From Post Colonial to Black British Literature.* Sesay, Kadija (ed) (Hertford: Hansib, 2005): 122–40.

Tolan, Fiona. 'Identifying the Precious in Zadie Smith's *On Beauty.' British Fiction Today.* Philip Tew and Rod Mengham (eds) (London, England: Continuum; 2006): 128–38.

Turner, Henry S. 'Empires of Objects: Accumulation and Entropy in E. M. Forster's *Howards End.' Twentieth Century Literature.* 46 (Fall 2000): 328–45; http://findarticles.com/p/articles/mi_m0403/is_3_46/ai_70907263.

Tynan, Maeve. '"Only Connect": Intertextuality and Identity in Zadie Smith's *On Beauty.' Zadie Smith: Critical Essays.* Tracey L. Walters (ed) (New York: Peter Lang, 2008): 73–89.

Volkan, Vamik D. *The Need to Have Enemies and Allies, from Clinical Practice to International Relationships* (Northvale, NJ: Aronson, 1994).

Wachinger, Tobias A. *Posing In-between: Postcolonial Englishness and the Commodification of Hybridity* (Frankfurt am Main and New York: Peter Lang, 2003).

Walden, Celia. 'More's the Pity.' *The Daily Telegraph* (9 August 2005): 20.

Walters, Tracey L. ' "We're All English Now Mate Like it or Lump It": The Black/Britishness of Zadie Smith's *White Teeth*.' *Write Black Write British: From Post Colonial to Black British Literature*. Kadija Sesay (ed) (London: Hansib. 2005): 314–22.

——. (ed) 'Still Mammies and Hos: Stereotypical Images of Black Women in Zadie Smith's Novels.' *Zadie Smith: Critical Essays* (New York: Peter Lang, 2008): 123–39.

——. (ed) *Zadie Smith: Critical Essays* (New York: Peter Lang, 2008).

Welsh, Irvine. *Trainspotting* (London: Secker & Warburg, 1993).

Westman, Karin E. 'Anatomy of a Dust Jacket: Deracination and British Identity in Zadie Smith's *White Teeth*.' Unpub. Paper 2002 MLA Convention n.p. http://www.cwru.edu/affil/sce/Texts_2002/Westman.htm.

Wieseltier, Leon. *Kaddishi*. (New York: Knopf, 1998).

Wilder, Billy (dir.); screenplay Charles Brackett. *The Lost Weekend*. Paramount Pictures (1945). starring Ray Milland.

Wilson, A. N. 'The Novel That Made A40 Life Pedestrian.' *The Daily Telegraph*. (12 November 2001).

Wood, James. 'Tell Me How Does it Feel?' *The Guardian* (6 October 2001): n.p. http://www.guardian.co.uk/books/2001/oct/06/fiction; accessed 8 January 2008.

——. 'Fundamentally Goyish.' *London Review of Books* (3 October 2002): n.p. http://www.lrb.co.uk/v24/n19/wood02_.html; accessed 8 January 2008.

——. *The Irresponsible Self: On Laughter and the Novel* (London: Pimlico, 2005).

Wyatt Mason 'White Knees: Zadie Smith's Novel Problem.' *Harper's Magazine* (October 2005): 83–8.

INDEX